T0356663

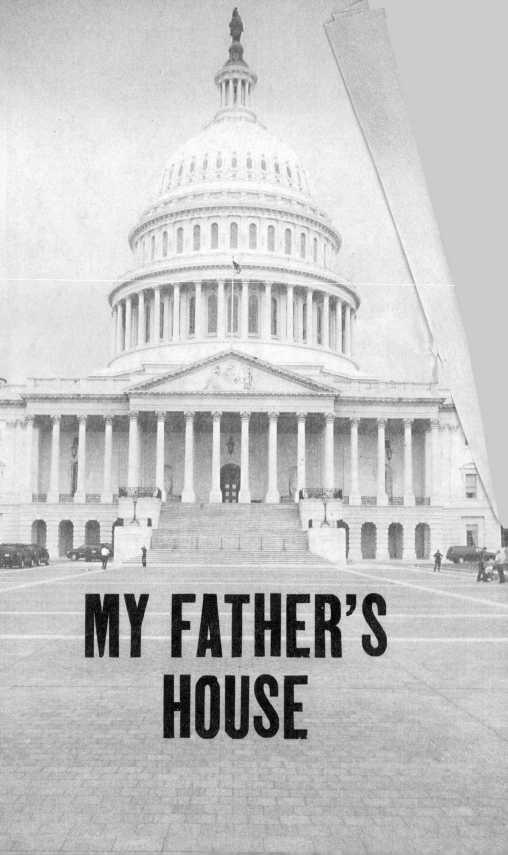

MY FATHER'S HOUSE

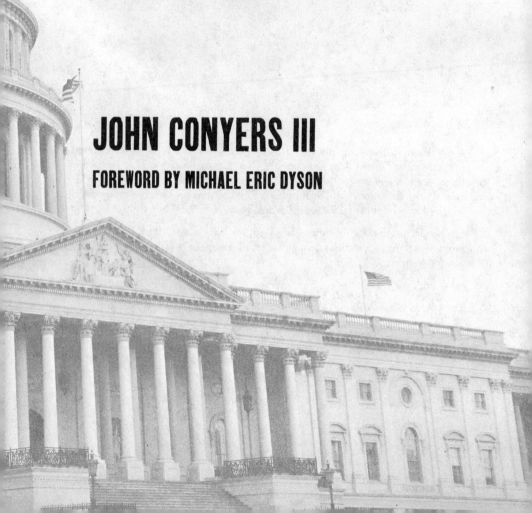

MY FATHER'S HOUSE

JOHN CONYERS III

FOREWORD BY MICHAEL ERIC DYSON

HarperCollins books may be purchased for educational, business, or sales promotional use. For information, please email the Special Markets Department at SPsales@harpercollins.com.

FIRST EDITION

Designed by Nancy Singer
Photographs on pages i–iii © Tupungato/stock.adobe.com
Insert photographs courtesy of the author unless otherwise noted

Library of Congress Cataloging-in-Publication Data has been applied for.

ISBN 978-0-06-333681-0

25 26 27 28 29 LBC 5 4 3 2 1

To the original John Conyers; his son (my father),
Congressman John Conyers Jr.; and MomCon: It's
been the honor of my life to tell our family's story.

To the unsung heroes of my journey:
Mrs. Tower, Mrs. Woodfin, Mrs. Mitchell,
Mr. Moore, Coach Rowley, and Ms. Shea.

To my agent, Will Lippincott, thank you for taking a chance
on me and sticking with this project despite setbacks and
uncertainty. Thank you for believing in my family's story.

My part has been to tell the story of the slave. The story of the master never wanted for narrators.

—Frederick Douglass

If you are silent about your pain, they'll kill you and say you enjoyed it.

—Zora Neale Hurston

CONTENTS

AIN'T NO CITY LIKE THE ONE I GOT

By Michael Eric Dyson

When I came up in Detroit in the sixties and seventies, giants stalked the earth. Kenneth Cockrel Sr. was an unashamedly Marxist lawyer who used mellifluous multisyllabic rhetoric to storm the cultural and political dominions of white supremacy. Cockrel cofounded the League of Revolutionary Black Workers to help working-class Black folks fight an automobile industry that exploited their labor. Even before he became a one-term council-man, he was also instrumental in galvanizing a movement to bring an end to the police department's brutal undercover unit STRESS (Stop The Robberies, Enjoy Safe Streets), which terrorized Black communities. Coleman Young, the man who pulled the plug on STRESS, was the colorful and delightfully profane first Black mayor of Detroit, taking office in 1974, a mere seven years after the urban rebellion of 1967.

There were preaching colossuses, too. Charles Adams, dubbed "the Harvard Whooper" because of his academic pedigree and homiletical style, fused spiritual ardor and political passion to assail racial disorders and other social sins at Hartford Memorial Baptist

Church. C. L. Franklin, Aretha's daddy and a pioneering evangelist who came to maturity in Mississippi and recorded more than seventy albums of sermons, broadcast his chanted homilies across the Detroit airwaves each Sunday night from his legendary pulpit in the New Bethel Baptist Church.

And there was my pastor, too, Frederick George Sampson, a towering Shakespearean figure who quoted W. E. B. Du Bois and Bertrand Russell alike, and from whose lips dripped the poetry of Langston Hughes and Thomas Gray. As pastor of the Tabernacle Missionary Baptist Church on the city's west side, Sampson was spiritual caretaker for people like me, a poor Black boy from the inner city.

But Sampson was the shepherd of prominent citizens like Elliott Hall, a renowned lawyer who became a vice president at Ford Motor Company. Sampson also watched over the spiritual pilgrimage of Damon J. Keith, who was appointed to the federal district bench in 1967 by President Lyndon Baines Johnson and who was elevated to the federal appeals court in 1977 by President Jimmy Carter. Keith presided over the 1976 tax evasion trial of famed mobster Anthony "Tony Jack" Giacalone. In the early seventies he also ruled against the Nixon administration's effort to carry out warrantless wiretapping, and when they sued him personally, the Supreme Court vindicated him in what became known as "the Keith case." Hall and Keith became my heroes and mentors and eventually my friends.

So did the remarkable John Conyers Jr., who was also a member of Tabernacle and an iconic politician who became the longest-serving Black member of Congress in the nation's history. I would spot Conyers at church, and grew enamored of his political gravitas, his serene disposition, his keen intelligence, his love for jazz, his calm yet eloquent declamation, and his moral decency. Conyers's handsome face was accented by a striking mustache that covered his upper lip in a slimmer version of Friedrich Nietzsche's dense whiskers. Conyers was a long-distance runner for justice, a venerable warrior for freedom, who made sure that Martin Luther King Jr. was honored with a national holiday and who repeatedly prodded Congress to at least study the prospect of Black reparations.

Detroit was a hotbed of Black organizing, particularly in mobilizing Black workers to fend for themselves and their hard-won right to enjoy social and political equality. It was a city that was unapologetically Black at its cultural roots, with the Motown record label symbolizing both its creative imagination and its hard work. Motown is a sly portmanteau of "motor" and "town," signifying the inspiration of the automobile industry in crafting, engineering, and producing music in similar fashion to the elegant cars that rolled off the assembly line. Motown founder Berry Gordy Jr. seized on the symphonic collage of labor and design in the automobile factory and transcribed it into the finesse, order, and structure of Black music humming on car radios. The automobile, after all, is how upwardly mobile Black citizens rode to work and where they spent a great deal of leisure time indulging their appetite for fashion, style, and sophistication.

The Great Migration had deposited Negroes into a seething cauldron of race and class in Detroit as they chased Henry Ford's promise of $5.00 a day in return for their labor in his factories. Detroit eventually became a Black cultural and political headquarters that drew Black citizens from the South from 1910 to 1930, and again during World War II, not only in search of greater economic opportunity but in pursuit of greater freedom from Jim Crow. My father came in the forties from Albany, Georgia, and my mother in the fifties from Hissop, Alabama, each searching for opportunity and freedom before they found each other. I was born in 1958, six years before the Civil Rights Act and seven years before the Voting Rights Act.

By the time I got to the fifth grade in my segregated elementary school, I was exposed to the radically uplifting pedagogy of Mrs. James, who taught us Black history and Black culture and gave us tremendous pride in our past. She insisted that we, too, could make history of our own. When Dr. King was murdered in Memphis in 1968, it was just a year after the urban uprising in Detroit sparked by police misconduct that was rooted in an ugly history of anti-Black violence. Detroit's Black community rose up to claim its rightful place in the city's political evolution, and Conyers led the charge in laying claim to the beauty and legitimacy of Black political power.

Those were high times. We heard Marvin Gaye asking "What's Going On?" from the jukebox, the home hi-fi record player, or the car radio, even as Coleman Young gave us a sense of pride in our Blackness. And John Conyers offered us a road map to increased political representation at the federal level. Before there was Barack Obama and Kamala Harris, there was in Detroit John Conyers, Congressman Charles Diggs, Coleman Young, Councilwoman Erma Henderson, and the great activist Rosa Parks, who migrated to Detroit after her rise to fame in Alabama.

John Conyers blew the trumpet of Black political triumph in the perilous but prosperous march to Black self-determination, especially in Detroit. He was beloved because he was loyal to his roots and to the Black milieu that helped lift Smokey Robinson, Aretha Franklin, Diana Ross, Martha Reeves, Stevie Wonder, and a choir of other soulful geniuses to epic achievement and dizzying artistic heights.

But Conyers also inspired the Black everyman and the everywoman, too, and dared to represent their interests, magnify their goals, glorify their struggle, and validate their citizenship. Along with Coleman Young and a host of Black mayors and council people and state representatives and statewide office holders and congress people since, Conyers helped to create a system of Black political privilege and opportunity that mirrored the sorts of political benefits and economic advantages that ethnic whites enjoyed in cities like Boston, Philadelphia, and Chicago.

Such a system was by no means perfect, and surely was susceptible to the same corruption that plagued white political structures. But it also offered a genuine chance for Black citizens to realize their ambitions in a fashion that didn't discount their desires as unnatural or unachievable. That is why Conyers was so beloved among Black folk until his death at ninety. And it is why it was one of the highest honors of my life to offer the eulogy at his funeral on November 4, 2019.

It is also a joy to publicly embrace his son John Conyers III as he seeks to extend his famous father's legacy by offering his own spin on Black life, Black struggle, Black political possibility, and the rewards and satisfactions of Black existence. A third-generation Conyers taking the baton and running his own race is a good thing, as we witness the emergence of a figure devoted to the same principles of fairness, justice, democracy, and economic opportunity that carried his father into immortality.

And at a moment when we are rejiggering racial identity, when we are re-litigating who counts as Black, and who doesn't, it is salutary that we are reminded of a legendary Black political figure who should be rediscovered for our age through the efforts of his son.

John Conyers III has joined the important debate about what Blackness is, about what we must do to ensure our survival, and how we must overcome the impediments to glory and the obstacles to liberation that his father so valiantly confronted and overcame. It's his turn now. May the spirit of his gallant father course through his veins and claim expression in his efforts to love Black folk into greater freedom and justice in our day.

LOOK WHAT YOU'VE DONE

There's an African proverb that goes "Until the lion learns to write, every story will glorify the hunter."

My father was a lion. Which makes me his cub. Even as a child, when I got lost in his shadow, I was privileged to be right there with him, witnessing the back half of his tenure in US politics, which he'd started straight out of the blocks as a rising, shining star. I was blessed to be by his side during his descent. To say it's important for me to tell the story of John Conyers Jr., the statesmanlike congressman and Everyman from Detroit, grossly underestimates my urgency to document my father's life and the paths he chose to take. For sure, Pop, on some level, knew he'd cemented a distinct place for himself in US history and some aspects of global history. He'd simply been too busy working—making history—to pen his own biography.

While writing this memoir—an ode to my father and a probe of my Black, male, millennial existence—I began to understand how prescient and imperative Pop's work remains. I've been weighing what his work has yielded and what it still asks of us. I've been studying the imprint left by my father, his closest comrades, and the countless others of their generation who enlisted in a war for every kind of justice on American soil. They helped make it possible for a woman of Black and South Asian ancestry to vie to become the first-ever person of her profile to move into the White House. And yes, they laid the foundation and provided a vocabulary for our rebuttal to every racist, sexist insult that continues to be thrown at her.

My father's work, and that of his peers, lives on a continuum. It goes on and on. It lives in me. Willingly, defiantly, and humbly, I have placed my heart, body, and mind on a path parallel to the one my father walked. Pop passed me the baton. He also implored me to be myself and that I never try to replicate him, measure for measure, or career move by career move. His journey has been my exhibit A. Exhibits B, C, D, and so on are the journeys and doings of civil rights, social, and economic justice leaders in Detroit, America's Blackest city and still a definite center of Black politics in the United States, as well as many leaders who hailed from other locales. I have gotten to sit at the feet of many of those leaders. I have been able to linger with them, to ponder their thoughts and strategies. Just as my United Auto Workers executive grandfather positioned Pop to listen, hear, and heed the Black elders of his era, Pop did the same for me. I started tagging along behind him when I was in pre-K. I still see myself in photos, hoisted on my proud father's hip at some political function or other, perhaps in the Motor City. Pop was sharp as a tack, button-downed, cuff-linked, peering into the camera's eyes through oversize eyeglasses with tinted lenses. I am not sure what possibly compares to being a Detroiter in that freeze-frame or hailing from a city where the janitor, the doctor, the judge, and the police officer—so, thankfully, often—have been Black. Blackness, in my hometown, during my lifetime, has always been multifaceted, multidimensional, and full of opportunity. That prevailing, predominant Blackness has allowed Detroiters to evaluate both the proficiency and deficiency of systems—political, economic, social, cultural—from a vantage point that does not readily exist for Black folks in many US cities and towns. Ever since Black Detroiters set our city on fire in 1967—a rebellion that helped contextualize an era when the Black Panthers and similar liberation organizations were also surfacing—we've uniquely grabbed hold of a considerable degree of local and regional governmental power and brought that power to scale, despite broader, systemic oppression that has not been abated.

Empowered Blacks, in 1973, made Coleman Young Detroit's first Black mayor. His policies benefited multitudes of Black people, businesses, civic groups, and political organizations. He modeled how a restructured government can enrich—and not just monetarily— Black people who'd previously, largely languished on the margins. The Detroit of that day, and of succeeding years, modeled systems change, pure and true. The change birthed Black leaders across many industries: investment banker Suzanne Shank; telecom and casino magnate Don Barden; automotive industry titan and philanthropist Bill Pickard; American Bar Association president Reginald Turner Jr.; former Michigan Supreme Court Justice Conrad Mallett, who also was a major player at Detroit City Hall; billion-dollar manufacturer Bruce Smith; Kiko Davis, who owns one of the largest Black banks in the country; and so many more. Many of them were friends of my father, who never strayed from Detroit, even as he was making major, national laws in health care, labor, criminal justice, entertainment, economics, and elsewhere.

While we must laud the good fortune of those on the roll call of Black wealth and power, perhaps we've taken some of that fortune for granted. More than we might want to admit, we've sometimes taken our eyes off the prize. We haven't focused enough on how our wealth might be shared and deployed to propel the progress of an entire Black nation within a nation. No matter the exaggerations and tropes about my generation and those following millennials being adrift, without a cause or legitimate care, many of us see what's happened. What we know about our history informs our critique of where this society now finds itself. So many in my generation are exploring pathways forward that stem directly, in several respects, from the blueprint my father and his peers constructed for us.

My father was old enough to be my grandfather. Except for the last seventeen years of his life, he lived in the twentieth century. Other than the first ten years of my life, I have been navigating the twenty-first. Pop's political activism addressed the immediate and explicit social needs of the times he came up in, times when a white supremacist police officer could brutalize a Black person with absolute impunity. In my times, when white supremacists and militia members help fill the ranks of sworn law enforcement officers, what lessons and tactics can be gleaned from my father, the first congressman—of any race—to call for radical police reform?

Sixty years removed from the Voting Rights Act of 1965, which Pop coauthored—and voting is a pathway to more than just a ballot—how and whom do we engage on every single front? For me, the political and economic arenas are inextricably linked. Combined, they form one great big battlefield. The victor gets the spoils and decides who, if anyone, might share in that bounty.

In this fraught political climate, we, of course, need more. We need more individuals with the same mindset and method as Maxine Waters and Jasmine Crockett to draft laws aimed at protecting our people. We need the Ketanji Brown Jacksons to fairly adjudicate the laws. We need more Ben Crumps and Johnnie Cochrans to try pivotal cases. We also must have more financial backers to flank the likes of John Rogers, Don Peebles, and Robert Smith, who put good chunks of their earned wealth toward supporting Black causes, political and economic.

"Even if it didn't necessarily look like it, your father also was a capitalist. He was part of the establishment, but more than any-thing, he was about making change that also was focused on the principle of economic inclusion."

Don, who'd been on my father's congressional staff before be-coming one of the country's major real estate developers, shared those thoughts with me. It was, in part, his agreement that we each have a role to play in our ongoing pursuit of a fully stocked and loaded Black liberation. A full-throated, unbound, multifaceted, and multidimensional freedom lets us—and us alone—define the many characteristics, strains, colors, and tones of Blackness. Black people are not a monolith, though forces within and outside our communities often try to reduce and constrain us to that. But, far from being one thing, we are all things. Good, bad, and indifferent. Embracing those realities itself is liberating. And liberation means we own ourselves, truly, in ways that Pop imagined and insisted on.

My father was a lion. I am his cub, armed with a pen, writing it down, and trying to make it plain. This is the perspective of the pride, not the hunter.

I'm aware that the legacies of too many Black leaders, ones with household names and those not in the public eye or under its scrutiny, sometimes get obscured. They get lost. Sometimes those legacies have been co-opted, whitewashed, watered down, and repurposed. Before today's FBI saluted the MLK holiday, a com-memoration my father made happen, J. Edgar Hoover's FBI was protractedly conspiring to undermine what Dr. King and Malcolm X, risking their very lives, were doing to foment Black liberation. Today, our annual salute to that activated, fearless preacher from Birmingham gets reduced to and summed up by his "I Have a Dream" speech, not his famous, strident "Letter from Birmingham Jail" or his internationally heralded protest of the US presence in Vietnam.

I'd be foolish to think that anyone can singularly control what history documents about lions like Martin or Malcolm or Pop. The very notion of control is illusory. It is elusive. Still, I do wonder. What if those with the most intimate knowledge of our revolutionaries took the first swipe at creating a public narrative about them before some outsider's facts, inaccuracies, and misrepresentations have calcified and become too hard to scrub clean? I wonder how much richer and more complete Martin's and Malcolm's stories would be if they had been allowed to live a bit longer. Or if their children had been a bit older when they started grappling with their interminably tragic, mortal losses and, from there, voiced their perspective on how we remember the fallen.

More than anything, though, I am grateful. I am blessed by this opportunity to offer my acknowledgment, analysis, and remembrance of the work my father, a lion, did for all of us. God bless these words.

JC3

CHAPTER 1

THE BLUEPRINT

My father used his voice like an instrument, hitting every note to keep people moving in the direction of progress. His even tone made his appeal. *Hello, folks. This is Congressman John Conyers Jr. with an important Election Day message. . . .*

He tweaked his prepared script in between takes as he broadcast on a local radio station during that long-ago day of campaigning in the Motor City. With each improvised revision of his pitch for 1968 presidential contender Hubert Humphrey, a political friend, and other Democrats, Pop was careful to repeat what had been a centerpiece of his campaign when he was first elected to Congress in 1964. *Let's overcome our powerlessness with vote power. Thank you very much.*

An acoustic guitarist, a pianist, and a drummer rendered a jazzy cover of Aretha Franklin's "I Say a Little Prayer" under Pop's request for voter support over the radio airwaves.

For my multi-instrumentalist father, the trumpet was the primary tool for melodymaking. The piano was his favorite fallback. On the piano bench, my younger brother, Carl, and I would sit on either side of Pop as the fingers of his old-man hands glided across the black-and-whites. He'd riff on jazzman Miles Davis's version of "Bye Bye Blackbird" or "My Cherie Amour," the chart-topper by

Stevie Wonder. Stevie was another of my father's good friends. He'd taught Pop to play that love song on the upright piano inside his apartment in Washington, DC. That residence became the epicenter of his serial absences from me, his firstborn boy; my brother, Carl; and my mother.

For Pop, music was his first love. It consoled, bolstered, and settled him. It stirred his joy and kept him company.

To this day, Pop's upright bass is in a corner of the living room of our family home on Seven Mile Road in Detroit. Satin curtains in a now slightly faded shade of taupe are a backdrop for that golden oak-stained bass, made of plywood, rather than a more expensive wood. Pop's bass is dusted often and polished to a sheen. Its upkeep is thanks to my mother, Pop's youngish widow, who, except for holidays, keeps our curated living room off-limits to anyone tempted to step foot inside.

It's not exactly a shrine to my legislating, trailblazing father, the US House of Representative's sixth-longest-serving member until his forced retirement in 2017, when he was eighty-eight years old and I was twenty-seven. A former "Dean of the House," my father was a gentleman and a hell-raiser. He remains the longest-serving Black member of Congress in American history in either chamber.

That living room, though, is a sacred place of memory and meaning for me: My mom is of a social class, mindset, and era in which striving Black folks who were barely up from sharecropping sometimes wrapped their newly acquired furniture in protective plastic covers, just in case you got it in your mind that couches and chairs were for sitting.

"Don't be playing in my living room!" was the first and final warning my mother gave whenever company was over or my brother and I got too turnt up.

As for Pop's lustrous bass, I don't remember it ever being anywhere except securely nestled in that corner of the out-of-bounds living room. When I walk through the front door of the family house on Seven Mile and glance up the foyer stairs toward that corner, I'm once again in my father's presence. When I pick up the saxophone Pop bought me when I was nine years old, maybe ten, my ears conjure the sound of him blowing that horn one last entertaining time, for me and my brother.

Though he died when I was twenty-nine and he was ninety, Pop looms. There are photographs and newsclippings and newsreels and film footage and YouTube videos and a freight-shipping container filled with files of research, papers, books, desks, desk lamps, congas, a different upright bass, and a host of other what-have-yous from Pop's old office on Capitol Hill. They were my father's maps of the world as he charted it. They became my guideposts.

I toggle between my father's worlds and my own when I'm circulating through Detroit, which is both a big city and a small, insular town. That, in part, is my observation. It's also an observation I've gleaned over time from an assortment of people, born and raised elsewhere, who've made Detroit home. Some of those transplants relocated to the heart of the city during yet another iteration of Detroit's off-and-on rebirth, cycles that started way before I was born and, these days, can get hamstrung by an unrelenting exodus of taxpayers, including Black people. Those transplants have told me this, summarily: The city is a marvel and a conundrum. Its Black power—cultural, social, and political—is mind-boggling. However, its grip on Black collective wealth and Black collectivism, period, has been precarious. Detroit teeters. Its academically credentialed professional class and unionized blue-collar workers, particularly in the dwindling auto industry, are connected, for sure. Yet, they're also separated. Some of those doctors, lawyers, architects, and such grew up in the same public housing or run-down neighborhoods of once stately art deco, midcentury modern, and other homes. They know poverty and how it feels to be sidelined. They may or may not be in the fight for the masses of blue-collar, working-poor, and outright destitute Black folks who, in the Motor City, with its inadequate public transit system, can't afford a car to get to work. As in so many parts of our nation, a disproportionate number of the Metro Detroit region's jobs also moved to the suburbs.

But trying to adapt to a place is quite different from growing up in it. Some of those outsiders' views, to me, have sounded a bit colonialist and a bit imperious. Do they think they know better than a native Detroiter what ails Detroit? I'm a third-generation son of my city. My observations about Detroit life are rooted in the facts of my birth. They are rooted in me being deeply grounded in the land that launched me and, before me, launched my father and his generation of Black elected officials during the Civil Rights Movement.

Black Detroiters moved from that period of what I call hope-in-action—voting Pop in as the second Black congressman from Michigan and his comrade, Coleman Young, as Detroit's first Black mayor—to what is today's somewhat dissipated hope. Starting in 2013, mostly Black Detroit, with its below-average voter turnout, elected a white man, Mike Duggan, to consecutive terms as mayor. Perhaps, that's a consequence of voters feeling as if Black leaders failed them. But the truth is more complicated than that. The truth, at least in part, is that Young and several Black mayors who followed him in leading Detroit City Hall were up against the whims and will of systems, including political ones, stretching from Lansing, Michigan's state capital, to Washington, DC.

My story traces and tracks my father's movements. The story of his political life and legacy, likewise, extends from Michigan to Washington to points beyond and between, until, finally, he retired and returned to our hometown. In Pop's last years, I had the honor and gift of enlisting myself, my days, my talents, and my time in service to my father. We'd kick it for hours in the comforts of the house on Seven Mile or shoot around Detroit to his favorite restaurants or community events, or we'd just be, doing much of nothing.

I store and keep one of my favorite photos of him and me in my iPhone; Pop's smile is big and easy. He bears no sign of the stress-induced devastation that made him violently ill and, we feared, would take him out right then and there. That hospitalization happened a few weeks after he was ousted—over the refutable, unadjudicated allegations of sexual harassment of a longtime female staffer—from the job he'd pledged himself to entirely and relished like no other.

In that photo, though, my handsome pop shows no sign of distress. He is a glowing, tested-and-proven old soldier, peering over his shoulder at me. My dandy of a father is wearing a navy pinstripe suit, a white handkerchief in the chest pocket. The subtle flex and nod to his more than a half century in the US House of Representatives is the pin in his left lapel, designating the 99th congressional session. It is something earned not given. It is a treasure someone as unassuming as the Dean cannot help but be proud of.

I wax poetic on the mic as Pop eyes me, I'm wearing a Lululemon jacket and polo shirt, denim jeans, and tweed and leather Alife high-top sneakers. I look straight ahead. I offer gratitude for my father's generous and forceful existence. It's amazing, I remind everyone, that we still have Pop and can revel in his delight over being celebrated on his ninetieth birthday. I am giving Pop his due.

My salutation repeats what I've said so many times before: "Pop, this country owes a lot to you. Not many people receive their flowers while they can smell them. We all gathered here to celebrate you and say thank you, for everything."

That was a summation of my salute to my father on that afternoon. Our gang of relatives and friends—regular folks from the neighborhood, stakeholders from news headlines, people from places near, far, and in between—was marking Pop's longevity at a party his baby brother, my uncle Nate, hosted in his home flanking what once was a whites-only golf course. I was twenty-eight years old on that day in 2019 when Pop finished his ninth decade. In 2019, the average lifespan for a Black man in America was seventy-two years, four years fewer than for white men. Pop had beaten those odds, and then some. And though I didn't dwell on it, I'd accepted that Pop, in the flesh, would not be with us for much longer.

On the day of his final birthday party, Pop had been out of Congress for almost two years. But, still, he was talking politics and policy, his favorite subjects. After fifty-three years of leaving his indelible mark on Washington, DC, the nation, and, by some measures, the world, lawmaker mode remained Pop's default. Here and there, he sprinkled mundane, everyday things into the birthday party convo. Mainly, though, he was making observations about what we confront, about the demons he thought our American motherland had exorcised and buried. He repeated the big, unanswered question: "What shall we do about all that's going on right now?"

No matter the topic, I loved listening to my father. On that particular occasion, I savored his nearness to me. Often without realizing it, I'd study him. As one in a first wave of modern Black American politicos, Pop's achievements were Herculean. I cannot evaluate myself by any similar metric. On Pop's birthday, I didn't ask how I could possibly follow his class act. No comparison could ever be made.

Yet I've lived my life in the shadow and light of my father's.

He and I were a mutually adoring duo. Philosophically, ideologically, and strategically, we were of the same mind on many matters. On others, we splintered, yet kept our common end goals in view. Among what we shared, as father and son, was a determination to help ensure equity for everyone, on every front of human existence, and focus our eyes and energies where we could make a reasonable, meaningful impact.

Pop took his ideals to Congress, winning each of his twenty-seven consecutive races for his congressional seat by a landslide. His lowest winning margin was 77 percent; his highest was 97 percent.

In my 2022 losing bid to fill my father's old congressional seat, I came in fourth in a field of nine candidates for the Democratic Party nomination. Eight of us candidates were Black. The winner—in a Democratic stronghold like Detroit, the nominee is all but assured victory in the general election—was Shri Thanedar. A pharmaceutical industry executive, he was born in India.

In 2019, Thanedar relocated from Ann Arbor, where 82 percent of the population is white, to Detroit's affluent Palmer Woods neighborhood, qualifying him to run for Pop's old seat. (In 2018, he'd lost the Democratic gubernatorial primary to Governor Gretchen Whitmer.) Blacks comprise three-quarters of Palmer Woods residents and slightly more than three-quarters of residents in Detroit. By the sheer numbers, Detroit is the largest majority-Black city in the United States.

I've spotlighted Thanedar's outsider status and wealth not because I'm anti-immigrant or anti-rich. (It bears noting that Pop, a public servant, had the seventh-lowest net worth of any among the 435 members of the House of Representatives. A few years before leaving Congress, he was in the red, with a negative net worth of $129,001. By comparison, $500.6 million was the highest net worth among House members.) I'm merely pointing out an irony of our present politics that allows a kindhearted and well-meaning carpetbagger, but a carpetbagger nonetheless, to become the congressman representing Detroit.

Should eight Black candidates—me being among them—have split Detroit's mainly Black vote so severely that Thanedar took the No. 1 slot with 28 percent of the primary vote? Maybe not.

Did I view my father's old seat as my birthright, as some of my detractors claim? Absolutely not. I also believe I've not gotten a fair shake. Precisely because I am not a pound for pound facsimile of Pop, because I am not of his generation, because I embrace different routes and methods toward achieving the same results that my father sought in terms of equity for everyone, some members of the old guard political establishment—but not only them—don't take me as seriously as I'd like and believe I deserve to be taken.

I was born at 11:49 a.m. on Thursday, July 5, 1990, at Detroit Women's Hospital. I'm from Seven Mile, or the Mile, as we refer to it in the city. I graduated from Detroit Renaissance High School (I'm a proud Phoenix), created lifetime friendships in Detroit, continue to help launch and support community groups and business enterprises in Detroit, pay taxes in Detroit, and commune, kneel, and pray at the altar of my preferred Detroit church. I have resided and worked elsewhere, including in Los Angeles and New York City. But I'm a Detroiter, to my core and in my soul.

Yet, my lived experiences in and observations of other places help to inform my assessment of my hometown—what it has, and what it lacks. Among the most glaring deficiencies: How is it that Detroit has no adequate public transit system? University of Michigan analysts calculated that a third of folks in the Motor City have no vehicle of their own. And yet, nearly 75 percent of all jobs in southeastern Michigan, the region dominated by Detroit, require a car to get to. How can we claim to be concerned about citizens' economic, social, and physical mobility if the aforementioned is true? If they have no reliable, affordable transportation to a job or a decent grocery store or a doctor's office or wherever? How much longer will we let decision-makers pay lip service to caring about Detroit's poor, disproportionately Black citizens but leave intact the structures that entrap so many?

Up until the day he died, these also were my father's questions. My father was the son of a pioneering Black United Auto Workers executive and a homemaker mom. They'd migrated to Detroit, a land of greater promise, from Jim Crow Georgia. They had expectations and dreams for their children. Pop, the second oldest of my paternal grandparents' five offspring, earned a bachelor's degree in history from Wayne State University and his jurisprudence doctorate from Wayne State University Law School. Later, a civil rights activist, lawyer, and legislator, he displayed a distinct style, combining elegance and gentility with cunning. If he was about to cut your throat, figuratively speaking, you'd never know it. He'd call you "sir" or "ma'am," address you by title and honorific. He had a certain, sure, square-shouldered posture. His voice was as calming as it was firm and commanding. He assumed his role among the many who've collaborated in an American Civil Rights Movement that is unending and circles back on itself. As governments and legislators in the New South try to out-MAGA the man who created that madness, they're also banning textbook lessons on this nation's bloody racial history. It's as if they think that Blacks will not challenge their newest acts of aggression. We've been shown how not to cower, how not to bow. As they try to erase the martyrs and leaders of our resistance from the national consciousness, they think we will forget our power. We won't.

We've amassed power before, even if our grip upon it has loosened, even if we've lost sight of its importance and find ourselves struggling to regain it. In his early years, Pop crisscrossed the country, litigating on behalf of, among others, Freedom Riders who were jailed en masse for defying the entrenched laws of the Jim Crow South. In the process, he struck up an enduring friendship with the Reverend Dr. Martin Luther King Jr., whose reputation rested on the words he wrote and lived as much as the ones he preached. Dr. King initiated a correspondence with my father that lasted until King was murdered. "Words fail me," Dr. King once wrote to Pop, "in expressing my deep and heartfelt thanks to you for your visit to Selma, Alabama last week. Your very presence there has had an electric effect on the voteless and beleaguered Negro citizens of this city, county, state, and nation."

After Alabama employers blackballed Rosa Parks for setting off the 1955 Montgomery bus boycott, Pop placed her on the payroll of his Detroit office, where she worked for two decades. Mrs. Parks arranged, on Pop's behalf, for Dr. King to show up during the 1964 election season: "You've got to come to Detroit and embrace Brother Conyers. We need you."

"He didn't give me a direct endorsement," Pop said, of MLK's nonetheless full-throated support for my father's congressional bid, "because, if he explicitly vouched for me or anyone else, he'd get a flood of requests from other candidates. But he made it obvious that he was in my corner."

Dr. King made a point of posing in photos with Pop. Dr. King and Pop sent messages back and forth through actor-singer Harry Belafonte, comedian Dick Gregory, and others among their mutual friends and activists. "And any time King was in Detroit," Pop said, "he and I would go together to visit churches, restaurants, and other spots where people in the community would gather."

Dr. King's final push for Pop's campaign came five days before the election. With a motorcade of local pastors, he wound through all of Black Detroit, along the great avenues and into the fourteen-story Brewster-Douglass Housing Projects, Detroit's biggest public housing complex. Reserved for people who had jobs but, neverthe-less, straddled the federal poverty line, it was the childhood home of Diana Ross, Florence Ballard, and Mary Wilson, before they were the Supremes, and of their fellow Motown superstar Smokey Robinson.

"Every few blocks," Pop said, of that final push in his first cam-paign, "Dr. King would step out, stand on top of a flatbed truck, and talk about how Black folks had to vote for candidates running to speed up the pace of change. He didn't say my name, but the message was clear. And these were the people, the streets, the neighborhoods that I was running to represent."

People poured out of their homes, barbershops, stores, wherever to look and listen. "Every one of them wanted to be in the presence of Dr. King," Pop said. "But King wasn't on the ballot. I was. And I knew that even with his backing, it was probably going to be a close election."

It would have been hard for my lawyer father and Dr. King to be unknown to each other. Almost everybody, Pop told me, who had anything to do with the Movement and getting white folks' feet off Black folks' necks, pretty much, knew everyone else who'd signed on for the heavy lifting. They were, Pop said, a small universe of people.

Ahead of June 1963's historic Detroit Walk to Freedom, Dr. King sermonized in my hometown about Black demands, refutations, and hopes. "Segregation is wrong because it is nothing but a new form of slavery covered up with certain niceties. . . ." That's what MLK proclaimed before a mainly Black but multiracial Motown crowd preceding the 250,000 who, two months later, would march right up to the steps of the Lincoln Memorial in Washington.

A rainbow of bodies—which, up until this moment in 1963, was unimaginable—descended on the National Mall that August for the same reasons that Pop and his fellow Detroiters had flooded their city's bustling Woodward Avenue in June. Blacks then comprised 40 percent of Detroit's population. They largely subsisted on the economic margins. They were subjected to routine aggressions by what were called the Big Four Patrols, baton-wielding, pistol-packing officers who rode four to a car and jumped out at random to accost Black people. Those same officers were sworn to protect the thousands upon thousands who peacefully poured onto Woodward (3 percent of police were Black at the time of that historic march in the Motor City; today, Blacks comprise more than half of the department's sworn officers).

MLK locked arms with Black Detroiters and the likes of then mayor Jerome Cavanagh, an anti-segregationist white who'd garnered 85 percent of the Black vote. Those marchers were televised worldwide, chanting and belting songs about deliverance.

"Those guys were trying to kill us," Pop told me, encapsulating a Black foreboding that clouded those times and, even now, hovers.

Pop wasn't insinuating that he, for a fact, knew he was under the immediate, premeditated threat of a bullet or a noose. He was conveying the stark reality of what every Black person felt the entire race was up against on any given day.

As a congressman working tirelessly to open doors of opportunity that had been deadbolted in the faces of our people, he introduced and collaborated on some of the most consequential laws this nation has ever enacted. From the House side of that chamber, Pop cosponsored the Voting Rights Act of 1965, laying the foundation for a wave of first-ever Black elected officials in Mississippi, Arkansas, Georgia, and other hotbeds of hyper-racism below and above the Mason–Dixon Line.

Likewise, Pop coauthored the Fair Housing Act of 1968, banning discrimination on the basis of race, religion, physicality, etc.

With the permission of widow Coretta Scott King, Pop blueprinted the MLK holiday in 1968, four days after a high-velocity, soft-point, metal-jacketed Remington-Peters bullet shot Dr. King dead on the balcony of the Lorraine Motel. That April in Memphis, Dr. King had landed to champion the workplace rights of and boost the morale of Black men hired at substandard wages as municipal garbage haulers. Two of them had been crushed to death by a malfunctioning machine. Their whole workforce had gone on strike.

Pop spent the fifteen years following the thirty-nine-year-old preacher's assassination agitating for MLK Day, determined to honor this global giant, the second Black American to be awarded the Nobel Peace Prize. In 1981, Pop's friend Stevie Wonder pecked out his jubilant "Happy Birthday" homage to MLK. In 1983, GOP president Ronald Reagan signed into law the holiday that Pop insisted upon.

Amid today's racism, classism, homophobia, transphobia, assorted otherings, and isms, the holiday's salute to one man and what he stood for takes on a whole other level of importance and imperatives.

The imperatives have been staring me, staring all of us, in the face. Like my father, I'd thought finding a place in politics would be one of the ways that I, a citizen, could fight back and try to fix a few things. Politics is a rarefied sphere, one where the love can often accentuate the hate. It's not inherently easy or logical. Not now, it isn't. Once while on the campaign trail in 2022, I was asked if I could name every standing committee in Congress. It was an inane question, designed, I think, to belittle me. But, when you have a name they say, these are the games they play. Pop had been my teacher. I'd studied him to the letter; my objective wasn't to do it the same but to do it better, where possible. I'd listened as he spoke, in particular, of Black Americans' need for a viable succession plan and a road map to pinpoint and concretize our place in politics. Pop and other policymakers like him tried to draft such a plan or, at least by example, show it to us. Mainly, they were practical. Pop, for example, considered former Klansman-turned-congressman Robert Byrd of West Virginia a political ally. The two of them were fortunate to land in Congress when Congress was a more serious, less partisan institution, seemingly more concerned about the present and future of every generation, not just themselves and their office. Congressman Byrd and Pop coalesced where they saw fit.

And they persevered in their efforts. Even if it took Pop years to make a thing happen, his labors did bear fruit for so many. Before there was Obamacare, there was my Pop's landmark legislation,

H.R.676, proposing free health care for all. Ultimately, it helped spawn President Obama's Affordable Care Act.

I know that Pop, Houston's Barbara Jordan, and Harlem's Charles Rangel were the crucial, barrier-breaking Black members of the twenty-one-person House Judiciary Committee during the historic Watergate Hearings, which prompted a lawbreaker president to resign from the Oval Office. Later, as chairman of the Judiciary Committee, Pop conducted hearings into everything from the first-ever House hearings on police brutality to the case of Lilly Ledbetter, an Alabama woman whose lawsuit against Goodyear Tire & Rubber Co. led to the nation's Fair Pay Act.

I know that three decades before the first-ever US House of Representatives subcommittee vote regarding reparations for slavery's descendants transpired in 2021—with every Republican opposing and every Democrat supporting it—Pop proposed the Commission to Study and Develop Reparation Proposals for African Americans Act. And with each new congressional session afterward, he reintroduced House Resolution 40 (H.R.40). It was named for the forty acres and a mule granted to just forty thousand freed slaves—four million had been officially emancipated in 1863—but returned to white people after President Lincoln was slain.

The commission would study how to repair, including through monetary compensation, atrocities against Blacks who landed in Virginia in August 1619. Late that month, an estimated twenty to thirty enslaved Africans were unloaded from *White Lion*, an English ship whose human cargo had been pilfered from Portuguese enslavers on a ship christened *São João Bautista*, or *Saint John the Baptist*. Between 1619 and 1865, an estimated 12.5 million African captives were transported across the Atlantic to thirty major ports stretching from New England in North America to the lower reaches of South America. An estimated 1.8 million captives died during what was a nightmarish two-month voyage and were hurled overboard into the ocean.

Five years before Lincoln's Emancipation Proclamation, enslaved Africans were this nation's largest capital asset, with a value estimated at roughly $4 billion. That would be $151.4 trillion today.

No amount of money can compensate us for the damages of slavery and its ongoing, residual effects. Not really. Not ever. But Duke University's Sandy Darity has come up with a baseline figure. "Our minimum estimate now is $16 trillion," he told me.

That figure, said Darity, the director of Duke's Samuel DuBois Cook Center on Social Equity, was based on federal data on consumer finances in 2019, which were the latest available, at the time. At that benchmark, the average white household in the United States had $1.15 million more in net worth than the average Black household. Per person, whites had about $400,000 more than Blacks. An estimated forty million Black Americans are descended from the enslaved—thus, the $16 trillion total indebted to us, if the goal is to balance the scales. "In our work, we've continued to argue that the minimum sum of a reparations payment must be an amount that's sufficient to eliminate the racial wealth gap in the United States," Darity said.

Before the start of Trump's second presidency, the national discussion about reparations was the most sustained since Reconstruction. And Darity noted what he called a "sea change in white attitudes about this." University of Chicago researchers found that 4 percent of whites supported monetary reparations for Blacks in 2000. A 2023 survey by the University of Massachusetts researchers found that 30 percent do. During the 2019–20 Democratic Party's presidential primary campaign, spiritualist author Marianne Williamson, former US Secretary of Housing and Urban Development Julián Castro, and hedge fund manager and philanthropist Tom Steyer each stated they were advocates of reparations. None of the three offered a detailed plan. Only Williamson put a price tag on reparations. "And it was very, very low," Darity recalled.

Reparations initiatives like those being pursued by local governments and local activists will not address the totality of what's owed, Darity told me emphatically. They are not an acceptable fix. Federal authorities, who control federal dollars, shouldn't be off the hook. The nation, not cities or counties, must account for and confess what it exacted from the enslaved and for the residue of slavery appearing, still, in Black bodies, Black communities, Black institutions, et al.

More than three years after Pop left Washington, in April 2021, with his signature reparations bill still heavy on his mind, my hometown newspaper wrote that the House Judiciary Committee had "advanced" H.R.40, with a vote that was along party lines. But the measure gained no traction at all in the US Senate. In the White House, President Biden reneged on a campaign promise to support reparations.

As she continued to take the lead in shepherding a reparations proposal through Washington, Texas congresswoman Sheila Jackson Lee, in early 2022, assumed the House had enough votes to pass something. But that something was a far cry from what Pop proposed. "This has been a thirty-plus-year journey," said Lee, who died in 2024. "We had to take a different approach. We had to go one by one to members explaining this does not generate a check." Should that new plan pass—it didn't—there would be hearings to gather testimony from those who are for and against reparations.

"This commission can be a healing process. Telling the truth can heal America," she said.

I am grateful that the congresswoman kept a fire lit on this. And I am shaking my head at the very idea of more formal hearings about what we already know, and at the suggestion that Black people not be paid even a fraction of what is past due to us. If it's even possible for us to be made whole, as some suggest, through reparations, the fixes must include a purely financial payment, some cash money.

Testifying before Congress in 2019, noted journalist, author, activist, and thought-leader Ta-Nehisi Coates had made it plain. "Yesterday, when asked about reparations," Coates said, "Senate Majority Leader Mitch McConnell offered a familiar reply: America should not be held liable for something that happened 150 years ago, since none of us currently alive are responsible. This rebuttal proffers a strange theory of governance, that American accounts are somehow bound by the lifetime of its generations. But well into this century, the United States was still paying out pensions to the heirs of Civil War soldiers. We honor treaties that date back some 200 years, despite no one being alive who signed those treaties."

Precisely. That's my thinking. It was my forward-thinking father's stated creed when he was still a relative newbie in Washington, working for his hometown. Way back in 1967, as Black Detroiters rebelled against injustice in their city and across the county, Pop had proposed a $30 billion fund for those who'd been systematically oppressed, dispossessed, disenfranchised, and, by other means, discriminated against.

I know my father's place in history, where he lands on the spectrum of egalitarians and of those who demand unmitigated justice for the gravely injured.

I feel, inhabit, cherish, weep at the very thought of Pop's wide-open love for me and my brother and all our kin and Detroit and slavery's children and humankind everywhere.

A favorite, instructive story about me and Pop, his love for me in full effect, is this: When I was a kindergartner, hanging out in my father's congressional office, one of his staffers asked me to do the favor of fetching a coffee. "I'm not your slaaaaavve," I shot back at Pop's employee, sounding every bit of the kindergartner that I was.

My father busted out laughing, looked me in the eye, and winked. He did not say a reprimanding word, though, in hindsight, I deserved to be chastised for "talking back" to an adult. Deference to another—a respect-commanding elder or not—is a heart-enlarging act of grace that, at times, I'm still endeavoring to extend. These days, as social-media bullying, brand building, and clout-chasing supplant good, old-fashioned hometraining and kindness, grace is a characteristic too many lack.

Pop, for the most part, was an easy, grace-giving man. By his chuckle and smile, he wasn't condoning my smart-mouthing of a grown-up. Mostly, he was signaling to a five-year-old that I had some degree of autonomy. It's a critical lesson for a Black boy growing up in a culture that, far too often, still expects Black boys to bend to the point of breaking.

And Pop did make me get that coffee. If I was going to be in his office—at the time, I had no clue of what Pop actually did for a living—I also had to somehow contribute to the work process. That do-your-part ethos? Pop drilled it into me, even as he indulged my immature, little-boy impulses.

As I've matured, I've begun to understand what Pop was trying to convey. We all—even and especially me—must extend grace. We all—even me—merit grace. How else do any of us help create some bit of heaven in this earthly realm? I conjure the sound of my father, a quietly but deeply spiritual man, planting that query and edict in my ear.

Five months after that ninetieth birthday bash, Pop did make his transition. He'd been an extraordinary man from an extraordinary era and subset of Black men, of all men. Within months of each other, Pop and civil rights giants Elijah Cummings and John Lewis, Black men who were my father's congressional colleagues and kindred spirits, also died. Only three of the thirteen original members of the pivotal Congressional Black Caucus, which Pop cofounded, were still alive on his dying day.

Whatever is true in me, whatever right intentions I possess, results largely from having studied a master, the blueprint, if you will, who surrounded himself with other tacticians in the fight for Black freedom and the liberation of all poor, cast-out, disregarded peoples. It results from sitting at my father's feet and, even when I wasn't aware, learning the lessons he taught.

CHAPTER 2

IN HIS FOOTSTEPS

Pop looked as if he was bracing himself against high wind. His torso was pitched at a slight right angle above his lower body. His head jutted up and forward, piloting us as we started our thirty-minute walk to Capitol Hill from his one-bedroom, waterfront apartment at Harbour Square co-op in Southwest Washington, DC.

Pop and I stepped out of apartment North 311 at the usual time, 9:30 a.m. We'd begun that mile-and-a-half stroll to the Rayburn House Office Building, where he and his staff were headquartered. I'd been coming to DC since the day I was born, especially during summers and holidays when I was a schoolboy. So we'd taken this walk hundreds of times together. That particular day marked my first time back in Washington since Mayor Adrian Fenty's revitalization campaign had gotten underway. Even without intending to, maybe, it was simultaneously fueling the demise of Chocolate City, as it were, and what some considered a desired renaissance of Washington, DC. Today, Black Americans have slipped into second place, behind white Americans, accounting for 45 percent of DC residents. Back home in Detroit, Black people accounted for 82 percent in 2010 and 77 percent in 2020, a downward spiral that hasn't stopped.

Pop chose to live in Southwest Washington, for its proximity to the Capitol. More than that, it kept him close to the poor and working-class Blacks residing in public housing projects that were a stone's throw from his waterfront apartment. That neighborhood was not a safe place at that juncture. It was not necessarily where one might expect someone with Pop's pedigree to reside. But he wanted it no other way. As some of his neighbors made their way to work or wherever by hopping the DC Metro's Green Line to more moneyed destinations, Pop chose to walk. He liked rubbing shoulders with his neighbors, even if just for those few blocks to the station. He asked about their well-being, about their children and their children's report cards, about what they needed from a society that had counted and pushed so many of them out. These were Pop's people. As a national lawmaker in the seat of the supposed democracy that we call America, he desperately sought to give them a voice, too.

An early sign that Pop's section of Southwest was morphing, ominously, into something else was the Safeway grocery store with shatterproof glass that went up. Another was the closing of Jenny's at the Wharf (Chinese food), one of my father's favorite restaurants. After forty years, it could no longer afford the rent.

Those calamities and the forces behind them were what drove Pop as, Monday through Friday, and often on weekends, he left Harbour Square for the US Capitol Complex. Usually, he exited that apartment building while gripping a canvas tote containing a mishmash of congressional reports and sections of the *New York Times*, *New York Review of Books*, *Mother Jones*, *Detroit Free Press*, or some miscellaneous publication he didn't finish reading between four a.m. and six a.m., the first of several cycles of his regimented workday.

Usually, my stride more closely mirrors that of an athlete. I'm quick. But on that headed-for-the-office walk, I downshifted. I matched Pop's moderate pace, partly in deference, partly because I wanted to practice Pop's pacing. He was an urgent man, but not an impulsive one. He was uber-strategic. He was studied. He was a keen observer. He cared and was concerned, chiefly but not exclusively, about Detroit and its people.

Pop had tracked an uptick in Detroit's Black population lasting all through the 1930s, 1940s, 1950s, and 1960s. It numbered almost 41,000 in 1920, the start of the decade when Pop was born, but 483,000 by 1960. (The surge continued, peaking in 1990, when roughly 780,000 of the city's one million or so residents were Black.) As he monitored Detroit's ebb and flow, Pop had gone off to serve in the US Armed Forces in the late 1940s, then returned home to finish college and law school during the 1950s. He'd further figure out his place in the Conyers family but also in American society and Detroit society. Under the one-person, one-vote proposition, Detroit should have been gaining another congressional district. The doubters, which included white Republicans with a dangerous degree of certitude and disbelieving Negroes, didn't think the area could send a second Black person to Congress. Charles Diggs, like Pop, a Democrat, was the first one. Starting in 1955, he was elected to twelve consecutive terms. No other region of the country had two Black congresspeople, the doubters argued. But my father, the young lawyer, sued to ensure that an additional district was carved out. In 1964, Michigan became the first state to have a Black duo in the House, Pop and Congressman Diggs.

The dynamic duo of Conyers and Diggs skillfully navigated the conflicts and alliances of their era, including with their own Black colleagues. When Congressman Adam Clayton Powell Jr., the famously flamboyant and whip-smart kingmaker minister from Harlem, tried to shoot down Diggs's proposal for what would become the Congressional Black Caucus, Pop was one of the main voices pushing back against Powell. "He said," Pop recalled of

Powell, "'I represent Black people. We don't need to form anything.' We said, 'Well, of course you do.' . . . There were so many issues that we couldn't keep track of unless we formed an association to report to each other what was going on in the areas of committees in the Congress upon which we were serving."

Powell had arrived in Washington two decades before Pop, the sixth Black person elected to the House in this modern era. By this time, that growing cadre of Black elected officials in Washington was expanding its focus beyond civil rights and into human rights.

On our walks, Pop shared all this history, not to boast, but as points of fact. When Pop paused, sometimes I posed a question. Sometimes I interjected, cutting him off mid-sentence. Sometimes inside our silences, I just waited. I tuned in to Pop's inhale-exhale. His walk to work also amounted to Pop's exercise.

One summer morning's walk I recall more than the others. I can't explain why it stands out, only that I felt like I was finally entering my father's universe. I'd begun to surrender some of my grievances over his many absences. I watched, during those walks, how my father set a pace. I'd never gotten to beat him in basketball, the sport I love above all. We'd never challenged each other to a game. Pop was too old, too busy, and too disinterested. It's hilarious, to me, that Pop was on the varsity basketball team at Northwestern High School, his alma mater. He couldn't have cared less about the team. Tennis was Pop's preference. He played it almost anytime, anywhere, with anyone. "I was out there just hitting the ball against a wall and watching other people play," said actor James Anderson, rapper Big Sean's dad, recalling meeting Pop on the Palmer Park courts back in the early 1990s. "The person your father had been playing with left, and your dad said, 'Hey, you wanna play?' I said, 'Oh, my God.' This is John Conyers, a Detroit icon, the quintessential politician. He gave me little pointers; he was so patient. It was a brief moment. We shook hands afterward.

It was surreal for me—because he was John Conyers, just a cool guy, a man of stature."

When I was five or six, my father bought me a racquetball racket, thinking it was best suited for a little kid learning the sport. But I couldn't care less about tennis. Not until I watched Andre Agassi and James Blake go head-to-head at the 2005 US Open did I begin to care about Pop's passion. After that match, I started watching tennis, with Pop and by myself. And what I wouldn't give, looking back on it, to have spent some time on the court with my father.

My extra-memorable day of walking with him happened in 2010. He was eighty-one; I was nineteen. He wore dress slacks, a linen shirt not buttoned all the way to the top, and a loose, lopsided necktie. His signature huarache lace-ups crafted of Mexico's signature woven leather were not, to paraphrase the iconic rapper Biggie, *pink gators* but were still *slicker than your average*. My dandy of a father overlooked my high-top Jordans and my turned-backward baseball cap. I was willfully, deliberately, dressed down.

Pop had requested that I show up in Washington that summer, boarding a slew of father-son flights between Detroit Metropolitan Airport and Reagan National Airport. It was a request unlike any of his prior invitations. He wanted me to really dig in, really observe his maneuvering around and through the Capitol, with its outsize sway in the world. He hoped I'd gain a better understanding of what droves his preoccupations inside the Beltway, along the banks of the Potomac. George Washington designated that river as the nation's river. Virginia-born Washington won his fight to make the District of Columbia, with its open-air auctioning of shackled Africans, the national capital with the help of two other Southerners, then secretary of state Thomas Jefferson and Virginia congressman James Madison. "An Act for Establishing the Temporary and Permanent Seat of the Government of the United States" was added to the Constitution in July 1790. Informally known as the Residence Act, it relocated the seat of the US government from Philadelphia to the District of Columbia. That, among other major reasons, was to appease Southern slaveholders whose ranks included Washington, Jefferson, and Madison, respectively, the first, third, and fourth US presidents.

Their embrace of chattel slavery and the evils on which it stood, concretized into the centuries-old laws, is a true-life tragedy, foundational to every legislative move Pop made. Those race hatreds, their genesis, their ongoing ground-zero devastations, and their collateral consequences are the topics Pop and I discussed when, finally, I eased up on this father of mine and agreed to not just shadow him on the job but truly heed the things that consumed him.

But as I leaned into my newly accepted apprenticeship, I still was not ready to give Pop a complete pass for missing basketball games, soccer games, a few birthdays, some hallmarks, and the low blows of my Detroit boyhood. My grievances were under the thinnest, top layer of my skin. As I shadowed my father, I also offered up my wounded, confused, combustible teen self for Pop's examination. One evening, roiling, I disrupted Pop's viewing of Bill Maher (or maybe it was Rachel Maddow). I went in on Pop: "Can we talk?"

"Sure," he answered, still fully focused on the television. "What's up?"

"You know," I said, "you were a terrible father. You were never around."

"Okay . . . So what . . . ?" was the gist of Pop's initial smackdown of my confrontation.

Years later, I made the same complaint, but with less venom: "I'm not saying you're the worst father in the world—or that you were a totally terrible father—only that you weren't there, really and truly there, all the time."

"I hear you," Pop responded, clearly hurting, too. "But I can't change that. Where do we go from here?"

Pop accepted responsibility. He made himself accountable. Holding a pint of Häagen-Dazs butter pecan ice cream in one hand and a tablespoon in the other, my father surveyed the damage. He acknowledged his truth and that of an oozing, aggrieved boy verging on manhood. And I started tiptoeing toward something like a healing.

Pop's apology also came by way of letting me be his No. 1 neophyte observer of politicians, their operatives and politics. My father was giving me space to flesh out my own thoughts and ideas. He was listening as I began trying to craft a cogent argument about this or that.

At his back, by his side, often pushing out front to open a door for him, I was gaining abundant insight into the business behind Pop's leavings from Detroit, me, my mom, and my little brother.

My resentments started melting away as I, maturing but hardly a man, relished how my father was letting me in. Along with his apologies, I picked up the pearls of wisdom he was putting down. I gleaned what I could from that soft-spoken, stately old rebel who'd, in several ways, seemed a man before his time.

"I'm backing Obama," Pop had told me, a couple of summers prior, when I was seventeen, during a morning stroll to Capitol Hill. "You know, the Clintons are our friends. Any other time, I would support Hillary. But Barack came to me asking for my support. I think he's really got a shot at this thing."

Like my father, I was a philomath. I'd been one since around the time I'd turned fifteen. I'd followed the stories. I knew Pop had broken ranks with many old guard, establishment Black leaders and rank-and-file Black voters who'd initially dismissed Barack Hussein Obama as an upstart with pipe dreams of leaping from Chi-town to the White House. They couldn't imagine that the United States of America was ready for a Black president. They did not see that we, too, merited a place in the West Wing. Black people also can operate that machine. Whether its machinations ever bend in a direction fully benefiting poor Black people and everybody remains to be seen.

But Pop dared to believe in the possibility. What might a young, Black, former community- and union-organizing, ascendant star like Obama mean for the unfinished efforts of Congressman John Conyers Jr. during his twilight?

My father's imaginings were unbridled, perhaps, especially while a Black man was in the White House. (Obama did formally endorse my father's last, winning bid for reelection.) "What we seek is not just a mere apology," Pop had insisted, as he, by then the House Judiciary Committee chairman, planned hearings on his years-old, still-pending House Resolution 40, proposing a "Commission to Study and Develop Reparation Proposals for African Americans."

"Apologies, to me, are a dime a dozen and are easily offered up," Pop had rightly argued. "But they don't change the hugely structural discrimination that has marked the history of the struggle of Black people in America.

"We want first an examination of this phenomena, and also a study of the circumstances that have led lead to structural discrimination and the great disparity statistically, in economics, employment, education, and housing in America that has created, in effect, two Americas."

My father had good reason to believe I'd someday want to pick up where he left off—he never got to conduct those reparations hearings—in improving Black and other people's quality of life. My dad was like most dads, maybe, who delight in the prospect that their offspring will carry the torch and finish the course. He did expect me to follow in his footsteps, somehow, but never to wholly emulate him. At any rate, that would have been impossible. Pop was born a decade before World War II. I showed up in 1990, a decade before the start of a new millennium. Our lives splintered in certain places, but they ran parallel in others. Shortly after Pop's high school years, my father spent time as a trumpet player in a jazz quartet. The gig paid him fifteen cents a show. "I knew I couldn't make a living that way," Pop told me.

I inherited my father's love of music. And, at first, I tried to make my way down that road. I've written for myself and others. I helped pen a Grammy-nominated song. I got no royalties for my contribution to that artistry. And the sticking point wasn't the money, it was the refusal to acknowledge my role.

In one of the last conversations I had with that performer, he thought it relevant to remind me that he was "a good-ass rapper." His skills were never in question—his response didn't settle the issue at hand. Furthermore, it did fuck all to address what I'd materially contributed to that song and three others on the album. No doubt, I was being exploited under the guise of friendship, and being denied compensation I'd earned. Songs in the pipeline that I'd contributed to would have been lucrative. At twenty-four, they would've put life-changing money in my pocket and set me up for a strong future. In the final hour of me pouring out my creative self, I was being robbed. I'd have to go back to the music publishers I'd been in talks with and tell them the work I'd actually done— work of my mind, heart, and hands—wouldn't be attributed to me. My appeal was futile. I put down the music business, just like Pop dropped his quartet.

My father went on to become a lawyer. I studied philosophy. I've been a consultant in business and entertainment. I was the founding partner of a Detroit-based, majority-Black, 100-percent-minority-owned hedge fund, set up to manage money for clients in the music and movie industries. We'd leverage connections I had in Hollywood, where Pop was a known entity and had connected me to people of influence. We'd leverage connections that one of the other partners had in the world of finance. Our third partner had worked with one of billionaire George Soros's sons. Cross Creek Pictures and DreamWorks were among the film studios we were in talks with. It was a master plan—subverted by Andrew Middlebrooks, my peer and the partner who ran off with all of what I and others had invested. The Office of the United States Attorney in Detroit charged him in 2022 with defrauding investors of more than $27 million.

I'd put every penny I had into that endeavor, which I'd severed ties with by the time federal investigators asked for my help in getting to the bottom of Andrew Middlebrooks's thievery. By then, I'd left Los Angeles for Detroit, where I prepared to run for Pop's old seat in Congress. Those two events have, at times, made me question my judgment of other people's character. But, as my peers say, "We move."

From the outside looking in, I appear to be just another person of privilege, with plenty of options in front of me. Probably, I've always appeared to be that. But, in fact, I have—like so many of my generation— at times struggled to find my footing. All that glitters, as they say, is not gold. When Pop was forced out of Congress—for his part in an unfortunate but, I'm convinced, consensual extramarital affair with the aforementioned longtime staffer—Pop's nuclear family still had a nice house on Seven Mile in Detroit. Tangibly and financially, we still have little else. Relatively speaking, we also exist paycheck to paycheck.

For my own part, I'm a capitalist, one who knows that every revolution must be financed. But Pop calculated his intrinsic value through the height, depth, and reach of the laws he made and hoped to make. Pop knew that his progressive and yet-to-be-passed Medicare for All legislation laid the foundation for Obama's Affordable Care Act in 2009, even if that disruptive law—it shook up parts of the for-profit American health care industry—still falls short of being the fuller corrective Pop desired for uninsured, under-insured, and disproportionately unhealthy Americans.

I'd lain back in the cut in Pop's congressional office one summer while Obama's then-proposed Affordable Care Act was being debated and whittled down. I watched a swarm of physicians from throughout the country show up in person to support Pop. I listened as they told Pop the reasons why they endorsed his more expansive Medicare for All, a universal health care proposal that would leave out no one. In the end, we'd be a less sick nation of people, they said. Someday, they said, Pop's bigger plan would, by necessity, become the law of the land.

I've been privy to such important discussions during those trips because I was present with Pop as we reconciled our disjointed past, honored each other, and accepted that mere men do fall short, we do fail.

A friendship blossomed. Pop and I opened up about any and everything. Business, my mother, my girlfriends, how sexually transmitted diseases of my day didn't exist in Pop's day. "Make sure you wear a condom," he cautioned.

The small talk mixed in with the heavier topics that enlivened our treks to and from Capitol Hill each day.

Returning from ten or twelve or fifteen hours spent with Pop navigating Congress and me, on many levels, trying to keep up with him, we settled into a rhythm. We took a load off. We let the night move in the opposite direction of a hurried dawn. We listened to John Coltrane, or Adele, or some other favorite of Pop's. We were together, granting each other space and grace.

When we switched off the lights and whatever night music Pop had chosen, I'd hit the pullout couch. Pop took to his bedroom, until his internal clock prodded him to rise again at four a.m. for what was his meditation: Poring over headlines and congressional reports, listening for his guiding God, throwing back a glass of cold milk.

At six a.m., he catnapped. At eight a.m., he answered his chief of staff's dial-in about that day's congressional committee agendas, floor votes, and whatnot. These cycles beckon me now, but I slept a lot more than him then.

"John Conyers Jr. and John Conyers III," Pop reminded me, "are two different individuals. We might have the same last name, but you're your own man."

When one door has closed, we seek entry by other means.

"What we do," Pop said, "is persist."

CHAPTER 3

UP FROM BLACK BOTTOM

"Those drumsticks are for your daddy. Do *not* touch them."

That was my mother's command at the start of Sunday supper. I was a child just starting to comprehend that Pop was not the average father. The one impenetrable rule at our family's Detroit dinner table was that the drumsticks were Pop's alone. There was flesh, bone, fat, muscle, and lived history in a chicken leg.

My pop's infatuation with drumsticks dated back to his boyhood in Detroit's legendary Black Bottom neighborhood, which, at its peak, was home to 150,000 middle- and working-class Black people. The adjacent Paradise Valley commercial district was comprised of three hundred largely Black-owned businesses. Hotels, bars, restaurants, doctors' offices, drug stores, dry cleaners, barbershops, hair salons. It was a self-sustaining, self-contained, self-determining community of people who'd, initially, been forced into Black Bottom and neighborhoods akin to it by laws banning them from white neighborhoods. Multiple families sometimes were packed into tiny homes for which they paid far too much in rent.

But deprivations intended to hold them back didn't stop Black strivers from bettering Black Bottom. In addition to Pop, that community catapulted such notables as world heavyweight champion

Joe Louis, United Nations' mediator and Nobel Peace Prize winner Ralph Bunche, singer and actress Della Reese, and Coleman Young, Detroit's first Black mayor.

My father was born in Black Bottom—a name given for the area's fertile soil, first farmed by the French but often misconstrued because of its majority-Black population—in 1929. That year, Charles Bowles, a white lawyer, was elected Detroit's mayor with major support from the Ku Klux Klan. Its surging Michigan membership, which included whites who'd also migrated up from the South, numbered up to thirty thousand during the 1920s and 1930s. That era was part of the sixty-year-long Great Migration of six million Black Southerners to the North, where factories were paying far more than a sharecropper would ever earn. The Detroit KKK's notorious Black Legion, which wore black robes instead of the Klan's signature white ones, killed fifty Black people between 1931 and 1936. "As a boy, I'd seen African Americans pulled off streetcars and beaten in the streets of Detroit," Pop recalled of horrors he, then a fourteen-year-old, witnessed during what I call the 1943 Detroit race rebellion. History books call it a "race riot," which almost always implies that Black people were running amok, rather than defending themselves against white aggression. Pop didn't take it lightly, he said, that he "somehow was able to avoid being lynched."

Ignited by dueling, false rumors of race-based crimes, including that a Black woman and her baby had been thrown into the Detroit River, the rebellion lasted for two days in June. Of the thirty-four people who were killed—mostly by white police—twenty-five were Black. Of the 433 who were wounded, 75 percent were Black.

As they've done throughout much of American history, white officials blamed Black people, and Black youth, in particular, for the mayhem. The National Association for the Advancement of Colored People (NAACP) cited, among other causes, job discrimination, housing shortages, and police brutality. Much later, an analysis concluded that the white rioters mainly were young and jobless, the very characteristics—except in reverse—white officials tried to pin on Black youth involved in the devastation.

My father had come from people who subsisted on the margins. Pop's father, John James Conyers Sr., was a Georgia-born school dropout and laborer. In Detroit, he excelled as few Black men of his time did. He got hired and fired from a small succession of jobs in a burgeoning auto industry where the color of one's skin sometimes determined one's salary. Henry Ford, Ford Motor Company's founder, was paying Black workers the same as whites, persuaded to do so by several Black pastors. When my grandfather's employer, Chrysler, didn't follow suit, he took his protest straight to the top boss's office. "Why," he asked titan Walter Chrysler, "does a Negro man earn less than a white man for the same day's work?"

My grandfather died on New Year's Day in 1986 before I was born. He had painted cars for Chrysler and was among Black workers earning ten cents less per hour than white Chrysler employees.

My grandfather would go on to become a founding father of the United Auto Workers, organizing and serving as steward of UAW Local 7. By the early 1940s—up against the ex-felons, ex-cops, and gangsters who were hired vigilantes for Ford Motors, which was hardly benevolent, after all— my grandfather had become the lead organizer of a campaign that unionized ninety thousand men and women at Ford's Dearborn, Michigan, plant. My father was eight years old when he watched his father get attacked. The hired thugs also battered my pioneering granddad, who retreated from combat on the work front into the safety of his household in Black Bottom.

The first time my grandfather saw Lucille Jane Simpson, who was up from her native Mississippi, she was wearing a fly, flashy pink coat, spending leisure time at Belle Isle Park. "She was like, 'Oh, that coat snagged me that one,'" my first cousin Ellen Conyers, a Michigan attorney, told me, recalling how Grandma Lucille caught my grandfather's eye.

"Lucille was a very, very strong woman," Ellen said of our grandmother, who bought me my first baseball bat and put a basketball in my toddler hands. She loved sports and was a die-hard fan of the Detroit Lions. "She'd grab Stinky, a stray cat she got off the golf course," Ellen said, "and crack open a brew and we'd watch the game with her right in the house on Seven Mile. This was long before Uncle John got married."

Lucille Simpson Conyers, my grandfather's wife and Pop's mom, was a pretty woman who was "strong, physically, psychologically, and emotionally," she said. "She cast a remarkable shadow. She had a husband that was often jailed. She was, in effect, a single parent raising four boys alone a lot of the time. 'He may be gone, but I've got this household, I've got this family.' She was making sure her boys were going to leave an imprint, a positive one, in their local community, in the wider community, and ultimately, perhaps unbeknownst at the time, nationally. They were going to do something to make a difference, first in their household, and, from there, the circle would continue to broaden."

Ellen, the fourth youngest of Uncle Nate's five children, remembers how our grandmother kept her house Easter Sunday clean. Every single day, it seemed, her kitchen stove spilled over with pots and pans of food she'd heap onto platters for the dining table. "Turkeys, hams, rolls, macaroni and cheese, everything was made from scratch. And she also had that plastic on the furniture in the living room. . . .

"Our grandmother saved soap chips, and I'm talking the size of a quarter. You couldn't do much with one, but if you've got a hundred of those suckers, you can make something happen with that."

When Uncle Nate was around five or six, my grandmother put him in charge of rolling a red wagon of vegetables and other groceries to and from their Black Bottom home on market day. "What I'm not going to do is let the handle on this wagon go," Uncle Nate, reminiscing, once told Ellen. "Somebody may be playing basketball over there, and I may really want to watch, but I'm not letting this handle go." That was the unspoken vibe he got from my grandmother.

Lucille Simpson Conyers was not the demure, silent type. She looked a person in the eye. She was confident. She loved to laugh. Her laughter came often, easily, and was full-bodied. "And they didn't grow up in a time when they had a lot to laugh and smile and joke about," Ellen reminded me. "They faced very serious, dire circumstances every day. Poverty, racism, economics. They had it coming at them at every angle."

Clarence L. Jones, Grandma Lucille's Mississippi-born nephew, the son of Allen Jones and Callie Simpson Jones, said he was twelve or thirteen when he went into the fields with others in his family. "Cotton, corn, potatoes, and peanuts . . . The white man owned the fields. We worked in August until school started in the fall," Cousin Clarence told me, encapsulating the place that birthed my grandmother.

Charlotte Simpson, my grandmother's mother, was a domestic. My grandmother's father, Cousin Clarence told me, was "ol' man Jess Robinson." Robinson was Charlotte's white employer, a man who owned a sheet metal business and leased his land to Black sharecroppers. "Aunt Lucille was my mama's sister, the second child. She grow'd up in Mississippi and left there as a little girl. Aunt Roxy, my mama's mama's sister, came down from Chicago and got Lucille. Later on, they moved to Detroit. This is the story my mama told me," said Cousin Clarence, who left Mississippi for New Orleans about a decade after he graduated from high school in 1963.

"My mama told me Aunt Lucille was a good child, but she didn't like to work. Their mama would say, 'Now you gone wash the dishes after e'r'body finishes.' And Lucille would just go to sleep." Cousin Clarence and I laughed at that.

Three of my great-grandmother Charlotte Simpson's seven children were by white men. She'd chosen them as fathers, Cousin Clarence said. I'd been told that my grandmother was the product of rape. "No, Lucille's mama was not forced. She went with that man. His wife musta know'd because, one time, she sent one of their workers, a Black man, down to take a look at Lucille. He went back and said, 'Naw, she dark.' If he hadn't, they woulda killed her.".

My grandmother did love hosting her Mississippi kin in Detroit, where, my elderly cousin figured, she'd decided to keep parts of history to herself. "When we'd go to Detroit, John and Nate used to ask my mama who was Lucille's daddy. My mama would say, 'Ask Lucille.' She knew who her daddy was and who her sisters and brothers were on the white side. We lived in the same neighborhood, in walking distance of each other. Even if they didn't know her, she knew them."

There were some hard truths in his aunt Lucille's story, said Cousin Clarence, whose mother was the first of Charlotte's seven and had a Black father. Charlotte did not like her appearance. "She was dark as soot and had short hair," he said.

There's something about disliking who you are that can make you do crazy things. It's why an increasing number of voters of color profess adoration and support for a person like Trump, who's won the backing of closeted and cloaked members of the KKK and other racist groups.

My grandmother was born forty-four years after Lincoln freed the slaves. She died in 2000. Her life is not far apart from my life; her time is not far apart from these times. The present facts of racism, overlaid with my grandmother's origin story, give me an overwhelming perspective, so many things to ponder and to act on. Her backstory must have been where so much of her strength came from.

My paternal grandfather and grandmother bore up against racism as a team. They came together in strength and cooperation. They were confidants, two parts of a brain trust. She, who'd later become a chief architect of Pop's winning congressional races by launching "Women for Conyers" in 1963, helped my grandfather problem-solve what he confronted as a worker and union organizer.

My homemaker grandmother doted on her man. She would often set aside my grandfather's favorite piece of chicken. They signified something about the young Conyers clan's slow but steadily rising social and financial status in their adopted hometown. Those drumsticks suggested something about my grandfather's role at work but also his position as the cherished servant and lord of his home.

There simply were not enough drumsticks to share evenly in what eventually would be a household of six. (When she was two years old, my grandparents' firstborn of five children, a girl, died of accidental burn wounds that got infected when my grandmother treated them with butter, a common home remedy of the time.) So the rationing of chicken also signified what remained of my grandparents' progression toward, someday, never lacking enough of what they needed. Like many other Black people of their time and place, the Depression-era Conyers family had one foot figuratively stuck in Southern fields of cotton, cane, tobacco, and indigo that they'd escaped. The other foot was kicking through doorways of opportunity up north that were often being shut in their faces. Up there, when segregationists leveled a threat akin to "boy, stay in your place," a Michigan accent may have been the only thing distinguishing them from Southern terrorists. Whatever Black folks got, too often, they had to take by force.

Saddling up to his father at the Conyers clan's Black Bottom dinner table, Pop, as a youngster, had fixated on the sight and sound of his father eating what he considered the best part of the chicken. (Pop and my grandmother handed down the story to my mom, Monica Ann Esters Conyers. She kept the tradition going.) That food symbolized much more than bodily nourishment.

He would need to draw from various reservoirs of strength, Pop said, for what lay ahead, from his boyhood onward. Watching white mobs drag Black people from streetcars and bludgeon them during that race rebellion in 1943 was an awakening for Pop. But, at fourteen years old, what more could he do but store away that trauma, making use of it at a later date?

He burrowed into school. He was exceptionally smart, even then. He breezed through his academics while skipping class to play pool some days. Sometimes, in the evenings, he'd sneak his underage self into one of Detroit's several bustling jazz clubs. He'd buy a beer as if to prove he was grown, but Pop never became much of a drinker.

With music his always-and-forever passion, his enduring first love, Pop played trumpet and lettered in that instrument as a member of the band at Northwestern High School. He also studied bass, piano, tenor saxophone, and trombone. He surrounded himself with musicians. His high school classmate Betty Carter's jazz vocals made her a star. Vibraphonist Milt Jackson was born in Detroit a half dozen years or so before Pop. Saxophonist Sonny Stitt was a regular on Detroit's jazz scene when Pop was a teen. (Years later, Pop's Wayne State University buddies, Detroiters, would include composer and pianist Tommy Flanagan and jazz guitarist Kenny Burrell. Ultimately, saxophonist John Coltrane would join Pop's roll call of friends in jazz.)

In 1954, with his high school diploma in hand but no money for college, my grandfather's influence got Pop a spot-welder job at a Lincoln auto plant. There, Pop also became the director of his UAW local unit.

When he wasn't at the plant, Pop took night classes to complete chemistry and physics basics he'd not obtained in high school. On a union scholarship in the late 1940s, he began studying civil engineering.

But the Korean War, on the other side of Pop's world, interrupted that.

From that war, Pop mailed an important typewritten letter, dated February 29, 1953, and postmarked from Kunsan, Korea, where Pop, a dispatched US serviceman, had been refusing to put himself on track toward becoming a US Army Corps of Engineers officer. He'd told me that his higher-ups in the military, in which he'd enlisted in 1948, initially as a Michigan National Guardsman, thought he could rise to their level. But that was their plan, not Pop's. That letter hinted at his desires.

Inked almost five years after President Eisenhower's executive order desegregating the US Armed Services, that missive was addressed to Uncle Nate, Pop's twenty-three-year-old baby brother. By 1945, as one global conflict tapered off and another was cranking up, 2.5 million Black men had registered for the draft, even as their homeland hung "Whites Only" bathroom or water fountain signs and other notices of race restrictions down south and imposed less flagrant but still stultifying limits across the fifty states. Of those military draft registrants, roughly 1 million—less than a tenth of the nation's then 12.6 million Blacks—were primed for battle and sent overseas.

Pop's four-paragraph note to Uncle Nate mentioned nothing of what was happening on that air force base, with its army soldiers, air force pilots, civilian workers, and so forth. Rather, that letter home to Detroit concerned family business. It made clear how much Pop, his brother, and their father were intent on building a Conyers dynasty: "As I type this letter now, I think of how obsolete and penny-ante this letter will become after we are established in a family enterprise toward which we are now striving. I have had the opportunity to do a lot of research—perhaps more than I would have been able to do had I not been in such a place as I am now. I have casually traced the causes and conditions which cause some families to become financially at ease. And in practically all cases, including those who became multimillionaires, their beginnings were extremely humble."

The further details of that letter were Pop's two cents about a leased apartment that the family owned and my grandfather oversaw. At that time, the tenant had slithered away without paying her rent. Pop wrote of his surprise that my grandfather was so anxious, bordering on fretful, about the real estate exam that he was prepping for. Pop mentioned the $300 that my grandfather and Uncle Nate had pooled to buy a new car. He urged Uncle Nate to also take the Realtor's exam.

When Pop returned from overseas, my grandfather continued to be instrumental in shaping Uncle Nate's and my father's careers. A coin toss determined which of those two boys would have the political career their dad might have sought in a less racialized America and which would be the businessman he'd dreamed of morphing into. "Heads or tails?" my grandfather asked, matter-of-factly, flinging a fifty-cent piece skyward as Uncle Nate's and Pop's eyes followed. It was a perfunctory, but punctuating gesture. By the time the coin landed, it was decided that Uncle Nate would be the politician. But his wife, Aunt Diana Howze Conyers, a teacher who'd put him through law school, wasn't having it. Uncle Nate would stay in Detroit to mind his growing, young family. Uncle Nate would continue on the course set with the joint purchase of that new car. Pop would run for elected office once he returned from Korea.

Both the brothers would earn degrees from Wayne State Law School, paying their way with what they'd earned as veterans eligible for the GI Bill. Nathan G. Conyers—the smart, funny, cool, charismatic counterpoint to the studied reserve of big brother John, the one bound ultimately to Washington—would go on to open several lucrative Ford auto dealerships and such spin-off ventures as an auto-body shop in the Motor City. He became the first president of the National Black Dealers Association, which he'd cofounded with my godfather, Jesse Jackson, in 1970. That same year, Uncle Nate opened his first dealerships on West Grand, smack dab in inner-city Detroit. There, systemically, residents had been economically redlined and refused.

In a Facebook post of remembrance, a photograph of my father's father, who eventually would join the UAW's international C-suite, did get shared among the Conyerses' circles upon circles of kin, friends, and associates. My grandfather's rise from shop steward to UAW executive made headlines in the *New York Times*, *Detroit Free Press*, *Detroit News*, and almost every publication of what then was a more vibrant Black press. They chronicled his solidarity with American workers and his special allegiance to Black people.

I can't begin to imagine how much his boys' coordinated endeavors, their separate and joint successes, confirmed for my grandfather that he'd been a fine parent and a fine example of Black manhood, of Black personhood. His boys were upstanding citizens and trusted stewards of the community.

What my grandparents set in motion, Pop and his brother kept going, though not always in ways I'd desire. Uncle Nate eventually sold his car dealership to folks with no blood ties to the Conyers clan whatsoever. Still, with this fitful family history as a catalyst, how best to steward our legacy remains my prime objective. Not long ago, I watched actor and director Erika Alexander's documentary about reparations, *The Big Payback*. It made mention of my father's name, almost anecdotally, as if his contribution to the movement via his pioneering legislation, H.R.40, was not the foundation of the efforts we see today. Furthermore, it failed to take into account his strategy and reasoning behind the call for a study, as opposed to legislation that actually sought financial relief for descendants of slaves. Not only, in my mind, is there an erasure of my father's imprint; his name also doesn't come up often or broadly enough in the ongoing discussion of Medicare for All or of the political history around police reform, sparked by police brutality, where he played such a substantial role. Ensuring the work done in my father's house is both my blessing and my burden—that work and example is a legacy he left for all of us, and I won't allow his part in history be erased.

CHAPTER 4

FAMILY WE CHOOSE

Beano struggled to form his words. He paused to clear his throat; his voice trembled. He tried again to speak but, instead, stammered. I knew something was very wrong. Beano had never, ever dialed me crying and struggling to collect himself.

Finally, he muttered the news that drop-kicked my heart into an ocean of sadness: "Bydia *self*-transitioned this morning."

"What? . . . Huh? How? . . . No!" A flash flood of tears poured from my eyes as I sent those frantic, rapid-fire questions across my phone line in Detroit to Beano's in New York City, where word came of Bydia's death by suicide.

My body bent forward, involuntarily. I slumped on the steps leading to my old bedroom in the house on Seven Mile, where I'd been sifting through some of Pop's congressional papers. Stunned, I waited for answers that would never come. Beano had gone silent. Right then, at 1:30 p.m. on a Monday in September 2023, a calendar alert sounded and surfaced on the face of my iPhone. *Call Bydia*, it read.

Nine months prior, on New Year's Day, I'd promised myself that I'd check in more often with each of my most intimate friends, folks I'd met, perhaps by serendipity, then deliberately clung to.

Our crew—we call ourselves the House of Homage—includes my contemporaries, a few of my elders, and me. We are a diverse group with commonly held but also divergent points of view. We nurture these connections. We ponder the disconnects sometimes. We give to and gain from each other. Everything that the treasured members of this group are and stand for, their attributes, and their faults, help to sharpen me. The House of Homage gets me closer to being my optimum self. My friends are the mirror I set before me. Every member, Bydia included, has been an essential person.

Sitting on the steps, as grief dug in deeper, I swatted at my tears with one hand. With the other, I held my cell phone in front of my face, staring point-blank at that calendar notification. *Call Bydia*. Thoughts and visions of my funny, flamboyant, fly-dressing, life-of-the-party brother-from-another-mother stampeded through my brain. Which of our shared ideas about music and entrepreneurship and community building could not come to fruition in his absence, in his permanently disappearing himself from this plane?

Bydia's death, when he was thirty-five, came during a prolonged period of staggering losses for me. Eleven months before Bydia, my cousin Deonte, who was thirty-one, also became one of the ancestors, ascending to where sheltering angels and gone-too-soon spirits reside. But my fuller season of being run down by death had started in 2016. Across a span of three years, I'd said a last goodbye to Aunt Rhonda and Aunt Gulinda, both of whom died of cancer. Liver failure from alcoholism took out Uncle Robert.

In 2019, the same year that we buried Pop, whose only frailty was old age, two of my cousins were shot to death. Antoine was twenty-nine. Marcel was twenty-seven. In that agonizing stretch of time, to borrow from Sade's "Soldier of Love" lyric, "I've lost the use of my heart but I'm still alive."

In 2021, as the pandemic was coming off its peak but still raging, COVID-19 killed Darryl, my bighearted, burly cousin.

Without me even asking him to, he had doubled as my trusted older brother for longer than I can even remember. Darryl, a fellow Detroiter, my aunt Gulinda's firstborn, was thirty-six. For me, Darryl modeled how to be a better big brother to my only sibling, Carl, who came into the world when I was five. Often, I had been clumsy and overbearing with Carl, a much gentler soul than I. Darryl helped me to understand a brother's juggling act, his roles as a protector, a sounding board, a partner who also gives a sibling room to be and to stand on his own.

Carl, others in my inner circle, and I share bonds greater than mere DNA. We comprise a special unit. We have chosen these relationships to be touchpoints for each other. This self-selecting, tightly woven, chosen family has helped me to own and grapple with every aspect of my being, the best and worst of it, the top-of-the-mountain me and the me who sometimes has been in the wilderness.

Bobbo, another Detroit cousin, reminds me I'd been *that* wild kid, from the jump. I was the one who sometimes needed to check myself. I was the one who'd throw a tantrum when things didn't go my way. I was spoiled, the crybaby in our tier of first cousins and family friends. I'd get frustrated if we'd been outside playing basketball—I am, today, still, a trash-talking, skilled hooper, despite being vertically challenged—and someone else decided we should head indoors for video games. If the video game happened to be mine and I wanted to play first, I'd snatch the controller from one of my cousins' hands. If I lost a battle, I'd unplug the game or dart from wherever I stood or sat and click the game off. If someone beat me, I'd insist on a do-over, again, and again, and again, however many times it took for me to win, or until I'd worn myself out. In my head, I had the same competitive fire as NBA great Michael Jeffrey Jordan. I'd been watching him since I was a boy. I'd been collecting every book and every VHS tape about him. As he helped to eulogize the late, great, gone-too-soon Kobe Bryant, Jordan described their level of competitiveness as a curse, a double-edged thing. That curse also has afflicted me.

"This shit is still going on. We just aren't playing video games no more," said Bobbo, laughing but only half joking about me. We were reflecting on our time as kids, how we were and how we have evolved into men.

Bobbo made that observation after I and the people dearest to me, who believe in me most, were in postmortem mode, regrouping still from my unsuccessful primary run in 2022 to be the Democratic candidate vying for Pop's old seat. Shortly after I announced my candidacy in March of that year, the initial polls slotted me as the No. 1 contender in a field of nine. It included a former state legislator, a former Detroit Police Department chief, a nonprofit executive, and a then state legislator/pharmaceutical executive/carpetbagger, Shri Thanedar. Based on responses from 43 percent of likely voters, according to pollsters, it was projected that I would garner 19 percent of the votes. Several pundits attributed that early lead to my name being Pop's name. I was, in that way, familiar to a large chunk of the electorate.

Five months later, though, things had switched up. When the primary election was over, I'd slipped to No. 4 among the nine, winning less than half of those initially projected votes, 8.6 percent. Thanedar, the victor, got 28.3 percent.

My defeat forced me to confront, as my father had explained, the long-range fallout of the US Supreme Court ruling in favor of the conservative nonprofit Citizens United. That 2010 decision allowed corporations and special interest groups to spend, without limits, on political races. A well-organized, well-messaged, and meaningful campaign is no match for a well-funded one, Pop had said. And I'd been exponentially outspent in 2022. My mentors and advisers tried to encourage me, during our election postmortem, by reminding me that I'd won more votes per dollar spent on the race. But they knew me better than that; I don't believe in moral or Pyrrhic victories. I lost.

Though that overly competitive kid still lives in me, Bobbo has noted how not winning has also proven to be instructive for me. Thanedar's surprise victory, for one, led me to dive into a trove of congressional documents, books, newspaper clippings, and archives that are part of my inheritance from Pop but also what Pop left for anyone else who might want to pore over and glean from what he'd methodically designed and etched as a politician. What was his focus while on the campaign trail? What might we borrow from that? Build upon?

As I create my road map, I share the blueprint Pop outlined in those recordings and such with Bobbo and everyone else in our close-knit circle of relatives and friends. Pop's blueprint shows how life and its inevitable losses do shape an individual.

En route to becoming a better me, the impulses that once unwittingly sabotaged the younger me are controlled. The passion that once unintentionally conveyed anger is now subdued, projecting the importance of a matter in only the strictest, most select circumstances. Constantly, I am studying myself as part of the process of refining my personhood and humanity. I do that with the indispensable counsel of my people, my community, my private party of confidants, creatives, thinkers, and doers. As a collective, we stretch from the East Coast to the West Coast, North to South. Mainly, we are Black. Mainly, we are men, but we count and welcome a few women among us. One of them is the entertainment-arts whiz I refer to as Cousin Sonya, though, technically, we aren't related. Her cousin was my mom's best friend in high school and, later, a college classmate. When I was marginally homeless in New York City—couch surfing while getting a taste of that metropolis and testing my chops as a songwriter, producer, and performer in rap music—Sonya found someone willing to rent me a room. That $700-a-month sublet was in the heart of Harlem, a spot on 149th Street and Broadway. Sonya advised me to be respectful of my temporary landlord's property to avoid the risk of overstaying my welcome: "It's not just about the rent you pay, it's really about the respect you give."

She was giving me rules to live by, gems that helped me cultivate a true Empire State Of Mind. They applied to much more than my one-room rental while I was in that legion of out-of-state transplants trying to find their way in New York, the concrete jungle where dreams are made and more often dashed.

So many people have generously imparted their wisdom to me. They have handed me their material, physical, and other support as I sort myself and my issues out. At fifteen, I was diagnosed with major depressive disorder, which I manage through a regimen of good food and exercise. While I do depend on a trusted, credentialed clinician for what will be a lifetime of mental health care, my tribe's counsel has proven critical to my well-being. Sometimes, I feel as though I barely deserve their generosity or that level of forbearance from my precious tribe. Still, they give it.

"Confess your sins to one another and pray for one another, that you may be healed." That's in the Bible. It's a creed, even if unspoken, that I and those dearest to me live by as we go along, shifting, stretching, bending, and growing.

Once, dashing through our dorm room door, I yelled over my shoulder to Terrence, my roommate, that I was late for a dinner date with one of my uncles.

"Which one?" he'd asked.

"Uncle Bill," I told Terrence, who has been a constant presence since we stepped on the grounds of Morehouse College in fall 2008 as members of its freshmen class.

"Uncle Bill?" Terrence batted back.

"Bill Clinton."

I dropped the detail like it was nothing special. Terrence, as he informed me later, was speechless.

But this was the norm for me. One of my two godfathers was the Honorable Damon Jerome Keith, a Black civil rights and civil liberties icon. Like Pop and his brother, my uncle Nate, Uncle Damon was a Wayne State Law alum. Uncle Damon went on to clock fifty years of breaking barriers while holding forth from the federal bench in Michigan. He was the one who'd ruled it unconstitutional for the Nixon administration's CIA to wiretap conversations of activists in Ann Arbor. He was the one who ordered Pontiac schools to bus students, a 1970 ruling that was a first of its kind up north. It paved the way for busing as a tool to desegregate schools throughout the region.

In May of 2016, when Uncle Nate accompanied Pop on a visit to the White House to celebrate his eighty-sixth birthday, President Obama overheard Nate mention that, before becoming a big-time auto dealer, he'd been a law partner of Damon Jerome Keith. "What!" Harvard Law–trained Obama had exclaimed. His earlier roles as an attorney in Chicago and Illinois state senator had given him ideological and regional proximity to that judge. Fascinated by Uncle Nate's connection to the judge, Obama took Nate aside for a whole separate conversation about Uncle Damon.

In the annals of American history, my godfather was that important. Like Pop, he didn't make much fuss about his work. They were of a time when the proof was in the work, as Pop would say, when public servants and leaders were not so obsessed with patting themselves on the back. In 2019, the judge died, at age ninety-six, six months before Pop did. Before he transitioned, I had several amazing years of getting to know him. He was earthy and approachable. Each year, he hosted an open house at the US District Court for the Eastern District of Michigan. The line of attendees for that soul food luncheon would spread down the block and around the corner in downtown Detroit. I saw that they were anybody and everybody and those who considered themselves to be somebody and those who were not quite sure. That courthouse belonged to taxpayers. Much like Pop's open-door policy at his office, Uncle Damon's annual luncheon was a way for the people to be in proximity to the law without being subjected to its penalties. The professionals running those courtrooms are charged with administering equal justice under the law; the people's job is ensuring that justice is served.

"Listen to your father," Uncle Damon, who was still in office on the day he died, used to tell me.

Pop, the lawmaker, and Uncle Damon, the law keeper, saw themselves as a team. They formed a brotherhood. Apart from each other, they could not perform their duties. And they knew that.

My other godfather is Rev. Jesse L. Jackson, former presidential candidate, former District of Columbia shadow representative in the US Senate, founder of Operation PUSH, and another extraordinary, history-making hell-raiser. Now an old man, he has kept his promise to Pop that he'd watch over and help shepherd me for as long as he's able. The last time I dialed just to check in and say hello, Uncle Jesse, slowed by Parkinson's disease, could muster little more than a mumble. I could hear him, feel him laboring to offer more. But it was enough for me that he took the time to pick up the phone. It's enough that I've committed Uncle Jesse's quick-witted quips to memory. And I do what he urged me to do, speaking with the preacher's cadence and cautions he's been known for: "Fight the good fight. Do the right thing. Don't get in your own way."

I'm honored to have ongoing access to that beloved man and, among others, President Clinton. When I couldn't attend Uncle Bill's February 1999 state dinner, where Ghanaian president Jerry John Rawlings was the honored guest, Uncle Bill wrote the kindest keepsake of a note on the place card that had been prepared for me:

To John III, I missed you tonight. Hoping you're well,
Bill Clinton.

Uncle Bill, the so-so saxophonist, and Pop shared a vibe. Music captivated them, mutually. They had charm, charisma, and appeal, but also a deference that made them appear as Everyman in other folks' eyes. Pop and Uncle Bill masterfully worked a room brimming with people; both finessed a one-on-one chat, whether on the campaign trail or in some quiet spot off the beaten track. Making genuine connections to average folks and the high-and-mighty alike came second nature to them.

In politics, Uncle Bill and Pop had some common causes. And sometimes they disagreed, famously. Clinton's full-throated embrace of the Violent Crime Control and Law Enforcement Act of 1994 was one seismic point of dispute between him and Pop. Authored by then congressman Joe Biden, it was supported, at the time, by several Black mayors and 58 percent of Black citizens, according to a Gallup Poll that couldn't possibly gauge or forecast what would happen next. Some Black folks can be as shortsighted and impressionable as anyone else when it comes to addressing the root of a problem, not just its most glaring and troublesome symptoms. The tough on crime policies of that landmark crime control law fueled a more-than-two-decades-long surge in the over-incarceration of Black bodies, most of them male. A disproportionate number were accused of nonviolent crimes, particularly drug-related ones.

At a 2016 campaign event for his wife, who was seeking the Democratic Party's presidential nomination, Clinton falsely claimed that the crime bill ushered in "a twenty-five-year low in crime, a thirty-three-year low in the murder rate." His embellishment was supposed to make it appear that he was making inroads against what was framed as an intractable crime problem whose accompanying spike in incarceration rates extended back to the 1960s. During the 1970s, as chairman of the House Subcommittee on Crime, Pop crisscrossed the country conducting hearings whose experts included elected officials, academics, grassroots organizers, and formerly incarcerated people. In city after city, he spotlighted FBI and federal Bureau of Labor Statistics research linking a whole array of crimes to joblessness, homelessness, lack of education, and a host of other social problems. On this fraught matter, on the sexual exploitation of children, on policing, on police misconduct, and on other issues of crime and criminal justice policy, Pop was prescient.

"Unemployment Is Killing Black People" is how Pop titled a 1977 Congressional Black Caucus report. "Homicide, most of it gun-related," Pop wrote, "has exceeded heart attack and accidents as the leading cause of death for black males between the ages of 15 and 44. . . . Of the 125,000 heroin addicts in New York City, it is estimated 46 percent are black. . . . The prison population is increasing 10 percent each year and by 1986, if present trends continue, over half a million persons will be incarcerated, 70 percent of them black. . . . Young people, under age 25, comprise 63 percent of total police arrests. . . .

"Is there any connection in these circumstances that are so destructive to the black community? Of course, there is. The single most important cause of homicide, narcotics addiction, teen-age crime, and overflowing prison population is the incredible desperation of millions who are without jobs, income, self-respect, and hope. Their frustration triggers desperation and violence."

The 1994 crime bill did include funds for preventive programs aimed at shielding young people from the degradations of poverty and other dysfunctions that can steer them down a path toward prison or result in police profiling that also takes them there. But too much of its emphasis was on combating crime through arrest, conviction, and incarceration. While some pundits and others argue that it's unfair to blame the 1994 law, in totality, for what is the world's highest rate of incarceration, the role that the crime bill continues to play cannot be dismissed. You don't allocate, as the crime bill did, $9.7 billion for state prison construction without expecting that those warehouses would operate at their per-prisoner capacity, if not over capacity.

Pop and a minority of Congressional Black Caucus members—twelve out of the thirty-eight—voted against that bill. (Overall, the Caucus had opposed the bill's support of capital punishment, which disproportionately is meted out against Black and Brown detainees.) Among them was "Auntie Maxine," otherwise known as California congresswoman Maxine Waters, a firebrand who, though not my blood relative, is part of the Conyers clan. To this day, her politics reflect much of what she and Pop held in common as legislators aiming, somehow, to be outsiders inside of Washington's Beltway.

Sometimes my friends ran around Washington with me and Pop. He loved sharing that place with them. He couldn't resist asking what they knew of Washington's effects on even the minutiae of their everyday lives, their families' lives, their neighbors' lives. Did they clearly understand how every single thing was connected? Pop listened for their answers. He chopped it up with them. He wanted to know, for real.

Most of my friends were born in the late 1980s. We were barely in our twenties when Occupy Wall Street burst through to challenge inequality, corporate greed, corporate money in politics, gazillionaire fat cats and their kind who, according to Federal Reserve data in 2023, had amassed wealth amounting to $38.7 trillion. That was 26.5 percent of all household wealth in the United States. The number of people worth more than $10 million doubled between

2000 and 2023, the same period when those worth more than $100 million quadrupled.

Twenty-six percent of the nation's wealth was held by the middle class, which comprised roughly 50 percent of US income earners in 2021, down from 60 percent in 1971. Three percent of that wealth belonged to the bottom fifth.

What's more, the US middle class dwindled in size every decade between 1971 and 2011. During that time, the share of adults across all races who were upper income increased by seven percentage points, rising to 21 percent from 14 percent. But those who were lower income spiked, rising to 29 percent from 25 percent of all US adults.

In 2012, as the middle class was declining and the tally of poor people was growing, Occupy Wall Street protests kicked off next to the eleven-foot tall, seven-thousand-pound Charging Bull anchoring the Financial District in New York City, which remains the No. 1 global financial center (ahead of No. 2 London and No. 3 Singapore, an international tax haven). A symbol of America's by-the-bootstraps, wealth-making ingenuity to many, that bronze sculpture of a rampaging bull is sacrilege. It reveres a sell-your-soul capitalism that's strictly bent on making a dollar—no matter who it crushes in the process—and excludes a whole heap of folks. It seems that there is a long list of china shop owners who could have warned us about bulls and things trampled. I wonder when they'll ban those books, too.

When Occupy Wall Street challenged the political and economic policies protecting the exorbitant wealth of this nation's ultra-rich, that movement's critics asked, absurdly, "What do they want?" As if Occupy's demands weren't obvious. Occupy Wall Street's argument for change is no less necessary today than it was back when it began, calling the American dream of homeownership and a well-paying job the farce that it is.

My friends and I battle the same fatigue, attrition, and misperception of our priorities that undid Occupy Wall Street. We're driven by the reality that our economic prospects are dimmer. In the lead-up to the 2024 presidential election, a survey by analysts for consumer finance–focused Experian debunked the lie that millennials and, behind us, Gen Zers don't care about our personal balance sheets, that we are frivolous with our wallets while expecting our parents to pick up the slack. On the contrary, 68 percent said the economic climate was handicapping their efforts to be financially independent adults.

And while 56 percent said they were optimistic about their financial future, it's far from certain that better days are ahead. Recent years' job growth has been concentrated in the service industry. It's a wide category of employees who probably shouldn't be lumped together. They range from comparatively well-paid solar panel installers and software developers to poorly paid home health aides, restaurant workers, and taxi drivers. Even in the fast-growing health care industry, with its mix of high and low wage employment, low wage job growth has dominated.

Roughly a decade before Pop was elected, 55 percent of US jobs were service jobs. By 1982, the rate was 69 percent. Today, it hovers around 80 percent. That trend, coupled with the declining tally of nine-to-five and other shift-work positions paying enough to rent an apartment for one or buy a home for an expanding, young family, fuels the gig economy. My generation and younger ones disproportionately fill those ranks. Even so, some of us gig by choice. We see it as a form of insurrection but in a good way. On the opposite end of the spectrum, the percentage of Americans age fifty-five and older who've had to delay retirement—because they cannot afford to kick back—has steadily increased. There's the story of the eighty-two-year-old Walmart cashier, a navy veteran whose old bones had rounded his spine and shoulders, forcing him to crane his neck upward and back in order to look a customer straight in the eye. A viral TikTok video and GoFundMe netted him $108,000. But how often does a Good Samaritan kick off that sort of fundraising for an elderly person who should no longer be doing shift work, let alone standing on his feet?

"It's something inherently antagonistic to the status quo under which we live right now," said my close friend Harry Davies, referring equally to his gigging as a bartender and fine art painter, calling his own shots. We met during my first two months of living in New York. He has his own art studio. He's determined to sell his work when and to whom he chooses, not just to the highest bidder. That resolve and sensibility permeates our whole crew and like-minded members of our generations and others.

While working at the same Italian restaurant in New York City—Harry as a bartender and me as a barback and waiter—he and I struck up another of those instantaneous friendships. This Black kid from Detroit and Harry, the white kid from a neighborhood of whites, Blacks, Puerto Ricans, and Jews on the Upper West Side, were raised on pop culture that, though not transracial as we came of age, seemed to draw audiences that were more racially mixed. (And more willing, perhaps, to hear each other, even as we've tried to drown out our critics.) We share a worldview: There should be food on every table. Starvation in one household is directly linked to overconsumption in another.

That ethos has prompted Harry to invest his energy, as a civically concerned voter, in local elections. He has a visceral and adverse reaction to presidential politics as they exist right now. In the lead-up to Election Day 2024, he was heavily considering, for the first time, not voting in the race for his district's representative in Congress: "Our congressman voted for more money and weapons to help the Israeli government kill babies in Gaza. That doesn't represent the wishes of the people of his district. Not at all."

The heart of Arab America is suburban Dearborn, one of Detroit's next-door neighbors. It has been drawing Yemeni, Syrian, Palestinian, Lebanese, and other Arab Americans since waves of them started immigrating to our home state in the 1880s. My father showed up for his Arab neighbors. In 2002, while the ranking member of the House Judiciary Committee—he'd be its chair from 2007 through 2011—Pop formally chastised US Attorney General John Ashcroft for violating the Sixth Amendment's guarantee of a public trial by illegally, secretly conducting the deportation hearings of Rabih Haddad. Lebanon-born Haddad immigrated to Ann Arbor, where he was an imam and founded the Global Relief Foundation. He was among those the US government rounded up, alleging they had a part in the 9/11 terror attacks on the Twin Towers. Though the government never proved its allegations that Haddad was a terrorist, it deported him for overstaying his US tourist visa. There is right, and there is wrong. That's what Pop emphasized and lived for.

It's a goal I shared with Pop, though I have encountered hurdles on my way toward reaching it. Without meaning to, I've created some of those obstacles. Here's a case in point: Pop's acquaintance with a famous and powerful music business attorney and my pursuit of a career in the music business meant that Terrence, my old roommate from Morehouse, and I got to sit in on a class taught by that lawyer in 2017 at the University of California, Los Angeles's extension program. Terrence and I, who'd been testing our capacity to make it as music industry artists on the West Coast, audited that class while my romantic life was unraveling. As Pop and several others saw it, I and the young woman in question should never have been together in the first place.

Terrence and I were laughing, joking, and mixing it up in the hallway as we waited for class to start one day. As the previous class ended and I moved toward the classroom door, I opened a highly unanticipated, official-looking letter.

Only Terrence can convey how stricken I was, spinning with embarrassment, fear, and self-disappointment. It showed on my face, in my blank, disbelieving, straight-ahead stare.

The story behind that legal order was only half told. My then girlfriend had charged at me with a knife.

"Get the fuck out!"

She was screaming, dead up on me, and ordering me to leave her apartment. I grabbed her forearm with both my hands, hoping to jar the knife from her grip. During the scuffle, she got nicked in the arm. When officers from the LAPD showed up, she claimed that I'd assaulted her. I had not. I was handcuffed and arrested and the charges were ultimately dropped. Many of the news headlines about that incident, however, barely scratched the surface. "John Conyers[:] Son and heir apparent arrested for felony domestic violence" still lives online at TMZ, the news site most known for reporting about entertainment. Below that blaring headline, with its boldfaced letters, is a photo of me in a suit and tie.

I'm not suggesting that I should be absolved of what happened in that Los Angeles apartment. I am stone-cold guilty of ramping up, not defusing, that last in a series of toxic face-offs between two young adults, both born into Detroit's Black upper crust but grappling, nevertheless, with childhood trauma and self-identity. She and I should have worked it out differently, peaceably. Probably, I should have led the peacemaking.

But we'd established a pattern of breaking up, then making up. She phoned even after I'd been served with that protective order. And as much as my heart wanted to, I knew I could never again call her back.

I couldn't help wondering if what I'd done had somehow tainted Pop's name and standing by appearing so unflatteringly in coast-to-coast headlines. I questioned if I could ever or, rather, how I would ever be able to date again. A breakup that public and that traumatic feels like the end of the world. About a year later, when I found the courage to ask him what he would have done in the same situation, Pop was mute. Intentionally, he said nothing as we drove along; he just let me squirm in my mess. I broke that uncomfortable silence with something like, "I guess what it comes down to is it's just not that deep. No relationship is ever that deep."

And Pop said, "I think that's right." We never spoke of it again.

Pop had a way of reducing things to their essence. He knew that my place, as the son of a political lion, had its perks and its hazards. I had to be ever mindful of that.

Cousin Sonya, the oldest of the surrogate kin inside my cipher, has helped me navigate that minefield as I try to be known not for my worst moments, but for my finer and most ennobling ones. Having collaborated with and advised the children and grandchildren of several notables—and produced documentaries on, among others, actress-activist Ruby Dee and, by extension, her famous husband Ossie Davis—Sonya has several observations about "children of legacy," as she calls us. We confront some of the same challenges and tensions. We might just easily benefit from carrying a certain last name or we can face a torrent of blowback. We come up against whatever the broad public perceives and misperceives about us. We are asked, endlessly, to account for ourselves.

We also, Sonya said, do a kind of shadowboxing with ourselves, the legacies we've inherited, and the cautionary living that attends that: "*Whatever you do, don't embarrass the family*" is how Sonya once encapsulated it.

"That is what is so very clear; that's the context," she told me. "There's shadow, cloud, opportunity, energy that children who are born into these traditions of leadership are flowing in. There's this sea, this current of possibility. At the same time, you're trying to find your own strokes, trying to keep your head safely above water.

"As for millennials, many people say they're not resilient or they're this or they're that. Many of those who criticize often come from a line of people who worked the same job for fifty years, then got the gold watch. But this is not the industrial age anymore. While attending church, especially in the Black community, has long been an expression of respectability politics, that's not so true anymore. So what does it look like to be a person of influence now? Being able to support questions around that—about how to show up in relationship to the legacy, how to own your humanity, how to look forward, and what it looks like for you to make a difference in the world, build a life, have a family—is a critical part of our relationship."

In other words, it's fair for me to explore what it means to be myself. To be a Black man, a millennial, a brother, a friend, a community person, a son who aspires, as my famous father did, to a life of changing lives, whether inside of politics or on its perimeter.

Terrance Woodbury, a senior at Morehouse College the year that Terrence Smalls and I were freshmen roommates, had a special, unobtrusive way of gathering in and sheltering kids, like me, from prominent families, on the hallowed grounds of Mother Morehouse, as the institution was dubbed. Terrance saw that I aspired to do something that intrinsically honored Pop, but bore my distinct imprint. I've wanted whatever that something is to be meaningful, to put money in my pocket and other people's pockets, to give Black people and poor people of every stripe a sense of the power and agency they might obtain in this society. Terrance saw these desires of mine when, as a Morehouse student and during the years immediately after I dropped out of Morehouse, I couldn't entirely pinpoint or articulate which direction I'd eventually go in.

"Robert Franklin, Morehouse's president at the time, included me in a group of what he considered Morehouse ambassadors, mentoring and adopting this new class of students," Terrance said. "I tried to afford you what the son of a very influential father should be afforded; I gave you room.

"The benefits of what many call nepotism are often transferred to and assumed by the children of white influential people. Too many Black people think we are not deserving of that. But, instead of us looking down on that kind of entitlement in Black children, I say Congressman Conyers earned a space for his son to walk through."

That notion offends many. And I get that, too. I also get that some fathers leave debt and some, fortunes. Mine left both. A fortunate name and network, a cost to pay, and lessons I'm still learning daily.

When they told me, mistakenly, that Pop was on death's door after the stress of being kicked out of Congress put him in the hospital, Terrance—at the time, he was working toward becoming a key analyst for Hit Strategies, the top pollster of Gen Z and millennials—found me sobbing in the hallway of Pop's Washington apartment building. Terrance, as my other friends have, gave me a shoulder to cry on.

"They're killing my father," I blubbered.

Terrance just held on while I wailed. He scraped me off the floor. He got me steady enough on my feet for me to make my way back to Pop's apartment and keep packing up his things to ship them home to Detroit.

My tribe is that devoted. It has never let me slip too far into the darkness that seems, always, to flank me, to be right on my heels.

The darkness is a trickster. It descends, dodges, and eludes. If it hinted that it had swallowed up our sweet Bydia, we totally missed the clues. We did not know he was so bereft. What we hear, still, is the sound of Bydia crossing a Harlem street, talking about the fly-ass, sun-colored suede shoes he was sporting or popping a fire-orange bucket hat on his head or pairing his "Morehouse Relays" cap with a T-shirt emblazoned with the face of Dick Gregory, our warrior comedian, a prototype of how to love and check and defend Black people.

"People with some of the biggest personalities also have some of the highest sensitivities. Bydia was empathetic in a way that most people simply are not." That's an apt assessment from Chris Thomas, another Morehouse man and a member of the House of Homage who happened to have grown up in Philly with Bydia.

Always, Bydia was smiling. Or so it seemed.

Several months into my nonstop mourning over Bydia's death, on a Sunday morning at my favorite Detroit church, the preacher titled his sermon "This Is Us." I texted the men who make up my private brotherhood while sitting in the pew.

"Aye. Today has been extremely tough for me. I wanna share the verses from church today because they reminded me of how special this group of friends is and how special Bydia was. I never cried in church before, but I was stuck. Love y'all boys."

The scriptures that the pastor referenced included these: *They devoted themselves to . . . the breaking of bread and to prayer . . . They sold property and possessions to give to anyone who had need. Every day they continued to meet together in the temple courts . . .*

If that didn't describe how my surrogate kin function toward each other, if that didn't describe my brother Bydia, I don't know what does. During my stint in New York, Bydia had gotten me a job as a paid intern at the then fledgling Barbarian Agency, a digital advertising agency in New York's fancy Tribeca neighborhood. Bydia, Chris, and brother-from-another-mother Pook let me sleep on their couch.

Bydia was the connective tissue. He brought me to Wes, Uzo, and DayDay and Mel and Kenny and Cory and me to them and all of us to each other. Bydia was the reason we are a beautiful thing.

I dream of, I wish for, Bydia still living and breathing, sure-footed and sharing whatever he chooses across a phone chat that we pick up, just, whenever. Just because. Without him, our cipher is incomplete. Still, we don't stop. We keep going. We tighten our grip on each other.

CHAPTER 5

CAMPAIGN SIGNS

Arthur Featherstone was a cherished friend of my father's. Outside of Pop's family, Featherstone was one of his earliest and most ardent political supporters. Featherstone was Pop's main man and eventually his congressional field director.

Before Detroit was immersed in an ongoing fight for the United States to settle its colossal debt to Black people, Featherstone was already a civil rights royal. Mississippi born and reared, he'd been a Freedom Rider, drawing attention to and protesting back of the bus, coloreds-only seating that flouted federal law governing interstate travel. His grandfather, a preacher who'd been born enslaved, was a lead organizer for the NAACP in Mississippi, where Vicksburg, in 1918, hosted the state's first chapter of the organization.

Vicksburg is a small city with an outsize history. There, on the branches of old cypress and elm trees, Black bodies—flesh shredded, bones broken and dislocated by volleys of bullets, limbs missing—were strung up with such frequency that Blacks reviled Vicksburg as a lynching capital in the lynching-est of all fifty states.

In Vicksburg, Union troops had overtaken Confederate soldiers during a siege lasting forty-seven days. But after the Civil War was won and lost, during Reconstruction, a rabid white mob murdered as many as three hundred Black freedmen—two white people were killed—in a monthlong massacre, sparked by the determination of those newly freed people to protect Vicksburg's duly elected sheriff, a Black and formerly enslaved man, Peter Crosby. Indignant whites, with their militarized armament, outgunned the defenders of Sheriff Crosby—the most powerful elected official in a county where Black people were gaining wealth and property at a pace threatening the white power structure. He was reinstated by US Army troops. Later, Crosby was shot in the head. Barely surviving and severely maimed, he was forced out of law enforcement.

Featherstone was two generations removed from that massacre. Yet, "I was born into the struggle," Featherstone told me, acknowledging a lineage that predates him and includes every generation thereafter. People like Featherstone quickly discerned the high costs of being on the front lines of that struggle. James Baldwin put it this way: "What one does realize is that when you try to stand up and look the world in the face as if you had a right to be here—when you do that without knowing the result of it—you have attacked the entire power structure of the Western world."

Featherstone echoed a version of that same message during one of my last visits to ask him about Pop, the father whose story I'd submerged myself in and was sussing out. Single-mindedly, I was determined to write it down. During that visit, Featherstone pulled from his private archives and trove of priceless keepsakes an 11½-by-18-inch scrapbook, showing and telling for my benefit and my brother Carl's.

"That Sunday morning when John Lewis went over the bridge in Selma, where they beat the civil rights people down to the ground, Andy Young called. Then, Dr. King called. Dr. King wanted John to come meet him in Montgomery. John had one of his assistants call the White House and ask President Johnson, 'John wants Air Force One.' And John got that plane," Featherstone said.

"Damn, that nigga wasn't lying," I thought to myself, as Featherstone kept talking. My father told me that and other facets of his activist politics, but not in the same impassioned way as Featherstone. Pop had told me about flying on Air Force One to Alabama and about his interactions with Jimmy Hoffa, the Teamsters union president who disappeared in 1975, about the behind the scenes and the who's who of his life. But I cannot begin to convey how startled and grateful I was to Featherstone for separately, independently confirming the factoids Pop had shared with me so matter-of-factly. For sure, Mr. Featherstone liked to talk. He could pontificate with the best of them. Perhaps, even more than I did, he knew how desperately we needed to tell my father's story and, consequently, the stories of countless others who facilitated the Civil Rights Movement.

Featherstone was born on December 28, 1928, a point in time when sharecropping had become the nation's new slavery. Indianola, his Mississippi hometown, had a majority-Black population of three thousand. Indianola's circumstance reflected that of the entire region. Before World War I, across the Deep South, there were more than 200,000 Black-owned farms, boasting a total of 1.6 million acres. They'd been kick-started with loans from Black-owned banks. But by 1928, the number of Black-owned farms was furiously in decline. As their property was lost, often due to the actions of corrupt elected officials and coconspiring, white private citizens, the number of landless Black sharecroppers rose. They planted and harvested in white-owned fields. They sold what they reaped to those white landowners. The landowners set the price for share-croppers' yields, forced them to shop from landowners' stores, and, then, shackled sharecroppers to ever-deepening arrearages that were all but impossible to zero out. Under cover of night, some share-croppers fled that bonded labor. They were betting on fair wages and better opportunities somewhere over the Mason–Dixon Line.

To avoid a field hand's lot and related forms of subjugation, Featherstone enrolled after high school at all-Black Alcorn State University. His college roommate was Medgar Evers, who would go on to become the NAACP's first field secretary in Mississippi and, when he was not much older than I am, a mere thirty-seven, another martyr of the Civil Rights Movement. Half past midnight on June 12, 1963, a member of the White Citizens' Council aimed a bartered 1917 Enfield rifle at Evers. Enfields were engineered for American soldiers to slay the US government's enemies during World War I. Ku Klux Klansman Byron De La Beckwith shot Evers straight through the heart in his driveway in Jackson. "I opened the door, and there was Medgar at the steps, face down in blood. The children ran out and were shouting, 'Daddy, get up! Please get up!'" Mrs. Evers recalled.

She has retold the horror of that evening, over and over, to journalists and public audiences during the whole, long lifetime after she was cannonballed into early widowhood. On that horrible night, ahead of greeting her husband when he walked through the door from another exhausting workday, she and the children had watched President Kennedy's televised address on the "moral crisis," "domestic crisis," and unconstitutionality of the nation's appalling failure to deliver equal rights to everyone. Overlaying that chaos was an economic crisis that still exists. Black people earned sixty-two cents for every dollar that white people earned, according to the National Community Reinvestment Coalition in 2023. At the current pace, it would take five hundred more years for us to close that gap.

In his speech, Kennedy lauded the two Black students who were allowed, by court order, to desegregate the University of Alabama and the National Guardsmen who were protecting them from a threatened assault by a white mob. The president lambasted white supremacy for its never-ending savageries. He called for peace in the streets, no matter how implausible that seemed, given how tired and fed up Black folks had become—and how angry some whites were at the progress, however slow and remedial, toward racial equality at that point. In May 1963, JFK ordered federal troops into Birmingham, where Black Alabamians set ablaze white businesses. Blacks fought the local police, hand to hand, and with sticks and stones. Members of the city's police department were said to be coconspirators with the KKK, which had planted bombs at the Black-owned A. G. Gaston Motel and the parsonage of Rev. A. D. King, MLK's baby brother. The two men were coleaders of the Southern Christian Leadership Conference's Birmingham campaign for racial justice. Four months after that Black uprising in downtown Birmingham, the KKK bombed the city's 16th Street Baptist Church. Four little Black girls lay dead in the rubble.

"Are we to say to the world," Kennedy intoned on TV on June 11, 1963, "and, much more importantly, to each other that this is 'the land of the free,' except for the Negroes? That we have no second-class citizens, except Negroes? That we have no class or caste system, no ghettoes, no master race, except with respect to Negroes?"

Seven days after that speech, Kennedy, who'd tapped Pop as an inaugural member of the Lawyers' Committee for Civil Rights Under the Law, sent Congress his Civil Rights Act proposal. That November, before he could get that legislation across the finish line, assassin Lee Harvey Oswald shot and killed Kennedy. In July 1964, JFK's successor, President Johnson, signed the landmark measure into law.

Featherstone was among those hoping and praying that Kennedy, and then Johnson, from the White House would spur on the racial progress that, in dribs and drabs and by force, Black people were ushering in. The change came at a steep price. Featherstone personally witnessed the sacrificial service of, among others, his Alcorn State classmate and fellow Mississippian Medgar. Featherstone had a front seat as Arlington National Cemetery received the remains of his friend, a US Army laborer and police officer during World War II. Featherstone and my father were among the many who stayed vigilant while waiting for justice for Medgar Evers. It came thirty years later when Klansman De La Beckwith—who'd left the rifle with his fingerprints on it at the crime scene—was found guilty of murder after what was his third trial. In 2001, at age eighty, he died, a paltry seven years into his sentence of life in prison without the possibility of parole.

There were too many such atrocities, too many unambiguous signs, too many indicators for those aggressions to be considered as isolated incidents. People of a certain bent and defiance had to respond. How could they not? Right is right. Wrong is wrong. The circumstances of our people are what compelled Featherstone, Pop, and their comrades to act in Detroit, which also had a Black uprising in 1963. Detroit's race troubles were not too dissimilar from those in Mississippi. The terrain was different. But the tenor was the same. White workers at Packard and elsewhere waged "hate strikes" against Black Southerners coming north. How dare they work alongside whites with good-paying jobs in car manufacturing? That was just one example of Northern-style bigotry.

As he continued leafing through the scrapbook of stapled, glued, taped, laminated newsclips and assorted important memorabilia, Featherstone was detailing how he'd routed MLK's telephone call through to Pop, whose whereabouts Featherstone took it upon himself to keep under wraps. Pop had been getting death threats.

"John got the white congressmen from New Jersey, New York, Pennsylvania and the five members of the Congressional Black Caucus, Adam Clayton Powell. They got on that plane and flew to Montgomery," Featherstone explained. "Dr. King told John, 'We need a rally. We need to raise some food and clothes 'cause they freezing the Black people out in Selma.' The white folks had said, 'Don't sell them niggahs nothing. We gone starve 'em to death.'

"John put on a full drive. From Detroit, we sent two tractor-trailer loads of canned goods and clothes and everything to Selma. Jimmy Hoffa told John, 'I'll drive the trucks.'

"I'd never seen nothing like it."

As Featherstone marveled, Carl sat to his right on the sofa of Featherstone's dark, dank home. I sat on a chair in front of those two, recording Featherstone with my cell phone. Carl and I traded looks at each other. We smiled and nodded, sort of shocked and awed by that story. Pop, in his matter-of-fact way, had given us the broad strokes of how he arranged that emergency flight on the president's plane. But he left out many of the details Featherstone offered up. Pop never mentioned the crackdown on Black people in Selma in the way that Featherstone had. Hearing the story with all his animation and color elevated it. The story somehow had more credence.

I've found that people with power and influence are quick to let you know that they are powerful and influential, particularly in Detroit, though this is true of many places. But Pop—and, by extension, Featherstone—was quieter. He had standing but he didn't flaunt it. He did what needed to be done. If he needed to pull strings, he did that. It was simple, matter-of-fact. Maybe that's why Pop didn't tell me and Carl the particulars of that ride on Air Force One.

Carl and I are Conyers men, sons of our father. But our lives, in substantial ways, are distinct from Pop's. Before we were old or mature enough to even begin grappling with what birthrights are and before we developed the strength to make our own way, we'd been issued a call to action on behalf of our people. Featherstone echoed that call while Carl and I sat inside his house.

I'm not at all sure how Featherstone and Pop met. I do know

that, along with Pop's younger brother, Bill, they roomed together for a while in a place at Dexter Avenue and Oakman Boulevard in the core of Black Detroit. (Bill would die of a rare cancer before realizing his dream of leaving the auto industry for law school.)

Featherstone had landed in Michigan when he was fresh out of serving US interests in the Korean War, his second military stint. His first, at the tail end of World War II, found him drafted and dispatched to Russia, then a US ally against Nazi Germany.

Being conscripted extracts from and disrupts a life, Pop had said. (He'd spent roughly a decade, alternately, in the US Army, Army Reserve, and Michigan National Guard.) For Featherstone, who was still trying to separate himself from the specter of those Southern fields where cotton was king, military service was further radicalizing: "I never got my degree. And I've been bitter about that ever since, man. I'm fighting in Korea, and Blacks couldn't vote in Mississippi. Blacks couldn't vote in Georgia, couldn't vote in Alabama."

I was speechless as he protested. Even if I'd wanted to interject, I had nothing of value to add. I had nothing that could meet Featherstone where he was at that moment. Featherstone was echoing complaints from countless other Black veterans of US military incursions onto other nations' turf and often into situations where this country had no business meddling. Those Black veterans presumed, correctly, that they'd be granted the full rights and privileges of American citizenship in exchange for following Uncle Sam's marching orders. Pop, Featherstone, and their kind didn't win that part of the battle. So they found other means and methods to make do and make change happen. They kept it moving.

Like Pop, Featherstone was also a Korean War veteran. He got hired on in Detroit's auto plants, where a war for equity was being fought within the broader battle for labor rights across the United States: "There was always racial tension in the union because there was white guys that didn't think Black people were supposed to have a position. The white guys controlled e-ve-ry-thang."

Featherstone worked on a Ford assembly line, molding steel car frames, throughout most of the 1950s. Much of what he earned went toward putting one of his brothers through veterinary school at all-Black Tuskegee Institute in Tennessee, another brother through undergraduate studies at all-Black Mississippi Valley State, and a sister through undergrad at Alcorn State.

During Ford's 1958 recession-driven downsizing, Featherstone was among those who got laid off. After that, he worked in food services at a Veterans Administration hospital, using skills he'd gained while stationed at Fort Chaffee and, later, while working in restaurants. Featherstone also began investing his considerable energies in running the local NAACP's efforts regarding ensuring fair access to housing for Black people and in collaborating on politics with Pop, the aspiring candidate. By then, my father had quit being a spot welder at a Lincoln auto plant. Pop had been there since returning from the Korean warfront to a position that my grandfather, the United Auto Workers executive, made sure Pop got. Even now, auto industry payrolls and retirement rosters list parents and their offspring, generation upon generation, sometimes side by side.

But Pop had no intention of spending his whole working life at the Lincoln plant. He stone-cold refused to be snapping vehicle parts into place until he retired and a pension kicked in.

"I'm going to be a lawyer," Pop had casually told a Lincoln co-worker, who immediately poo-pooed the idea.

"That's what they all say. We're making good money at this plant," the dubious listener replied. "You might not make it to law school."

Pop, cool as could be, just smiled.

Pop had this thing about him. If you doubted his capacity to achieve, he was going to prove you wrong. No doubt about it. Our people, Pop believed, needed to insert ourselves in almost every aspect of America's many obstacle-laden systems. The law—good and bad—governs almost every aspect of American life in some form or fashion. Pop had watched the signs. He knew what Black folks were up against. He also knew what they had achieved, racism be damned. Pop saw himself as a template, just as he had followed other people's examples. Not the least of which was his own father, my granddad, who, as one in his succession of wins for union workers, made racist whites at Packard see and reckon with Black people as their co-workers. If Pop could finish law school and pass the bar exam, other Blacks could, too. And we needed—still need—an unbroken chain of Black lawyers.

Even though Featherstone did enroll for a while at Michigan State during his initial years of carving a place for himself and his ideals in Detroit, he never earned a bachelor's degree. He didn't attain an academic pedigree commensurate with that of Pop, the Wayne State Law grad, or many of Detroit's studied and scripted Black up-and-comers. But Featherstone didn't let his collegiate lapse stop him. By no means did he stop. He brought the fiercest parts of his self-taught and institutionally learned intelligence, his real-world savvy, his street creds, and his passions to movement work. Oh to be a fly on the wall in that home at the intersection of Dexter and Oakman shared by those three young men. To hear Featherstone, Pop, and Uncle Bill Conyers batting around big ideas? Solving problems? Strategizing over all sorts of issues as they dove headfirst into activism, advocacy, and lawmaking? Pop the politician and his first lieutenant, Featherstone.

"Lorraine was a young lady that your father dated at the time," Featherstone told me, smiling just a little, his raw, rough-hewn voice turning wistful. "She was the first person to tell me, 'John's gonna run for Congress.' She also told me that John's mother was from Jackson, Mississippi."

It was a rare mention of my grandmother, Lucille Conyers, who'd been instrumental in refining my father, the would-be politician, and in campaigning for him on the street, in churches, in Black-owned shops and restaurants, door-to-door in Black Detroit. She'd launched "Women for Conyers." The mention of my grandmother reminded me of what I learned in my studies on the pursuit of Black freedoms in America. Even when women were on the front lines, they too often had been relegated to minor roles in the master narratives of this movement for equality among the sexes, geographical regions, races, and so forth. That movement has never ended, even if its embers sometimes burn deceptively low.

For Featherstone, the bloodline of the Black American experience traces back to Mississippi. From there, it courses every which way. For him, this genesis is irrefutable. It is not up for debate.

"Well, John's campaign manager was from Mississippi," Featherstone said. He was testing me with that voice, making a proclamation, rather than stating a supposition.

Featherstone's voice was inflected, I'm sure, with the toil, sweat, and dirt of those cotton fields. So many Black Michiganders, especially the old folks, sound like Featherstone to me, except that his words were more rapid-fire. He talked fast, whether he was being interviewed on TV or radio, giving directions at a community meeting, or speaking to me and my brother. His urgency about winning Black freedoms made him do that, I guess.

"Bob Millender? He was the kingmaker," Featherstone continued, starting to rattle off the politicians who owed their status as Black Firsts to Millender, an attorney born in Chicora, Mississippi, near the Alabama state line. Though Featherstone harped on Millender being a Southerner by birth, Millender, who died in 1978, was transplanted to Detroit when he was five years old. His father had gotten a job at a Ford plant.

"Bob Millender ran Coleman's campaign; he ran Robert Tindal's and Erma Henderson's and Claudia Morcom's campaigns. He ran John's campaign," Featherstone said, referring to Coleman Young, Detroit's first Black mayor, and Pop, the second Black Michigander elected to the US House. "He ran Richard Austin's campaign for Michigan's secretary of state. . . . He ran everybody's campaign. That's why we called him kingmaker.

"You know, they tried to get him a job at the circuit court—because Bob was electing too many Black people and they wanted to get him off the scene. But Bob turned it down. Bob said, 'Why should I go work for the circuit court?' He say he can make $200,000 more a year in that law firm than he can make being a judge. And Bob stayed in that law firm. Bob was a brilliant lawyer."

That firm, Goodman, Eden, Millender and Bedrosian, was the successor to Goodman, Crockett, Eden and Robb, said to be the first integrated law firm in the nation. George Crockett, the Black man in that quartet, had been a UAW lawyer and, during President Franklin Delano Roosevelt's administration, the US Labor Department's first Black attorney.

Featherstone was getting amped as he talked about those Black Detroiter breakthroughs. He was full-on animated discussing how and why Coleman Young, Robert Millender, George Crockett, Pop, and the rest in their constellation of Black pioneers were prompted to take action. Nothing they did was willy-nilly. Nothing was accidental. They'd been triggered by what they'd personally witnessed or secondhandedly obtained proof of.

Featherstone was excited, telling me and Carl about how woke his generation of activists had been. It excited Carl; it excited me. I wished my whole crew, all the homies, especially my boy Wes, could have been in that room. The idea that Featherstone had retired was just that. An idea, a technicality. It was a function of his age, which, on the day of our visit with him, was eighty-eight. But Featherstone was still on the warpath. He was still trying to win.

He was signaling that Carl and I had an obligation to finish what he, Pop, and others in their generation had begun. We had to grab the baton that those fathers and mothers were handing off.

For the most part, in Pop's day, those individuals were not people with notoriety or wealth. Mostly, they weren't after money or fame. They stayed in the race for our rights because they had to. They knew how essential to this war everyone was. So there was a place for everyone. The big guns and the little guy, the person with no college degree and the person with multiple degrees, the domestic worker, and the dogcatcher. Before volunteers on Pop's first congressional campaign even knew what big-time attorney Bob Millender looked like or met him face-to-face, he'd go to campaign headquarters in the wee hours to clean toilets and empty trash cans. You cannot fake that sort of commitment or work ethic. Millender was modeling what it meant for each man and each woman to be on deck, completing whatever task needed attention. They didn't pull rank. They didn't set themselves above the other. They put purpose over ego.

In 1964, when Pop was in the throes of that neck and neck campaign to be the Democratic congressional candidate in his district, volunteers for Richard Austin, Pop's Black competitor, were removing my father's campaign signs almost as fast as they were posted. It didn't matter to them that their campaign had more resources, more signs and billboards, and more support from local businesses. Still, they were stealing Pop's campaign signs all over the city.

"What did y'all do?" I asked Featherstone.

"We just put 'em back. Me, John's uncle, John's baby brother, Bill, Joyce Miller, Homer Matthews, all of us. We'd work until three in the morning, putting out new signs. Our mission was to restore or repost every sign that the enemy camp—campaign, I mean—had torn down. But, see, Austin and his people would be sitting at the bar while we were out there campaigning, kinda like the rabbit and the turtle."

The rabbit and turtle reference threw me off, at first. For some odd reason, I thought, "The Rabbit and the Turtle? That must be the bigwigs' bar where the Austin campaign hung out after work, puffing on cigars, drinking cheap brown liquor, whatever was the Crown Royal or Henny of their day." That camp was getting high on its overconfidence. They were, as Black people of a certain generation might say, smelling themselves.

Oral history is part of the Black tradition; so much of the game comes from the elders like hand-me-downs. And so, Featherstone put me on. He was talking allegory, folktales, symbolism, and parables: The speedy rabbit had challenged the glacially slow turtle to a race. The rabbit flew out of the starting block, leaving the turtle so far back in the dust that the rabbit couldn't see him. But the rabbit peaked early. By the halfway mark, he'd worn himself out. While the rabbit napped to regain his momentum, the turtle cruised on by, crossing the finish line first. The referee, a fox, flag-waved the winner across the finish line.

Featherstone had gone backward and forward in time. In that first campaign, Pop had been endorsed by the little guys, including the Trade Union Leadership Council, whose blue-collar Black members were influential among what were Detroit's hordes of working-poor and middle-class voters. "But the bigwigs? All of them guys endorsed Dick Austin, who considered himself a big shot," Featherstone said.

He'd drifted into full strategist mode, sitting there between me and Carl: "The rabbit thought he had all day to beat the turtle. I've still got Conyers signs on my truck [right now]. You seen the signs. They were a big part of how we won the election."

Up until he died a couple of weeks before Christmas in 2022, Featherstone's yard was filled with all kinds of campaign signs and not just ones promoting Pop. His old red Mustang, folks used to say, seemed held together by campaign stickers. He believed that when your neighbor planted a sign on their lawn it was a declaration of support that shaped a neighborhood's visual and cultural landscape and its thought. It swayed voters.

Forty-three voters took my father over the line to beat Richard "Dick" Austin in 1964 and be handed his first certificate of election, dated January 2, 1965. The forty-three-vote margin is one of the most striking parts of my father's story and my own to-be-determined story, whether I am inside of politics or on its periphery. A tiny margin, a few citizens, can turn a situation. It can redirect. It can shift the paradigm and set the outcome.

I considered that as Featherstone, during one of our visits, was basking in the golden age that he and Pop shared, the one that made them such intimate friends and costrategists.

"Man, let me tell you something. We were always somewhere else. We went to Cleveland when Carl Stokes ran."

"Mm-hmm," I answered.

"We went to Chicago when Harold Washington ran."

"Wow," I said, sort of cheering Featherstone and Pop for being cheerleaders of those first-ever Black mayors in those important cities.

"We went to Newark when Gibson ran. . . . We worked on that campaign."

Then, he circled back to 1965. Pop had partnered with US representative Charlie Diggs, the first Black man Michiganders elected to Congress, and sixteen other congresspeople to prevent Mississippi's all-white congressional delegation from being seated on the House floor or voting on House business. The mostly Black Mississippi Freedom Democratic Party, which had fielded a trio of female candidates, including the legendary Fannie Lou Hamer, decried the state's 1964 elections because white Mississippians had blocked Black Mississippians from registering and voting. Of the Black adults who were eligible to vote, the Mississippi Freedom Democratic Party wrote in a filing to Congress, just 2.97 percent were allowed to register. "It was illegal," Featherstone said, of Black voters being blocked.

In addition to Hamer, Freedom Party candidates Annie Devine and Victoria Gray, all of them Black women, had vied for three of what then were five congressional seats in Mississippi, where Blacks comprised 42 percent of the state's 2.2 million residents.

"Few Americans can doubt," New York congressman William Fitts Ryan, spokesman for those seventeen rebelling House members, had said, "that Mississippi has systematically, through unconstitutional laws, illegal administration, and violence, denied American citizens the right to vote."

Five busloads of Black Mississippians had lined both sides of an underground passageway so that the sixty-eight delegates from the Mississippi Freedom Democratic Party could get up to that higher ground of the House chambers. They stood strong, Pop recalled.

Testifying before Congress on behalf of the Mississippi Freedom Democratic Party and all that it sought were MLK and the young widow of Congress of Racial Equality (CORE) worker Michael Schwerner, who'd disappeared near Philadelphia, Mississippi, alongside CORE's James Chaney and Andrew Goodman. Age twenty-four, twenty-one, and twenty, respectively, they later were found dead after an FBI investigation. The involvement of federal law enforcement, Schwerner's widow noted, likely owed to the reality that Goodman and her husband were white.

It was as though Mrs. Hamer's presence unnerved President Johnson, historians have said. Preempting her as she prepared to testify, Johnson called a nonsensical, spur-of-the-moment press conference to announce it had been nine months to the day since President Kennedy and Texas governor John Connally had been shot in Dallas. Mrs. Hamer's testimony was over by the end of Johnson's press conference, which the TV and radio news networks all cut to. But Johnson's blackout of her at the mic and on camera backfired. For days, there were replays upon replays of the testimony from Mrs. Hamer, a sharecropper from Ruleville who'd been evicted from her family's sharecropper's shack because she refused her plantation owner's demand to withdraw her voter registration: "Chairman and Credentials Committee . . . It was the 31st of August in 1962 that eighteen of us traveled twenty-six miles to the county courthouse in Indianola to try to register to become first-class citizens. We was met in Indianola by policemen, highway patrolmen. And they only allowed two of us in to take the literacy test at the time. . . .

"When the man told me I was under arrest, he kicked me. I was carried to the county jail . . . I could hear the sounds of licks and horrible screams. And I could hear somebody say, 'can you say, "Yessuh," niggah? . . . She would say, 'Yes, I can say "yessuh."' [He said,] 'So, well, say it.' She said, 'I don't know you well enough.' They beat her, I don't know how long. And after a while, she began to pray . . . And it wasn't too long before three white men came to my cell. One of these men was a state highway patrolman. . . . He said, 'We're going to make you wish you was dead.'"

Those white law enforcement officers, who'd taken a sworn oath to serve and protect, made two Black men beat Mrs. Hamer with police batons until they were too weak to beat her any longer.

Eventually, those white Mississippi congressmen got seated. Who really, reasonably expected that they would not be? But not before 149 members of the House, Pop among them, voted by roll call to make those white officials wait. Forty days were allotted for both sides to provide evidence to make their case. There in Mississippi, forced by congressional subpoena, those white officials had to show up in Black communities to tell their lies in front of the people's faces.

There were no words to describe the teeth-gritting pain of what Mrs. Hamer had endured, Pop said. She was a single individual among the throngs of battered Blacks down in Mississippi but also God knows where else all across America. Most of them never got a congressional hearing. They never got time in front of a microphone.

Throughout much of the Black man and woman's history in this land, a handful of us were granted—or, more precisely, seized—a platform to amplify our lived experience and the narratives surrounding them. We've been relaying to our people what it costs to, first of all, stay alive and, second, to make progress. Two decades before I began probing Featherstone about Pop, he was peeling back the layers of Black people throwing off successive forms of bondage for a University of Michigan historian who happened to be white: "My grandfather was Gordon G. Featherstone. Born enslaved. September 5th, 1856 . . . He used to travel [around Mississippi] in a white horse and a buggy. They called him an uppity N-word. They thought he was just preaching. But they would organize and have prayer meetings. He was organizing NAACP chapters all over the Delta."

"There is almost no evidence," the historian began, before Featherstone quickly deflected the interruption, "of that in books about the NAACP or about Blacks in Mississippi—"

"It was dangerous," Featherstone interjected. "They kept it undercover. . . . When Roy Wilkins and Walter White n'em ran the NAACP during the lynching period in the South, it was dangerous. My father and n'em used to pay white reporters to go and take pictures of lynchings for the *Pittsburgh Courier* and the *Chicago Defender*. The Klan used to wonder how they got those pictures."

Published in those Black-owned newspapers, among other publications, those photos were powerful. They didn't lie. The interviewer's research was fodder for his planned writing on Rev.

C. L. Franklin, famous Aretha's activist father. Hailing from Sunflower, Mississippi, Franklin was born in 1917 to sharecropper parents. The interviewer was armed with his prepared questions about Franklin, the preacher, activist, and music producer. But when the researcher's questioning veered off course, Featherstone got the researcher back on track. Featherstone provided the arc of the story, debunking some of the researcher's presumptions and, perhaps, arrogance. Featherstone's preacher grandfather and later Reverend Franklin, MLK, and the others in their circles and lineage stuck close, Featherstone explained, just riffing away about the Black story as he knew it.

Reverend Featherstone, the grandfather, had whooped, preached, and prophesied with the best of them. He preached in small pulpits and large ones, including Chicago's Ebenezer Missionary Baptist Church, a major, mid-America meeting house for Black activists. Billed as the birthplace of gospel music, pianist Ike Cole would play there all night, Featherstone told the historian. Ike's brother Nat sang sanctified songs about holy ghosts and other intercessors before his silky ballads and crossover appeal made him famous. The Cole family lived about three blocks over from historic Ebenezer, right behind Parkway Ballroom, which hosted those who were royals of entertainment and often took their music to the movement's front lines, in both protest and divine praise.

Pop and other early Black politicians had benefited from what was a collective effort. Church and community leaders would, for example, host fundraisers on the West Coast for someone seeking office down south or in the Midwest. Detroit, Los Angeles, Chicago, New York, and such were especially instrumental in those pioneering races by Black candidates.

Featherstone credited Pop's first win, in part, to his campaign's civil rights tactics and how Pop, even before announcing his candidacy, already had been traveling south to provide legal counsel and get Freedom Riders out of jails where they'd been unlawfully detained and brutalized.

"The Civil Rights Movement was electrifying," Pop said.

The movement captivated him, Pop told me. He was grateful to his parents and his parents' parents' generation for setting him up and giving him leeway, for giving him room to be in that movement. He couldn't remember when he wasn't a politicized, activated person. As a boy, he had walked a UAW picket line with my grandfather. As a boy, Pop read those picket signs: "UAW on Strike for Increased Pensions." "UAW on Strike for Justice." Pop had brandished a picket sign himself.

"I was drawn to the struggle because my dad was a labor organizer for the UAW. He'd been in the labor organizing at Chrysler even before the UAW—when it was illegal to be in the union . . . where you'd get beat up before you got fired for trying to join the union," said Pop, who, following his 1958 graduation from Wayne State Law, spent a year as an aide to US representative John Dingell. After that, starting his own law firm, Pop spent a dozen years as general counsel to three labor union locals in Detroit. He wanted to serve the individuals he'd stood alongside in that plant, before reporting for duty wherever Jim Crow racism was doing its dirty work.

Pop was the legal mind. Featherstone was a different kind of mastermind. Among other things, he made sure the stories got told straight. In a report Featherstone submitted to Pop during Detroit's 1967 uprising by tired and fed up Black Detroiters, he'd etched in pencil, "Incidents reported at the time of the Detroit rebellion to Congressman John Conyers and the Detroit NAACP. Compiled by Arthur Featherstone, aide to Conyers."

Below his handwriting on that document, the typed snippets included this: "Adams, a wheelchair patient, was struck in the leg by National Guard bullets . . . shooting into the upper floor apartment.

The Detroit police refused to send an ambulance to take Adams to the hospital. . . . As far as Adams knows he may still have two bullets in his left leg."

And this: "Mrs. Austin stated that her son was arrested for entering without looting. He is home on a (40) days from the service. He was listed as A.W.O.L. Military police refused to get him out. He will be punished here and there."

Over their decades of sharing a seat in some pew at Tabernacle Missionary Baptist Church in Detroit, Featherstone and Pop contemplated those insanities of the nation that both of them served, militarily and civically. They understood their activism and critique of an undemocratic America to be equally, supremely patriotic acts. On Sundays at Tabernacle Church, they contemplated the miracles, signs, and wonders, the North Stars that Black people seemed to be forever searching the skies for. At Tabernacle, Featherstone and Pop sought renewal. They went to be replenished. White persecution of the Black masses was triggering. But they couldn't sit idly by as the persecution happened.

"I think the defense case was much better this time," the white Mississippi prosecutor told news reporters in 1964, following the second of two murder trials for Medgar Evers's killer. "I don't see any reason to assume we can put on a better case." In both trials, all-white, all-male juries deadlocked, claiming that they could not reach a verdict. Learning this fact compels me to implore my peers not to skirt jury duty, inconvenient though it may be. If we don't serve our peers, how can we ever be tried by a jury of them?

Today De La Beckwith's killer rifle is on display at the Mississippi Civil Rights Museum in Jackson.

Today a block away from the beautiful white sand beaches of Biloxi, a tourist destination in Mississippi, 734 miniature Confederate flags mark the graves of 784 Confederate soldiers, wives, and widows at the Beauvoir Cemetery on the grounds of the meticulously maintained, historic home of Confederate president Jefferson Davis. To keep the flags waving in the Gulf's breeze year-round, caretakers of those graves secure thousands of dollars from willing donors. White supremacy and its symbols have made a record resurgence, say those who keep such official tallies. I say supremacy never hid too far underground anyhow.

I cannot ignore these ongoing signs and the toxic parts of whiteness, hell-bent on staying alive. "There are days—this is one of them—when I wonder, how precisely are you going to reconcile yourself to your situation here?" James Baldwin piercingly asked in 1963. "And how are you going to communicate to the vast heedless, unthinking, cruel white majority that you are here?" And we're asking the same questions today. These triggering, here-and-now injustices prompt a response.

Leaving Featherstone's home after my final visit, I again took in his collection of campaign signs, those that were fairly recent and older ones that had been there for a minute, their colors and slogans faded. I read the ones bearing a single word, "Conyers," my father's well-known name. Heading into Featherstone's home that day, I realized I had read the campaign signs the wrong way. I'd interpreted them as self-promotional tokens, as Featherstone somehow projecting his ego onto the names of the various individuals with whom he had worked and for whom he had campaigned. But those signs weren't Featherstone's braggadocio. Not that he couldn't be a braggart—he could. No, it was the other way around. The signs reflected how much those candidates understood Featherstone's value, and he wanted to highlight their association with him.

Sign-stealing is a common practice in Detroit. But even if Featherstone plunked a competitor's sign on his lawn, no one from that campaign would dare to steal that competing sign from that old man's property. Featherstone might shoot a thief.

"He was known for carrying a revolver," Pop once told me, laughing a bit about that.

Saying goodbye to my father's longtime friend that afternoon, I got the feeling that many of those past and present politicos asked Featherstone if he would honor them by featuring their signs on his private landscape, where they lingered political cycle after political cycle, calendar year after calendar year, untouched.

Having your campaign sign in Featherstone's front yard was a feather in your cap—not his.

CHAPTER 6

MOMCON

Someone she was dating bought my mother her very first fur coat when she was in her early twenties. After she married Pop, he added several to her collection. And later, with her own money, she purchased several more. They were practical, of course, a defense against Detroit's long and brutally cold winters. Also, they were gorgeous, something for my mother to flaunt. To paraphrase Kanye West, MomCon as a *mink-dragging-on-the-floor* kind of woman.

One day she, a lover of luxury and a bargain, was browsing at a pawn shop when she caught sight of several furs that she wanted to add to her collection. She ran her hand over them to ensure they had no holes or tears and were properly preserved. As she was checking the seams and linings, she noticed the name embroidered on each of those coats.

"You have to give me these," she said, point-blank, to the pawn shop's proprietor. She didn't argue with them. "I am taking them with me," she said. "I know who they belong to." And that was that. She walked out of there with those coats.

Their grateful owner happened to be the grandmother of a local judge from a prominent family. The furs had been stolen. My mom's rescue of those heirloom furs was a prime example of what any decent person does. It was that simple, no more and no less. That's how my mother's mother summed it up.

So many acts of kindness had been modeled for Monica Ann Esters, the second oldest of my grandmother's seven kids. Back when my mom was an itty-bitty girl in a rough-and-tumble section of Detroit's West Side, she saw the extreme lengths that many in an extended family of neighbors and kinfolks went to while looking out for each other. They passed the hat to ensure the lights stayed lit, or the water kept running, or the landlord got what was due. My mom had seen her community's myriad ways of helping, despite their robbing-Peter-to-pay-Paul existence or the mayhem often fed by a lack of money. More than just a habit, helping was a reflex. No one had to explain it; it was understood. It had been cultivated. There must be something about having unmet needs—let alone unfulfilled desires for nonnecessities—that sharpens the instinct to step in and make a way for someone else. In my mom's eyes that was love in action.

When it comes to making a way, Alice Garrett Esters, my mother's mother, had been exemplary. Grandma bought her first house and her first car when she was a seventeen-year-old mom. Her pension accrued over decades of being employed at Michigan Bell Telephone Company, where with Yvonne Woodward, one of Malcolm X's sisters, she was among Detroit's first Black telephone operators. Later on, Grandma hardwire-installed office phone systems. Almost always, she worked a main job and one or two side-gigs. "I cleaned office buildings, I did clerical work, I worked at Crowley's department store. I did whatever I had to do to take care of my kids. I was never on welfare. None of that. My parents were not on welfare. And I am proud of my kids, all seven of them."

Hustling, as a discipline and skill, is what Grandma learned from her father, David Garrett. When she was six months old, he and his wife, Mairie Garrett, brought my grandmother, their first-born, to Detroit from Phenix City, Alabama. The Garretts had descended from sharecroppers in and around Phenix City, which is about a dozen miles from the Army base formerly known as Fort Benning, Georgia. (To dislodge it from the Confederate general, lawyer, legislator, and judge for whom it was christened originally, that military installation was renamed Fort Moore in 2023 as some memorials to racists were being dismantled.) On the books, my great-grandfather worked alternately at a Chrysler auto plant and for Budd, an auto parts fabricator and supplier. On the side, he owned a cleaning business and drove a cab. He did whatever it took to help his domestic worker wife feed, clothe, shelter, and otherwise care for their big bunch of eleven offspring.

The first of my mother's two childhood homes, the one on Buchanan Street, was a four-bedroom, one-bath, two-story residence occupying one side of a duplex rowhouse. Louise Esters, my mom's paternal grandmother, lived on the other side. Under the bait-and-switch nonsense that government officials labeled as urban renewal, the residence where MomCon's parents, Robert Esters and Alice Esters, had been raising kids was torn down to make room for I-96. It stretches from Detroit to the waterfront beaches and cruise ship and commercial ports of Lake Michigan. MomCon—my Finally Famous (a company run by my high school friends and me) friends gave her that nickname when we were in high school—and her friends rode their bicycles over dirt mounds that were an interim part of the demolition advancing the new roadway. For Mom, those bike rides in a vanishing neighborhood were a bittersweet memory.

My mother adored her grandma Louise, who I imagine gave my mother some of her free-for-all candor. "I used to see some of the prettiest ladies going into one of the houses on our block," MomCon recalled. "I remember telling my grandmother, 'Oooh, they soooo pretty.' But Grandma cut me off: 'They prostitutes and hoes.' At the time, I must have been around eight years old. I had no idea what my grandma meant. All I knew was those women were pretty, wearing fine clothes, and furs. Later on, I found out that a pimp lived across the street in that house."

My great-grandmother Louise was determined to keep her grandbabies on the straight and narrow. She kept a sharp eye out for MomCon, who, as our family members will tell you, has sometimes inserted herself into situations she maybe should have run from. "Grandma was a snitch," MomCon said. "If I got in trouble in school, I'd say, 'Grandma, please don't tell my mama.' The principal, Miss Edwards, who knew my mom, had already called my grandmother and told her what I was doing. By the time I got home, my mama was ready for me. . . ."

Tired of being bullied in school, MomCon told me she'd started speaking up for herself. If it came to it, she was willing to throw some hands, knuckle up. "I was arguing with some girls. Me and my girlfriends were about to give them the business. Miss Edwards was trying to prevent us from fighting."

MomCon wound up transferring to a different school and neighborhood. One day when she was in second grade, she and her stair-step of siblings came home to find that their mother had arranged a whole new living setup for them. "I saved my money up and bought me a house," Grandma Alice told me. "I went home and said, 'We moving.' We left everything there and I bought everything new. I didn't even take their beds. . . . I left their dad and I left the neighborhood. It wasn't a hard decision. I was just tired of living over there."

Alice and the kids moved fifteen minutes away to Crocuslawn, a three-block avenue off the intersection of West Chicago and Wyoming, desegregating what had been an all-white neighborhood. It morphed to predominantly Black as white folks took flight. My grandfather Robert, Alice's husband, was not part of the move. To put it nicely, Grandma and my grandfather, whom I never met, were not getting along. Grandma had watched and listened to her parents brawling, taking it toe-to-toe, cuss-for-cuss, no holds barred. "I grew up with my mother and father fighting. All the time. And that's a hurting feeling. It is such a hurting, hurting feeling."

"My father," MomCon told me, "was a heroin addict. He was not kind to my mother, and my grandparents didn't say anything about how he treated her. Neither did his brothers and sisters. One day, when I was little, I grabbed a cast-iron skillet and hit him in the head with it and busted his head.

"And it wasn't just my father who was on drugs. My father's cousin also was an addict. Maybe it was the thing to do back in that time."

I can only go by the history. A lot of people turn to drugs once they return from an actual war, traumatized; or when they are waging internal, emotional, or psychological warfare. For many people with a mental illness, illicit drugs are a method to self-medicate, numbing the pain. I wonder what might have ailed my maternal grandfather to make him turn violently against those whom, I choose to believe, he really did love.

Especially after they moved, MomCon's father wasn't around very much.

A brother of his who lived in New York parachuted into Detroit to move MomCon's grandma Louise off Buchanan Street to rescue her. MomCon's dad got an apartment somewhere, no one really knows. And he died relatively young. "I'm not sure if he was in his thirties or forties. I don't know if it was drugs or his heart gave out. My mom just said he was dead.

"My mom was my everything. She shielded us from a lot of the chaos of my father."

Consciously or not, flagrantly or undercover, with temperance or unruliness, we bring where we come from to where we are.

Everything I have seen, done, committed to, walked away from, loved, hated, messed up, refined, cloaked myself in, struggled to shake off—all of that and then some—factors into who I am and how I operate day to day. The same is true for MomCon. The same is true for every mom.

While I love my mother and we have some major differences, some major points of departure on a whole host of issues, anyone would be ill-advised to act or speak out of turn, in my presence, regarding MomCon. It doesn't matter that MomCon and I have been estranged intermittently, including during periods when we lived under the same roof. Speak on what you know and leave the rest alone. Leave my mother alone.

In his book, journalist Charlie LeDuff hypothesized the rise of a declining Detroit. At a bookstore reading, he implied that my mother was the kind of woman he could take home. In his book, LeDuff wrote that MomCon grabbed his testicles, searching him for a wiretap, during what he said was a meeting he called to give her advice about how to be a better Detroit city councilwoman and a more sensible human being. During that meeting between the two of them at a popular jazz club on Livernois, not far from our house on Seven Mile, he wrote that MomCon batted her eyelashes, crossed her legs, and wore red polish and a shirt with a plunging neckline. He wrote that she was coy and coquettish. As if she was putting on a show for him. As if he was her audience. I had to suppress the urge to ring his doorbell and knock him the fuck out. For a brief moment, I had the mind to have someone else do it on my behalf. Public figures have too few protections, as I see it. Especially in these days of nonstop news coverage and armchair quarterbacking, some journalists feel they have a right and duty to tell any kind of story in any kind of way, for clicks and views. They shape the narrative as they see fit regardless of who gets hurt. The unethical among them hide behind the fact that they are journalists, using that excuse to say what they might never have the courage to speak directly to a person's face.

LeDuff objectified my Black mother. This was misogynoir, not your run-of-the-mill misogyny. It was as rooted in race as in gender. LeDuff purposely seized an opportunity, at my mother's expense, to promote himself. She was the butt of his jokes before white audiences of book-buyers. They laughed when he prompted them to laugh at my mother's shortcomings, as if she were not a real person with real failings, no matter how off the charts those failings. LeDuff, I'm sure, is the type of white dude who has considered himself conscientious and one of the least racist people of all. But, quite frankly, I have had my fill of white men getting away with mocking and despoiling Black women—from American Founding Father Thomas Jefferson repeatedly raping his slave Sally Hemings to entertainment talk-show host Don Imus calling Rutgers University's women basketball stars "nappy-headed hoes" to Justin Timberlake infamously exposing Janet Jackson's nipple-shielded right breast during what some said was a planned publicity stunt during a Super Bowl halftime show. Ms. Jackson—not Timberlake—ultimately was the scapegoat. She wound up penalized and blackballed by the industry. Years later, comedian Andrew Schulz added to that run-on of misogynoir when he joked about Black women, as love interests and partners, being uber-violent and hyper-argumentative.

I do recognize that LeDuff's brand of journalism also is performative. By the time he made his way from newspapers including the *New York Times* and *Detroit Free Press* to the FOX network's local affiliate in my hometown—his last stop before becoming a freelance podcaster—he was reporting on camera in sunglasses, his hair uncombed, and a five-o'clock shadow of a beard on his face. This was deliberate. He was taking unmerited liberties, this guy who was born in the suburbs and who returned to the suburbs, where he was living a not-so-tidy life. After that book came out, his wife had

LeDuff arrested and charged with domestic violence. His former colleagues at FOX's Detroit station ran footage of LeDuff, a non-Detroiter, behind bars, wearing those jail-issued orange clothes.

And it's not that MomCon or any public official should get a pass from journalists. But I'd prefer to get the news, even about my mother—and about Black people, in general—straight, no chaser.

I, of course, have my own particular and much more personal observations of MomCon. They are based on how we relate, mother to son. Some of my observations are far from positive. None are dispassionate. And all of them are charged with the emotion and intimacy of sharing the same bloodline. A nuclear family can become reactive, combustible. It can implode. For starters, my mother yelled a lot when I was growing up. I mean, honestly, too much, if you ask me or my brother. Yelling had been MomCon's default, a method of exerting control. MomCon could, and still can, be incredibly rigid. She can be unyielding. When I was a little boy suffering from ADHD—this was abundantly clear to my private school teachers—my mom's rote response whenever the symptoms flared was to yell "Shut the fuck up" or "Boy, act like you got some sense." My mom was my first and only bully—when I was a little boy with limited agency and no capacity to reasonably defend myself. I decided if I couldn't do anything about what was happening at home, I wasn't going to let it happen anywhere else. When I was a boy, I had no rebuttal, at least not one that I could express or that could combat what I was dealing with. As an adult, I set boundaries and at times I remove myself from her for however long it takes. I wouldn't let anyone else talk to me like that, let alone stay in my life. I'm not going to allow that just because she is my mother.

"There is only so much grace I can extend to my mother," I once said to Porscha Barnaby, my college sweetheart, who has become a dear friend. I was venting to her, struggling to understand MomCon's brand of love and my in-spite-of-it-all love for her.

MomCon also had cussed out Porscha, probably for just another of those innocuous things that set my mother off. "The way she spoke to you, the way she spoke to me, I'd never been talked to like that before," Porscha said.

"Her attitude is 'You're an adult when I say you can be adult.' She creates a false environment. When you start to settle into that environment, she's like, 'Hold up!' She tries to put you back in a child's place when she doesn't like your opinions."

But there's only so much a son can forgive. To me, my mother's verbal assaults were her way of pretending a problem did not exist. To her, a tongue-lashing was the fix, the cure for a predicament she had no clue how to comprehend, let alone solve. It was her way of having the last word. It was how she handled what vexed her and tested her patience.

To me, her hollering and cussing were signs of her refusal to accept what were my lived experiences and my shortcomings. MomCon seemingly viewed my mess-ups as reflections of me and not her deficiency as a parent. While my ADHD had nothing to do with her, the treatment I was denied did. What I was living was beyond her control and, without medical help, beyond mine. MomCon drew a hard line; she would not let me take prescription medicines to help me manage whatever was going on that had me in the principal's office for garden-variety classroom disruptions or for fighting in school or whatever. The compromise between her and Pop, though, was that I, then in elementary school, would start seeing a child psychologist.

My ADHD wasn't officially diagnosed until I was twenty-five years old, in charge of my own care. I took initiative and found a clinician who could help me figure out what was going on with me. Looking critically at how I was raised was hard. Recognizing and accepting that parts of my mother's child-rearing fucked me up was hard. It zapped my confidence, especially when MomCon reduced me, and her gauge of who she was as a mother, to me, her son, being "where I should be," literally, on development charts and in everyday interactions. For me, it showed a lack of accountability on my mother's part. Because of my mother's temperament, even today, I'm still triggered when I hear and see kids belittled for making simple, understandable mistakes. I wish more adults would give kids grace, teaching them the right way, instead of yelling.

My father's absence very much made my mom a single parent, which she didn't appreciate. "John and I didn't argue about much. But we did argue one day, down in the basement, about him breaking his promise to me. He said he would not be like the other congressmen, that he would come home every weekend. The first month that he didn't come home, I told him I didn't sign up to be a mama by myself, not all the time anyhow. He said he had to go to Haiti. I told him I didn't care. Making trips to Haiti is part of what he did. How did any of that matter to whether or not he came home?"

My father's schedule did make MomCon the primary, 24/7 fever-tamer, nose-wiper, chef, disciplinarian, and comforter, even if coddling a kid like me wasn't her forte. Her imprint on me—like her, I could be brash, confrontational, and aggressive—dominated until I went to boarding school. It dissipated when I was a young adult by choosing to spend more time with Pop. I started becoming, at least in my mind, more thoughtful and more strategic. I began to really give a fuck about relationships and preserving them.

Pop, maybe in defense of my mom and maybe to absolve himself of the problems that his absence aggravated, would implore me not to argue with her. And our arguing could be fierce. More often than I care to recount, MomCon and I have gone in on each other, hashing out a myriad of conflicts via extended threads of text messages well into my adulthood.

Way, way before that, we'd had some explosive, in-person

standoffs. Like the time she accused me of misplacing one of her favorite CDs. Now, I have loved music for as long as I can remember; it has been shown to ease depression and increase focus in people with ADHD. Knowing how territorial my mother was about her music collection, I had learned early on to leave her collection alone. The CD in question that afternoon, I'd never touched. I told MomCon so. Insistent and enraged, she blasted me out in front of an SUV full of kids—me, Carl, my cousins Carl, Aaron, Robert, and Tasha—returning from what, as best I recall, was a playdate.

"Oh, the infamous tire iron story," my cousin Robert began, recalling what I still can't, not accurately anyhow.

"Your mom had the CDs with the cover art; it was all in alphabetical order," Robert reminded me. "She was meticulous about her stuff. You would listen to her music, mainly her Tupac. You'd take her music and listen to it and sometimes not put it back. One day we were in the car coming down Seven Mile; we'd just crossed Wyoming.

"She was like, 'John, where is my Tupac CD?!'"

"You were like, 'I don't have it. I don't know.'"

"She said, 'Find my CD.'"

"You said, 'I can't find it. I didn't have it.'"

"Eeeeeerrrrhhh!" Robert mimicked the sound of MomCon slamming hard on the brakes.

"She said," Robert told me, "'Muthafucka lie to me again and I'm gone beat you with this tire iron.' The tire iron was in the trunk. But all of us, well, we were all wild-eyed, like a deer in headlights. We never saw nobody get beat, never saw no abuse, but . . . in the Black community, sometimes adults don't talk to kids like kids. But it was a different time; people were parenting differently."

Robert doesn't talk to his two kids in any way resembling that. He is disciplined and purposeful. Only in the rarest of circumstances—when, say, his little ones dart out into the street—does he spank them. "I was scared of my dad as a kid," my cousin told me. "I don't want my children to be scared of me."

In my most generous moments, I try to take MomCon's life story into account. Not only had her father died young, he'd also been arrested for burglary. What does that do to a person? Was my mom ever granted the time, mercy, and space to fully develop emotionally? Mentally? In her interpersonal relationships? And did her relatively early marriage to a man who could have been her grandfather stunt what might have been her richer, more robust development?

In theory and from a hopeful distance, I get why Black mothers, as a group, have been all but deified. Many have earned their place on a pedestal. They earned the accolades often reserved for mothers, whether they bore children or helped kids who, though not theirs biologically, were grafted into their lives. Black mothers are the backbone of Black churches, which still collectively do more than most other Black institutions to meet our people's daily needs. Black mothers head many a Black family. Too many Black moms are overworked and overwhelmed, shouldering too heavy a load when fathers have checked out emotionally or been absent altogether. Too many Black moms juggle too much. My mom juggled too much. I knew that; yet, she still didn't get a pass from me. It's not uncommon for people to say that until you have children of your own you can't speak on parenting. I disagree. Every living adult has been someone's child. I remember how I was made to feel. In fact, I can't forget it.

Some of my friends say they would never have succeeded without their superwoman moms. I wish I'd felt their feelings, experienced what they experienced. I imagine my mother also placed herself in a league with supermoms. But maybe if we eliminated the idea of anyone being a super anything, maybe if we stopped deifying Black moms, in particular, Black children would be better off. Deifying anyone strips them of their humanity. Humans are fallible and, as such, are open to critique. The wise person receives a righteous critique as a tool to improve.

"I tried my best" is what subpar parents might say to excuse their shortcomings. As a kid playing sports and, later, as I navigated adulthood, I learned trying your best does not always yield the desired result. A person's best can be insufficient. "It takes a village to raise a child," goes the African proverb. Other people gave me so much of what a child needs. They gave me essential ear time, counsel, and comfort, a reality that my mother took personally and as an insult. My mother provided more than enough, if not too much, materially. But she lacked the introspection and capacity for the emotional provision I needed and craved. At least partly, I traced what, as a child especially, was my emotional underdevelopment back to my mother. My brother has said that MomCon and I have spent what seems like my entire lifetime clashing, mainly because, in so many ways, we are alike. But if my mother and I mirror each other in this or that personality trait, it is a murky reflection. For we are not exactly the same. Even in rubbing people the wrong way, in being abrasive, we differ dramatically. My mom and I—how we move through life, how we deal with people, our vision and strategies—remain polar opposites. I would contend that we are more different than the same. MomCon and I confront reality differently. We view the world and our respective places in it from opposing vantage points, with opposing contexts and complexities.

MomCon is smart. But she has a stripped-down, bare-bones approach that, in the main, I do not. Even when it came to snagging Pop, she kept it simple. Those who knew Pop in his prime would tell you that my father was a fly guy. Jazz great Nancy Wilson and Pop had been a thing. Pop had done his share of romancing and being romanced. "The ladies loved him," Democratic Party high-roller Virgie Rollins, a Detroiter, told me. "Yes, John had his pick. And he knew he did."

MomCon also knew. At least by name, she was aware of a number of those who'd been in real or rumored relationships with Pop. "But most of them couldn't have no babies for him," she said, stating a fact and a boast.

Before they became a committed couple, MomCon had been to social gatherings and other functions that Pop hosted. She'd been tickled to death by how some women, eyeing my dad, behaved. "I wasn't thinking about men at that point. I was just trying to get my master's. I was working and teaching school. . . . I saw all these people at his house, so many men and so many women, jockeying for a spot. A woman would get tired of waiting and she'd leave. Another woman would get tired of waiting and she'd leave. I saw their disappointment."

Back when my parents first met, MomCon's best friend was dating a guy whose best friend's girlfriend worked for Pop. He, like every other member of the Congressional Black Caucus, was filling slots for interns. MomCon, then a grad student at Central Michigan University's public administration program, applied and got an internship placement in Pop's office. She answered phones, took dictation, and did constituent servicing.

When she caught the first hint that Pop had feelings for her, she went with it. She was giddy. During that internship, Pop had dialed her at five o'clock one morning, asking if she would help him at the polls. She realized, in that moment, that she wasn't just the enthusiastic, task-oriented, tagalong intern. She couldn't put her finger on it, but she knew something was going on. She knew something was afoot.

On one of her and Pop's first date nights, he steered his 1989 Ford Crown Victoria curbside in front of the house where twenty-something MomCon still lived with her mother. Pop tooted his horn, signaling to MomCon. Grandma threw open the front door: "Hey! Don't no hoes live in this house. If you gone try to date my daughter, you gone have to knock on the door and come in the house. I suggest you come back tomorrow and try it again.'"

Pop checked himself real quick. He did come back the next day. He pulled his car to the curb, parked it, switched off his engine, and proceeded to properly fetch Alice's daughter. Though Pop was a hotshot congressman, his position didn't win him any deference from the Esters family and their extended circle of relatives. Pop loved them, their lack of pretense, verve, boisterousness, and lively backyard barbecues. And the Esters family loved him.

"All I remember is that Monica said, 'I am going out with John, John Conyers.' I said, 'John Conyers who?' I didn't put it together at first," Grandma said, "'cause there was this other guy she'd been seeing."

Grandma didn't care who Monica had a liking for, as long as that person treated her well and as she was accustomed. "Age ain't nothing but a number if you really like someone," Grandma said, nonplussed by the fact that Pop was older than her and her daughter. "All I say is just don't hit her.

"I spoiled Monica when she was little. I took her everywhere. She demanded more. She wanted more than everybody, more of everything, more clothes and, I guess, more attention."

Pop, Grandma said, was "a nice guy. I only think I fussed at him one time. I just stood there and looked at him. It was something he did or said, something dumb, probably, though I don't remember. I just stood there and looked at him. He just looked at me and got up and walked away. Whatever it was he didn't do it no more."

Alice's daughter was drawn to what she saw in Pop. He seemed calm and so very decent. He seemed like such a nice, nice man:

"One day, I had this thought. 'What a legacy he has, but no one to leave it to.' I told him I wanted to have his kid. He said, 'Okay.'"

They married for the first time on June 4, 1990. Pop was sixty-one and MomCon was twenty-five. One month later, MomCon was delightfully and proudly and humbly—if those two feelings can exist at once—pregnant with me. She was delivering on her pledge to make a father out of Pop. It was sort of transactional, despite how much my mother loved Pop. It also might have been a bit naive. Pregnant with me, MomCon carried to Washington her usual outlook, which sometimes was too black-and-white. MomCon was too willing to make a quick move before getting the lay of the land. She remained that around-the-way girl from Detroit, unrestrained and not concerned enough about gauging how Washington works or how being savvy about its workings might benefit her, the congressional spouse, and Pop, too. Often, there was little consideration for how to make, nurture, and manage friendships or professional relationships in this new and unfamiliar world.

So she wound up feasting on what I view as low-hanging fruit, the small and inconsequential stuff. Like how Lillian Lewis and Alma Rangel, wives of legendary congressmen John Lewis and Charles Rangel, bought baby clothes when she was pregnant with me. My mother reveled in such gestures that, on the surface, appeared to welcome her into Beltway society. She was so grateful to Mrs. Rangel and Mrs. Lewis. They were among the few congressional spouses who did much of anything, in my mother's mind, to make her feel at home in the District. Many of the other Black spouses seemed entangled in a weird, perverted power struggle. They wanted to be in the spotlight, MomCon said. But a spotlight can't shine on everyone at once. The white wives? My mother quickly dismissed them as catty, among themselves, and hardly worth her time to engage. Those were the perceptions that MomCon clung to.

But Mrs. Lewis and Mrs. Rangel, they were different. They

bought baby gifts for my expectant mother and father. MomCon appreciated their kindness. Having said "I do" to Pop, an old man, she knew that she, a young woman, was an oddity, even suspect to some. She'd landed in a town that was, by turns, international and dangerously parochial, cliquish, and applied the same rules to everyone, even people who, like MomCon, didn't want to be boxed in. My mom liked being her own person. She liked standing out in a crowd. She liked having her own spectacular shine. She liked a certain kind of freedom. She was the epitome of a free spirit.

On one of her first visits to the White House, a party that the Clintons were hosting, MomCon started grooving to the music. She loved to dance, but Pop wasn't much of a dancer. And it was fine by him if his wife hit the dance floor with someone other than him. Standing near Pop and MomCon, a fellow congressman was snapping his fingers, grooving, too. When MomCon asked him if he wanted to shake a leg alongside her, he was blunt: "I don't dance with young women."

"But he was right there, popping his fingers to the music just like I was," MomCon said. "I was like, 'Okay.' And I walked off."

Where my mother came from, a party was just a party. A dance was just a dance. You might not even ask a momentary dance partner his or her name. You just had fun until the music stopped. You float on that revelry all the way home; you chitchatted the next morning about the good time you had. MomCon was earthy in that way.

"I wished I'd had a mentor back then. I should have had that," MomCon told me. "I wish the older women who were wives to congressmen had embraced me more. I wish they'd shown me the ropes a little bit more.

"I didn't really care what they presumed about me that wasn't true. But I didn't appreciate the way that some of them were just mean to me. I was the youngest one in this group of wives. I wish they had done more to take me under their wing. I talked to my pastor about how I was being treated, especially by spouses whose husbands had cheated on them with younger women. I suspect that my being a young woman reminded them of that."

To MomCon, too many people inside the bubble of the Washington Beltway feared being their authentic selves, at least in public. But she was determined to stay true to who she was and to represent the Detroit she loved. She'd also keep living her dreams. Not even her new status as a congressman's wife would impede that.

Though they may have disagreed on the finer points of how to approach a certain issue, politics was my parents' initial touchpoint. It was what they kept in common. Before becoming one of Pop's interns, Monica Ann Esters already was eyeing a career in the public sector, possibly as an elected official. She'd announced to her family, as a little girl, that she'd someday be a lawyer. Watching Pop in action fed her aspirations. "If you lived in his district," MomCon said, "he was going to help you if you asked for it. It wasn't just the big stuff he was doing in Washington—on prisoners' rights, or lowering the income ceiling on financial aid for college students, or laws to shield rape victims' identities—it was the small stuff he did behind the scenes at home in Detroit and in Washington. The folks with sick grannies in the hospital, the folks who needed a job or a reference to get into college, they were just as much on his radar."

She wanted to make a difference in people's lives, too. I'm still impressed by her efforts in that direction. MomCon began her professional career as a school teacher of, among others, special education students. On the way to eventually earning her jurisprudence doctorate from the University of the District of Columbia Law, she started her law studies by shuttling among Detroit, DC, and Oklahoma, where she'd enrolled at Oklahoma City University School of Law. Mind you, she was still a young mother. She and

Pop agreed that I, then a seven-year-old, would be with her in Oklahoma City and he'd take charge of Carl. Hilariously—sort of—and famously, Pop once lost track of Carl, who was two at the time. "I wasn't worried. You remember!" MomCon told me. "I just told your dad he better find my fucking baby." In hyperdrive at work, we suspect, my father had handed Carl off to some wonderful, trustworthy person who took good care of him while Pop legislated. Momentarily, Pop couldn't remember in whose hands Carl was. But he recovered his boy, safe and sound. "He better had found your brother," MomCon said.

Law degree in hand, she got elected in 2005 to the Detroit City Council, and chosen by her council colleagues as that body's president pro tempore. Her style was take-no-prisoners. To be sure, she often voted in the best interests of the city and its people. She told a Teamsters union official, flat-out, that too few staffers at its yearly international auto show were people of color and too many were white. She was the lone opponent of a measure resulting in Detroit selling off a good chunk of its water rights to the suburbs—leaving Detroiters with higher water bills than any municipality in our region.

On occasion, MomCon also publicly and vehemently broke ranks with the Michigan Democratic Party and the council. During one heated council debate, she dismissed one of her councilmates as "Shrek," Disney's fictional, animated ogre.

"Volatile" was how the *Detroit Free Press* editorial board described MomCon's tenure. She never lived down the Shrek outburst. Many Detroiters would not let her forget, even though many Detroiters also still loved MomCon. They have appreciated her I-don't-give-a-damn attitude. I sometimes wonder how she would fare in today's political climate. It's such a long, long way from being congenial. It is hostile. It is combative beyond combative, beyond what anyone during my mother's political heyday and, certainly, Pop's might ever have imagined.

ALL THE RIGHT NOTES.

◄

John Conyers Jr. with his beloved upright bass on March 25, 1980. *Susan Bowser/Detroit Free Press/ ZUMA Wire*

Whether he was **making music** or **making policy**, Pop always knew just the right strings to pull.

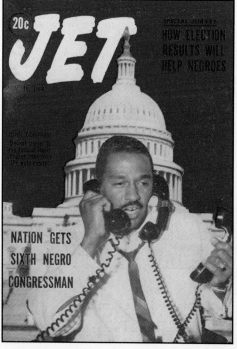

20c JET

SPECIAL SURVEY

HOW ELECTION RESULTS WILL HELP NEGROES

NATION GETS SIXTH NEGRO CONGRESSMAN

◄

John Conyers Jr. phone banking during his inaugural campaign for United States Congress in 1964.

Lucille Conyers at home on 3351 Charlevoix in Black Bottom. ▶

He always had the **support** of his **family** . . .

(Left to right) John Conyers Sr., Lucille Conyers, and Congressman John Conyers Jr. at swearing in of John Conyers Jr. in Washington, DC. ▶

(Left to right) Nathan Conyers, John Conyers Sr., and Congressman John Conyers Jr. ▶

John Conyers Sr. and union members on boardwalk in Atlantic City, New Jersey, for seventeenth UAW Constitutional Convention in 1959.

A young congressman John Conyers Jr. attempting to quell the crowd during the 1967 Rebellion on 12th Street.

. . . and the **strength** to fight for **the people.**

John Conyers Sr.

Pop was
not only
witness
to
history but
integral to
so much.

John Conyers and Jesse
Jackson at the March
on Washington ten-year
anniversary.

Congressman
John Conyers Jr.
and Congresswoman
Shirley Chisholm.
Bettman Archive ▼

Congressman
John Conyers Jr.
and Martin
Luther King Jr.

Stevie Wonder and Congressman John Conyers Jr. at the unveiling of Stevie Wonder Avenue on E. Milwaukee Avenue, December 21, 2016. *Romain Blanquart*

◀

(Left to right) Attorney Nathan Conyers, Mayor Coleman Young, and Congressman John Conyers Jr.

My parents were about this life and for us it was a *family affair.*

(Clockwise) Monica, John III, John Jr., and Carl Conyers.

(Left to right) Carl Conyers, Congressman John Conyers Jr., and John Conyers III.

(Left to right) John Conyers III, Councilwoman Monica Conyers, and Congresswoman Maxine Waters.

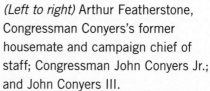

(Left to right) Arthur Featherstone, Congressman Conyers's former housemate and campaign chief of staff; Congressman John Conyers Jr.; and John Conyers III.

Rosa Parks and Detroit ▶ Public Schools Assistant Superintendent Eugene Gilmer presenting Congressman John Conyers Jr. with an award as John Conyers III takes center stage.

(Left to right) Congressman John Conyers Jr., John Conyers III, and Coretta Scott King.

◀

I may not have realized it at the time, but as a young boy it meant a lot for me to be included and present to see the great man that my father was, alongside many other greats. I was learning what a life of civic duty meant.

Pop always made sure I understood the assignment. And I know it's mine to complete.

◀

(Left to right) President Bill Clinton, Congressman John Conyers Jr., and John Conyers III touring parts of Congresswoman Brenda Lawrence and Congressman Conyers's congressional districts while campaigning for Hillary Clinton during the 2016 election cycle.

John Conyers III marching with protesters for reproductive rights.

▶

◀

John Conyers III and Congressman John Conyers Jr. at the Michigan Democratic State Convention in 2018 before the congressman endorsed Pat Miles for attorney general. *Michael Bardwell-Scott*

Monica Conyers left her seat on Detroit City Council under a cloud. On September 10, 2010, when I was twenty years old, my mother, newly convicted for admittedly accepting a $6,000 bribe from Synagro Technologies, surrendered to US marshals. It was the culmination of an FBI investigation resulting in several city officials, including then mayor Kwame Kilpatrick, also being convicted. My mother left our home on Seven Mile for Alderson Federal Prison Camp in West Virginia. She'd been sentenced to thirty-seven months at that minimum-security federal prison for women, nicknamed Camp Cupcake. Its famous inmates included food and lifestyle maven Martha Stewart, who'd been convicted in 2004 for illegally selling stock based on insider information, and jazz giant Billie Holiday, convicted in the 1940s for heroin possession.

Holiday, a dozen years after her yearlong incarceration, died of heart failure in 1959, when she was forty-four.

Eighty-something Stewart, upon release from five months of incarceration in 2004, kept banking millions of dollars.

MomCon, nearing sixty, is seeking something akin to redemption and a second chance, still. She is making a way for herself. She's got some rental properties and is engrossed in creating what will double as a home for Pop's archives and a community space where Black Detroit can chart a future for itself. She watches politics, locally and nationally, and does wonder how she can help make a difference for our people, still.

"I went to see her when she was in there," Grandma told me, referring to when her second-born was in West Virginia, while many Detroiters were complaining about how she'd made herself and her city look bad.

"We all were supportive of her," Grandma said. "Still, it was hard for any mother to go see her child like that, in a place like that.

"My child is a good daughter. She is a good mother. She is a giving person. She is the same person now that she was all along; she just got older. When she went to prison someone tried to stand in my face and say she was always like that. And I asked her, 'What does that mean? What about your son? Ain't he locked up? What did he do?' That woman ain't say nothing else. You come to me and say something about somebody, make sure you ain't got no skeletons in your closet. . . . I am still proud of my daughter."

MomCon called Alderson Federal Prison Camp "the People's Place," as if she were a wrongfully detained dissenter against some grave injustice against humanity. To me, it seemed like her way of deflecting the truth of her conviction and how she wound up in trouble.

Euphemisms were part of MomCon's bravado and blustering in public, including in front of TV news cameras. They were her attempt to conceal what her favorite cousin, Vonda Cooley, insisted was my mother's profound pain and disappointment in herself. When it became apparent that my mother would be unseated from Detroit City Council and be locked down at a prison five hundred miles from Motown, our cousin walked through the door of our home on Seven Mile to see about MomCon. "She was sitting there in the dark. By herself. She asked me, 'Are those TV cameras still outside?' I'd never seen her like that before."

In her Monica Conyers way, my mom did rebound, with her defense of herself and Detroit and her political aspirations still intact. After my unsuccessful bid to win Pop's old seat, MomCon tossed around the idea of running. In 2022, she filed to run for executive of Wayne County, the top elected position in the county that includes Detroit. She did so even after the county clerk ruled that state law prohibited convicted persons from holding an elected office until the conviction was at least twenty years old. MomCon's lawyer, Pamela Campbell, countered the clerk: "Until an election is completed, and a winner announced, Mrs. Conyers is merely a candidate for office. . . . The attempts to disqualify her based on the assumption that her prior conviction renders her constitutionally ineligible to hold the aforementioned position is premature and constitutes a substantive constitutional challenge."

Several local legal scholars and practicing lawyers agreed with that assessment. The law banned her from holding office, not from running. MomCon could maneuver. Sometimes it didn't work in her favor, sometimes it did, even if she was the only one who viewed it that way.

My mother's reality was my mother's reality.

"There remains no reasonable likelihood that the marriage can be preserved."

That declaration had been in MomCon's 2015 divorce court disavowal of the mutual, forever-after promises that she and Pop made to each other at their 1990 wedding. My father preferred to keep his marriage, said his attorney, Arnold Reed, whose other prominent clients included superstar Aretha Franklin. Except for periods that Pop spent in Washington without her and MomCon's months in federal prison, my parents mainly lived without animus under the same roof, Pop's lawyer told news reporters.

Which was a lie. My parents argued on the regular. Emotions frequently ran high at our house. For several protracted periods, MomCon and Pop did keep each other at a distance. I remember my mother's understandable fury over not being adequately tended to as a wife and as a woman. She was angst-ridden over the loss of soul-deep intimacies that seemed present during her and Pop's courtship and the earlier, sweeter years of their marriage. When they were no longer physically intimate, MomCon, rejected and sad, I think, explicitly cussed Pop out about it. At the top of her lungs, she yelled her complaint. Maybe, she didn't realize it, but my baby brother and I were within earshot. We heard it all. Maybe I should have felt some level of sympathy for her right then. Maybe I should have ached right then for MomCon. But I didn't. My sorrow was directed inward, toward my baby brother and me. We didn't deserve to be exposed to their troubles, which, I suppose, only got worse over time.

From my perspective, my parents were a mismatch. Pop, as a spouse, never was the type who complimented his wife the way I believe a husband ought. He didn't dote. Pop expressed whatever might have been his affections for MomCon in his incontrovertibly understated style, clearly insufficient for MomCon, given who she is. He was never an "Awww, baby, you look good in that dress" type, not as far as I saw and heard. I do remember reading a letter my father had handwritten to my mother about looking forward to going to the movies. It was dated 1994.

And I do know that MomCon loved Pop, perhaps lavishly of all, by cooking whatever he wanted to eat. And MomCon worked magic for her man in the kitchen. Pop had taught my mom how to pick the best cuts of meat when, while in DC, they shopped at the butcher shop near his condo. "I didn't become a big cook until I got married," MomCon told me. "Whatever he wanted, I made it. Chitlins, pork chops, beef sausage, sweet potato pie with butter pecan ice cream, creams, and raisin bran cereal and stew and milk."

The bougie Blacks and the regular folks alike know about my mama's incomparable cooking skills and how her food is the love she seems unable to express in words. Food is Monica Ann Esters's purest ministry. Cooking is what she learned, first, by watching her mother, then from my grandma Lucille, who thought, MomCon told me, a woman's place was in the home. "Though we had a nanny, my mother-in-law used to call me every day while I was at school teaching with some excuse for why I should come home. I had to have my husband put a stop to that."

After Pop's father died in 1986, Pop moved his mother in with him. From day one, after MomCon joined that household on Seven

Mile, a spectacular friendship sprouted between the two women, with MomCon listening intently to Grandma's tales about coming of age down in Jackson, Mississippi; about meeting her husband in Detroit; about rearing children; about not letting grief swallow you whole when a child dies. Grandma Lucille had laid three of her five offspring in early graves.

Grandma Lucille bought me my first miniature, portable basketball hoop and got me on track toward my lifelong love of the game. She taught MomCon how to prepare Pop's dinnertime chicken drumsticks, a favorite of his, a million different ways. And MomCon enjoyed dishing them up for "The Congressman," her pet name for Pop, spelled with a capital T and a capital C.

Because I considered it strictly grown folks' business, I never asked my parents about when or how their relationship morphed into such a massive, unpredictable roller-coaster ride. But they must have retreated into an earlier, more blissful, if not more loving, version of themselves when, almost a year to the day after that divorce filing, the two of them, instead, renewed their vows outdoors in a park. I was one of their handful of witnesses. But I cannot recall what they were promising each other. I'd zoned out, baffled by the motions they were going through. As if the motions made up for whatever they'd messed up. How many times had MomCon bluntly asked me and Carl, who were still schoolboys, whether or not she should divorce Pop? We'd answered her. "Yes, you should" or "Your happiness is what's most important," making supportive statements along those lines.

During their vow renewal, I was scratching my head. I was at a loss. Yet, in no way would my mother allow anyone, including me, to minimize what she and Pop had. "We built a family and a political collaboration and a life together, even if it wasn't picture-perfect," she said. "The best part was loving my husband and knowing what it was to have a good husband."

MomCon's devotion to Pop and to Detroit, in signature ways, has not wavered. The builder's license she went after, post–Camp Cupcake, was one of the ways she redirected herself. It is part of her plan to make sure Pop's musical instruments, artwork, congressional archives, and so forth someday have a solid, physical home. It's also part of her plan to build affordable housing and grow her real estate holdings. She is entitled to all of that, just as she is entitled to her versions of our family's truths. I hope that someday she will own her story. I hope she will take full possession of her story, then tell it, without hesitation or shame.

"All the people in Detroit know that I am here to help," she told me. "And if they don't know that, there is nothing I can really do about that."

CHAPTER 7

BROTHERHOOD

They say a picture is worth a thousand words. In one photo that's stuck in my brain, Carl is in the foreground, sitting to my right in his high chair. He is a gorgeous, curious baby, staring straight at the camera. His lips are slightly agape, moist with drool. He is pure sweetness, innocence, and lovability. I'm the wild child in that photo. I am wide-eyed and grinning ear to ear, looking every bit the boundless bundle of trouble I already was proving myself to be. I looked like I'd paused just long enough from doing something I shouldn't have done to pose for that photo. I looked like my first-grade self, ready to pounce, ready to make more mischief as soon as the person behind the camera finished snapping shots.

The photo is a telling illustration of two brothers, together and separate, born of the same seed but, by personality and behavior, are studies in contrast. Carl is five years younger than I am. Much more than I do, he has Pop's tenderness, tolerance, and an almost extraordinary ability to watch, listen, and wait. He is rarely knee-jerk. Figuratively speaking, Carl tends to look both ways before he sets off across a busy intersection, and clears his throat before he says a word. He is, like our father, measured and thoughtful.

Of course, I understood none of that when we were children.

I appreciated none of that. I was too caught up in being me and trying to have my way. I was hell on Carl, and hell on myself.

"I'm not sure how you feel about me having more of Dad's disposition," Carl remarked, in 2021, while we were living together in my LA apartment. "But I do have his disposition and I'm grateful for that. It really took something for him to lose his temper and I only saw that happen a couple of times. He might have said 'damn' or 'shit' if he stubbed his toe, but the only time I'd heard him swear in anger, it was directed at someone on his staff. And the anger, I think, probably came out of the fact that he took the work so, so seriously."

He was absorbed in it. So much so that Carl found out from his mostly white boarding school classmates, not from Pop, that our father was responsible for, say, the federal Martin Luther King holiday.

"Dad just never talked about it. He might have told me about the stuff he was doing currently but not the big historic stuff. And, for sure, I'd be bragging to my children, if I'd gotten them the day off school. He didn't, which provides so much perspective on who he was.

"Our father was kind—so is Mom in her own way—and he had that calmness. He was easily approachable. Part of that probably had to do with being a public figure for as long as he was."

Just once, Carl said, he remembers Pop being as red-hot angry at me as Pop was capable of becoming with anyone. Our dad was trying to show me or teach me something, though neither Carl nor I remember what that something was. Whatever it was, it was important to Pop, who said his piece to me and walked away to cool off. I'd stirred up something in our father that he didn't like. I'd pushed him toward a discomfort he wasn't accustomed to. In our house, MomCon doled out most of the discipline. She did not believe in sparing the rod. She was the reactionary.

"When we had a mold problem," Carl said, "and had to move out of our house for a year, half of that we spent with Grandma and half at a hotel. One night, Mom woke me up out of my sleep, whispering that I should get up and get out of the way."

MomCon was about to start swinging. She didn't want to swat Carl accidentally. I, the rebel child, was about to get my ass whupped. Again. MomCon would wake me up out of my good sleep. As Carl remembered it, I'd again broken some rule or offended someone, somewhere, somehow. Maybe I'd done something wrong at Vaughn, an all-boys middle school that is part of and feeds students into Cranbrook Schools' coed high school. I remember a few meetings with Mr. Reynolds, a science teacher who doubled as head of students for Vaughn's seventh-graders. I rarely did homework; I still think there are better, more engaging ways for young people to learn. With hindsight and an ADHD diagnosis, I wonder what could have been, academically, for me, if evidence-based support had been granted, even back then, to a bright kid who, medically speaking, had a tough time paying attention and sitting still. Maybe the lack of accommodations for my ADHD and, consequently, the lack of intellectual stimulation are part of why I found myself running amok—and later, stealing cash from Pop to place bets with a sports bookie. Carl has managed to find the humor in that and in others among my biggest blunders. I can, too, now that we're a safer distance from them, working toward inner healing.

Nevertheless, my immaturity also has caused Carl some anguish. My imperfection caused him some genuine pain. I'd traumatized my baby brother, without realizing I had and, I hope, without intending to. I yelled at Carl. I bullied him. I sometimes punched him. I did all sorts of things to him. When, without asking me, he took my prized basketball—stitched out of 100 percent leather—outside to play some hoops with his friends in our driveway, I raged out on Carl. I screamed bloody murder. I embarrassed Carl in front of his friends. "Wow! Was that me?" I've worked hard to not feel shame, as I sometimes do, reflecting on that time. "Had I transferred onto Carl the violence our mother meted out against me?" I'm convinced, to this day, that Carl eventually shunned basketball because of me. Because of my browbeating and because of the way I sweated him about sports—as if they were the measure of a Black man and a brother. Mind you, Carl has been the far better, natural athlete. He is more graceful, stronger, and four inches taller than I am. When he was old enough, big enough, and fast enough to try and outrun me, he developed the habit of challenging me to race to our car after MomCon finished her weekly shopping and was directing us home again. What helped lay the foundation for my brother and me to mend fences was that I found a semilocal AAU team where he could train year-round, not just during his high school track season. Two or three times a week, our aunt Sunceria or I drove Carl eighty miles round trip to Ann Arbor to train. Slowly, my brother began to realize how much I was trying to really, really see him. Also, I was giving him what I'd not gotten. As a teen, my coach, a former NBA player, thought I was polished enough to at least play overseas. And though I was an avid athlete all through my childhood, neither my mother nor father saw the need to push me further down that path. They didn't pay much attention at all to that part of me. Why, I'm not sure. Maybe because Pop wasn't around, overwhelming MomCon as she did double duty on the parenting front. She'd enrolled me in summer basketball camps to help me improve my skills, but that, for me, fell short of being on the AAU summer circuit, where teams competed against each other. To me, too often my mother gave us what she wanted to give us, not what we needed.

Carl veered in the opposite direction from the ones I careened toward for so many of our growing-up years. "Sure," Carl told me, "there were times that we bonded over how ridiculous Mom could be when whatever we'd said or done was not at all egregious. She has gotten a lot better now. But she used to not differentiate. When somebody made her upset, she was mad at everybody. If you acted out, it was like, 'Now, I got to deal with the backlash.' I just made sure to kind of be out of the way, not be in trouble. I saw the effects of you being in trouble. I didn't want to deal with any of that."

Leaving Detroit for Morehouse College, which has turned out generations of Black male graduates, clued me in on how much I'd failed as a brother. There are circles upon circles of successful students and alumni from that predominantly Black, all-male institution, where I showed up as something of a blank slate. Morehouse has received Black men of every stripe. There it didn't matter what my last name was or whether that name could be used as currency. What mattered on that campus was my competence, deference, and dedication to Morehouse, which in and of itself was a fraternity. What mattered was whether I could prove myself worthy to be called a Morehouse man. The brothers there held you to a standard worthy of Mother Morehouse. Morehouse students exuded a brotherly connection that forced me to man up and be better in that role with my classmates and, more importantly, with Carl. He was fourteen years old and, in my anxious mind, still the wide-eyed innocent from that old baby picture when we dropped MomCon off at prison. For the 475 miles from Detroit to Alderson, West Virginia, Aunt Gulinda, who drove, and Judge Vonda Evans, my mother's friend from high school, were up front. Carl, my grandmother, and MomCon took up the middle seats.

In the rear seat with me was Porscha, my high school girlfriend. If my mother was weighed down by what was happening, she didn't show it at all, Porscha said, giving at once an insider's and outsider's view of the situation: "It didn't seem like we were going to do what we were going to do. It wasn't somber. There was a good amount of joy. The elder women in the car had their moments, but even that was very much, kind of, the fussing you see in Black families; you are going to have some moments of spice when you're driving quite a distance, talking, and reminiscing on old times. It was not a sad, crying journey. It was a lot of laughter and love. It was nice to witness."

Whenever she has recapped for others her story of helping to escort the wife of Congressman Conyers to prison, Porscha realizes what a big deal that was. "When I tell someone we did that, they say, 'What?!'"

That my mother maintained herself during the ride didn't surprise Porscha, who views my mother with clarity and empathy.

"She has a soft side to her that I don't think a lot of people get to experience and see," Porscha told me. "I hug on my kids, kiss on my kids, but that is not how your mother loves. Now that I'm a mother, I understand the need to protect your children from your emotions sometimes.

"And because I've been to therapy myself, I would say that concealing parts of yourself is a safety mechanism. Your mom will rustle and tussle with the best of them. Letting that guard down is probably very uncomfortable for her. It is probably better for her to have a hard shell. She's gone upside my head a few times but I know she keeps me in her heart."

As for me on that drive, Porscha told me, "You did a good job of putting on armor before you walked out the door every day, during that time. As much as you might have been feeling whatever you felt, you did a good job of compartmentalizing for the sake of the moment and for the sake of everyone in that car. You have a very complicated relationship with your mother. But you love her so much. Love helped you laugh and have your usual contagious joy during that day."

When MomCon went on lockdown down south, I left Atlanta and went home, right before what was to have been the start of my junior year. Though I did not know for sure at the time, I was forfeiting my dream of being certified as a Morehouse man. My name would not be in a roll call including MLK, Julian Bond, Maynard Jackson, Spike Lee, and other titans Pop had known personally.

Since Pop couldn't rejigger his schedule to suddenly become a hands-on single dad to Carl, I'd stand in Pop's place—even if this was an inflated view of who I was and what I could do for my brother. Even if I gave Carl no say in whether he even wanted me back in Detroit. I was not yet twenty years old. I was feeling every imaginable regret over having bullied my little brother. As I packed up my Atlanta apartment to head home, I figured that, by hook or crook, I'd be feeling my way through a new role as Carl's part-time guardian. It was, at once, a really tough and a really easy snap judgment. I was hoping to build some strong muscle memory of how to be the flip side of the piss-poor brother I had, thus far, been to Carl. What I decided is that, with MomCon carted off to prison, Carl was hardly old enough or steely enough to navigate our hometown on his own.

And it's not that he didn't have a network of capable, loving support in Detroit. He had his own little village. Aunt Sunceria, Grandma Alice's youngest sister, already functioned as a second mother to Carl. She picked him up after class, dropped him off to spend time with friends, and sheltered him on his weekends away from a boarding and day school, Cranbrook, in suburban Bloomfield Hills. At one point, he moved a bunch of his belongings into her house. Sometimes, our auntie served as a necessary buffer between me and Carl; especially when he found me too abrasive and too domineering.

But an aunt isn't a big brother, and a big brother isn't a mother or father. While Carl viewed—and maybe still views—me as overbearing, my main concern back then was over how he was handling the damage done by MomCon being our holy mess of a mother,

her good qualities notwithstanding. All these years later, Carl says, he maintained some semblance of inner peace by blocking from his mind what had transpired with MomCon and been played out in the headlines, not just in Detroit but around the country. But I knew what depression felt like. I'd already seen signs of it in Carl, one of the most empathic people I know. Empathy, if not judiciously dished out, could make him a target. If any troubles were to threaten Carl, I wanted to help him triumph over those demons.

As for my feelings about MomCon's crime, conviction, and imprisonment, I was kind of indifferent. If anything, my frustration was over her flat-out denial that her major situation had a major impact on me and Carl. Once again, we were collateral damage in MomCon's battle with demons she had not admitted she was warring against. I had a level of what I can only call acceptance about her being incarcerated. Her imprisonment was hers. How I reacted to it was my responsibility. Saying, "Oh, my God, my mom is going to prison!" wasn't going to help me. I had to stay clearheaded: "This is happening. How do I deal with it?" When I was twelve, Joel Segal, who'd been one of Pop's legislative assistants, gave me a copy of *The Analects*. It's a collection of sayings from Confucius about patience, wisdom, understanding, and detaching from some of what's happening around us. I gleaned that we are supposed to engage with the world without becoming like the world, taking on the worst parts of the world. Though I may not have been aware of it, I was working harder to put that guidance into practice while my mother was away.

My newfound protectiveness regarding Carl during that period stemmed from the pressures I'd experienced precisely because I happened to be the Black son of the son of a prominent, yet reputed, local elected official and bore the name of a legendary Black politician operating on the national level. He had set a baseline and benchmark; he lived and breathed lawmaking and policymaking on a national level. Starting in middle school, long before I consciously fathomed that being a congressman's kid set me apart in some people's eyes, I got peppered with questions: "What's it like to have a dad in Congress? . . . Are you gonna run for office? . . . You have big shoes to fill!" But I was trying to inhabit my own life, be my own person, make my own decisions, and find my own way.

My father didn't apply the pressure one might have expected of him. Maybe he'd noticed my defiance and my struggle. "Be the person you have to be," Pop told me, aware that I could not be a carbon copy of him. He neither wanted nor needed me to be just like him.

Carl, now an executive for an indie film and music production company in Los Angeles, has reminded me of Pop's hands-off approach to how his sons would earn a living and, in the process, make a mark. "Mom wanted us to be lawyers. But Dad did a good job of not forcing that on us," he said. "As I've gotten older, I've been more aware of all the groups we've gotten into, the people we've been able to meet because of our father. But not until my midtwenties did I make peace with the reality that I could never be as influential as him. That is not a put-down of myself, and I will have an impact. But Dad and his legacy—for this nation—if you try to compare yourself to that, it can cause a lot of issues."

Those persistent questions from my classmates and, later, assorted others about how or whether a son like me follows in his famous father's footsteps did not stop coming. Depending on who was asking, the questions could be intrusive. Other people's curiosities about the Conyers boys' plans for the future were part of the reason Carl chose to go to college in Houston. He assumed his peers in Texas would find nothing remarkable about his last name. "My classmates didn't know who Dad was, but a bunch of older people I came across did," Carl said.

As Carl's awareness of who Pop was grew, so did his belief

that, for me, being John Conyers III, firstborn of John Conyers Jr., Esquire, I'd have a harder time in the world.

"It can be a hindrance," Carl said, referring to my name.

My brother's few words were weighted. As we came of age, he bore the brunt of some of my issues, of some of my acting out, perhaps, because I took ownership of being Pop's namesake as I saw fit—not as the world thought I should or wanted me to.

"There was definitely a good bit of time when I did not like you."

Carl has said that to my face enough for me to know that somehow I'm indebted to him. And I will be indebted "Until the End of Time," as I'm reminded by one of Pop's favorite contemporary songs. I was every bit aware of how unbrotherly I had been when I dropped out of Morehouse, heading straight in Carl's direction, compelled to do what I could to care for him and to make amends. I'd literally made Carl one of my punching bags when he was barely old enough to walk. It took me too long to develop the emotional intelligence to recognize my cruelty and, simultaneously, start to comprehend my brother's spirit and his heart. He remains the fiercest and purest person I know. He has been the soft counterpoint to rigid me. Our cousins Robert and Aaron, who have been like brothers to us, used to tease Carl for playing with toys far longer than we thought a growing boy should. But that prolonged child's play was an outgrowth of Carl's imagination. Maybe he was creating a world where his brother didn't go through an extended phase of being an asshole. Maybe he was doing something that had nothing to do with me. Maybe he, regardless of what the rest of us thought, was walking toward the creative and the man he has become. His attributes—his imagination, his childlike openness to everything—are among what drives his success in his industry.

I couldn't go back and reverse the tyranny I'd rained down on my brother. I do not remember exactly how I mistreated him. Carl remembers one time when I punched him in the arm. But I'm sure I landed more punches than that. And worse than the body blows was my below-the-belt verbal abuse, my seething anger over hurts he had not caused. Being with me made Carl extremely unhappy with me. He'd ask to play ball with me, just for the fun of the game. But I, there to win, talked smack until Carl walked off the court. He got sick of my mouthing off. For my little brother, not everything was a competition. Looking back, I know he just wanted us to spend time together. I couldn't undo those many wrongs. But, as our mother left for prison, I could drop everything and go to Carl. I could give him the best of myself, now that I was a young adult, vying to be a better me. So I went.

Concerning how I might help support Carl in MomCon's absence, as one of his guardians in Detroit, I was practical. I used what was at my ready disposal. For twelve months after landing back in our hometown, I searched futilely for a job. Many who'd professed to be so in love with and so grateful to Congressman Conyers didn't step up in his family's, his son's, time of need. We were not wealthy. Not even the UAW administrative office or the shops it represented—no one—would give me a job, not even on a trial basis. I needed help and was not afraid to ask. If I asked for help, those in a position to help should have at least considered it. I shouldn't have had to beg. I shouldn't have suffered that misery.

Nevertheless, the experience softened me. It raised my level of empathy another notch. It also made me get down to brass tacks. I started selling weed, legally and illegally. Drug dealing wasn't a foreign concept to me. I'd watched my uncles do it a decade or so prior when I was a boy. So I wasn't thinking to myself, "What am I doing?!" If anything, that decision fortified my belief in a bare-bones fact I first consciously heard from my father: "Life isn't fair." No one, including a congressman's son and family, was exempt from hardship. How to overcome the hardship was the issue at hand.

A childhood friend and I partnered, obtaining separate

medicinal marijuana cards. One of them was a patient's card; the other was a card for caregivers supplying several patients with medicinal weed. My partner and I each secured the maximum number of marijuana plants legally allowed to cardholders. We had a grow house off East Outer Drive. We harvested what we grew. To look legit and avoid suspicion, we sold some of our product to dispensaries to help patients who needed it to sleep, manage pain, alleviate illness-induced nausea, or what have you. With the rest, I hit the road and hopped on Interstate 75 to and from Atlanta, where we had a steady, dependable clientele. I never smoked our product. I tried every variation. Indicas, sativas, hybrids, even edibles. All of them were suggested to me by folks I trusted. No matter, though; all of them made me scarily paranoid. Paranoia is a scientifically proven side effect for a small percentage of weed users. I didn't want to mess with my mental health or be so whacked out that I threatened our enterprise or my future on the other side of a temporary means of bringing in some cash.

In the midst of that moneymaking, I encountered other, unexpected trouble. Twenty-year-old me drove my father's congressional-issue Cadillac Escalade SUV to one of many rap concerts produced by Finally Famous, a company run by my high school friends and me. A then up-and-coming rapper named Big Sean—the main attraction of our Finally Famous crew—was the headliner. The vehicle was ransacked. Now, there are a million rules in Congress. I can't imagine that Pop was thinking to himself, "Oh, this is a congressional car. . . ." His son, who didn't have a car, needed to get to work. Pop just gave me the keys. The car was ransacked. That was the infraction. But my father and I became the headline.

My father made a public apology. He reimbursed taxpayers a few thousand dollars for my unauthorized use of that car. I wasn't aware, at the time, that the car didn't actually belong to my father. Pop owned what was his to own in the situation. And rather than harshly chastise me, he calmly offered this: "It doesn't matter whose fault is. It is a matter of taking accountability."

There is nothing I would ever have done, intentionally, to tarnish Pop's reputation of being unflinchingly forthright and aboveboard. I was savvy enough to know that he, like many mighty Black men, faced a whole other level of constant scrutiny, but sometimes even when you know something, you have to learn it all over again. The Escalade being ransacked wasn't the only time I'd been found out by journalists—a breed I often have a visceral, adverse reaction to—doing what they consider to be their jobs.

Once, news reports chided me for posting a social-media selfie and flashing an unopened bottle of Moët champagne, while behind the wheel of a car, outside some social event. If journalists who republished the photo were trying to make me look like an entitled, wayward kid, they succeeded. What they omitted was context, nuance, and the complete facts. In the selfie, I do appear carefree and, perhaps especially to those looking for the worst in me, overly privileged and wayward. Purposely, I highlight that moment. I was a young man simply seeking joy at a time when it felt like much of my family's world and my world were crashing down. I'm not proud of everything I've done before or since that episode, either. I hoped back then—and still hope—that even my most painful life lessons and the pain would prove instructive for Carl.

But what credibility did I even have with my brother? That's the question I finally had to ask myself after Pop, banished from Congress, came back to Detroit and the three of us were spending our evenings in MomCon's kitchen on Seven Mile. I was slinging pots and cooking the delectable things that my mom had shown me how to cook. We ate and talked and passed the time and let ourselves just be, as our gentle giant of a father was slow-walking toward the sunset of his life.

Before Pop died, I wanted to help shore up the parts of my

brother and myself and our relationship that were adrift, flotsam on the sea where we'd been cast. I wanted to show Pop that his boys were much more in sync, the way he desired us to be. I wanted to show my brother that I could be a newer, more improved version—someone I was proud of him looking up to. Before Pop transitioned out of this life we, his precious sons, wanted to grant him that wish that all good parents wish: "Make sure you take care of each other." I asked Carl if he would go to therapy with me. It was a bid to make amends. It was a bid to draw us nearer to each other and, by extension, to Pop and to MomCon. Without taking too much time to ponder my request, my sweet, sweet brother said, "Sure, let's do that." I couldn't have been more pleased or more humbled.

What Carl and I said, specifically, to each other or in answering the therapist is a misty memory, a fog. "All I know is that you apologized a lot and cried a lot," my brother told me.

What I remember is that we both wept, at times inconsolably and at times with tremendous belief that we would make it over the mountain that I, the older of us, was largely responsible for erecting. I'd made mountains out of many a molehill.

In 2021, amid COVID-19, Uncle Nate, Pop's baby brother and last living sibling, shared with me one of his most vivid, earliest memories of his childhood. Before he retold it, my uncle, who was eighty-nine years old on that day, offered that recollecting was no longer his "strongest suit." But he laid out the story without skipping a beat. He didn't stammer, not once. To me, he seemed as sharp as a tack, lucid, and overflowing with details. It was like yesterday, for him, at that moment.

"I might have been in the fifth grade. We were standing before our mother and father, us four boys. And our father was chiding us four boys to stay in school, get ourselves as much education as we could. John always had a leaning toward the political life. I always seemed to have a leaning toward the business life. We kind of grew up in our own space. . . . Because we grew up in Detroit, were well-known in Detroit, had gone to Sampson Elementary . . . when we went into business as Conyers Ford, we had a lot of people who were glad to see us in business."

Carl and Bill, two in that foursome of Conyers sons, died young. They left here one after the other, far too soon. The remaining were Pop and Uncle Nate, a determined duo. Uncle Nate made so much money at those car dealerships—"We had one on the boulevard, one downtown, one way out on Jefferson," my uncle said—that he could help my father achieve his political goals. "Being well-known was one thing, being rich was something else. John wanted to be well-known in politics. I made the money and supported everyone [with political aspirations] at one time or another. . . . My brother and I both had gone to Wayne Law. I'd go and watch John in court. If there was a jury, they couldn't take their eyes off of him. They were watching him, listening to him, agreeing with everything he was saying. He just had that facility.

"Slowly, we began to build a reputation. We opened a law firm called Keith, Conyers, Anderson, Brown, and Walls. We were the most successful Black law firm in the city of Detroit."

They were defense attorneys, initially, with a lot of criminal work, then, with civil work, then, with probate work. "People who were sick, people who had lost someone . . ." Uncle Nate said. Those people, almost entirely Black, were trying to keep their razor-thin grip on what they had, their mamas' and grandmamas' and grand-daddies' hard-won possessions.

And I took a note from that memory of Uncle Nate's, that lesson from Uncle Nate, whose mother and father, my grandparents, allowed their children space while also making demands from which they would not budge and providing guidance.

I aim for what Uncle Nate and Pop modeled. I want me and

Carl to cross the finish line, if you will, together, leaning on and into each other, backing each other, loving each other. I see myself and Carl in the context that Uncle Nate laid out. Carl and I also are a dynamic duo. One of us cannot function without the other if indeed we are to meet our father's expectations that the two of us, separate and together, achieve our self-defined, self-determined goals.

That requires me to let Carl be Carl. It has required that I relinquish my relatively brief, but deeply held and affecting standing as, at least in my eyes, a part-time parent of my baby brother, deflecting and protecting him from threats of the chaos engulfing me when I was in my twenties and Carl in his teens. It has required that I let Carl speak for himself and say what he needs to say about me to my face. His assessments have been telling. For example—and I stridently disagree with Carl on this—I'd made him feel that his Black identity wasn't Black enough. But I've never held Black people to that yardstick. I don't find that debate constructive. Carl may simply have been sharply aware that, because he attended boarding school, he hung out with and befriended his white classmates. Naturally, that would be the case.

When he was well away from Cranbrook, a grown man building a life in California, Carl clapped back at what he imagined I thought of him: "You have dated more white women than I even thought about dating," Carl said, getting straight to the point and laughing. Since leaving boarding school, every woman he has dated or loved, including the one with whom he's shared a deeply committed relationship for several years, is a bona fide Black beauty with brains.

By then, we were having our most candid conversations ever.

"You need to focus on your mental health," Carl told me, knowing, I hope, that I finally was amenable to listening to and learning from and about my baby brother. "There are too many common themes in your relationships for it to always be the other person's fault. Which isn't saying it's your fault. But if you shored up some things, you'd attract someone who helps bring the two of you into a different kind of situation."

If ever he moved back to Detroit and I were still a Michigan resident, I wouldn't be my brother's No. 1 friend. He has stayed more regularly in touch with Robert, our cousin who was as devoted to Carl as a brother should be. Robert was gentle with Carl and showered him with a niceness that, back then, I didn't have to give.

Carl and I love each other. No doubt. My baby brother is my dude. We have a closeness, a brotherhood. That we are not closer, not thick-as-thieves close, hurts my heart. I've wished for more. I've continued to reach for it.

CHAPTER 8

POLITICAL LIMELIGHT

Inside Greater Grace Temple, in the lead-up to celebrity professor and preacher Michael Eric Dyson's official eulogy of Pop, I sat in a center-front pew. A protecting hedge of relatives and friends surrounded me, my mother, my brother, and the last remaining of Pop's siblings, Uncle Nate. I'd walked into that megachurch—perched on acreage my father had helped that influential congregation secure—sleepless and bone-tired. The rims of my eyes showed exhaustion and an expected but bewildering grief.

All the way up to that moment on that November morning, I'd been fending off last-minute requests from individuals whom my family, for efficiency's sake, had not slated to be on the mic during what would unavoidably be a mini-marathon of a homegoing celebration for my politically famous father. "Pretty please," several individuals asked, summarily, "might I say a few words about the congressman, a man so pivotal, so instrumental, so kind, so grand."

He had toiled on their behalf, and they were grateful. Maybe I was too anxious to be annoyed or flustered by their eleventh-hour solicitations. My brain was on autopilot. My heart throbbed with a nameless, elusive ache. My laser focus, however, was on a flawless finale to our days of nonstop preparation for a fitting send-off for

Pop, a culminating celebration of his life. "God, let everything flow smoothly," I prayed. "Let every story they tell about Pop be true. Let this be what he deserves."

When Uncle Bill walked forward for his turn behind the pulpit podium at Greater Grace, I fixed on his left hand. His thumb and third and fourth digits trembled as he turned the pages of his prepared words of praise for my father. The sight of that tremor jarred me. Strangely, perhaps, it also soothed. We do grow old. We do wither. From the time we are born until we die, we can build a meaningful life or squander the gift of that chance to make meaning.

President William Jefferson Clinton, the man I'd referred to as Uncle Bill since I was a kid, had partnered with Pop on certain policies and parted with him on others. Still, come what may, those two men respected each other. No doubt. In 1998, after the US House of Representatives' Republican majority impeached Clinton, charging him with perjury and obstructing justice in the grand juried case of his sexual dalliances with White House intern Monica Lewinsky, Clinton conferred with Pop. He relied on Pop. As the House Judiciary Committee's ranking Democrat, my father helped set the tone for the impeachment hearings. Eloquently and rationally, Pop slapped down shot after shot that his GOP colleagues took at Clinton.

"The president is on the phone," I'd overheard my mother say, handing my father the receiver. Pop was helping engineer Clinton's ultimate acquittal on what my father considered trumped-up charges. That exchange of presidential woes and lawyerly advice rambled on, sometimes toward the midnight hour.

Seated behind the nation's 42nd commander in chief, as Uncle Bill took his turn at Greater Grace's pulpit lectern, were Dyson; my godfather, Rev. Jesse Jackson; Rev. Alan Tumpkin of LifeChurch Southfield; Rev. Dr. Nathan Johnson of Tabernacle Missionary

Baptist Church, the church my father grew up in; Bishop J. Drew Sheard of Greater Emmanuel Institutional Church; and Rev. Dr. Wendell Anthony of Fellowship Chapel. Uncle Bill held a cordless mic in his right hand, which also trembled a bit.

"I want to thank Monica, John, Carl, Nathan, the entire Conyers family for inviting me to come and pay tribute to my friend," he began. ". . . I'd like to thank the people of Detroit for electing him twenty-seven times . . . for giving him the space and the support, not just to faithfully represent his district, but to represent people all across our country, and even around the world, on the things that we should all care about.

"He was out there banging the drum against apartheid in South Africa long before it was a widely popular cause. He always supported the people of Haiti, even when he could not support their government. He said the people deserved a better deal and the United States should be a good neighbor. He worked for all of our cities. For jobs and employment and opportunity and peace and justice everywhere.

"When somebody served as long and as well as John did, it's tempting to make sure you list every last bill that he sponsored or cosponsored or had something to do with. In a way, that's a big mistake. Because it tends to turn history into dry bones. The most important thing is to remember how different the playing field was when he began than when he ended, how steep the mountains he climbed were, how long the battles lasted, and how many real lives were improved by his labors."

Those honoring words brought me back to myself as I sat in that pew. I was there, in body but not in spirit, until those words snapped me out of my haze. Those actionable words brought me back to Pop. Ezekiel, a visionary in the Bible, saw those dry bones in a valley being miraculously brought back to life. That wordplay by Uncle Bill, who'd been reared in the Southern Baptist church and twice elected governor of Arkansas back when it was an unam-biguously blue state, alluded to Pop's many efforts to restore what was desecrated, dried up, and threatened with being windblown into oblivion.

"A Record of Progress: A Summary of Legislative & Related Achievements" is the title Pop attached to his careful, abbreviated catalog of his endeavors in Washington. I call it the "Library of Conyers." It is 132 annotated pages listing laws and policies Pop tackled, and legislation he initiated from the 89th through the 113th congressional sessions. (He retired in the middle of the 115th Congress.) "Rep. Conyers' numerous legislative and related activities have continued," Pop wrote in the overview of that sum-mary, "whether he was a junior member, committee chairman or ranking member, as he always sought to work across the aisle and with other members whenever possible. In addition, throughout his legislative career, Rep. Conyers has served as a singular beacon of hope for those facing poverty and injustice and in pursuing critical legislative causes. Whether it was being the first member to offer a Martin Luther King holiday bill after his 1968 assassination or more recently being the first member to introduce legislation to rein in abuses by the National Security Agency and reacting to the 2014 water cutoff crisis in Detroit, Rep. Conyers never shied from a difficult legislative challenge."

The cover page of the Library of Conyers bears a collage of pho-tographs. They are a partial timeline of Pop's career. He's framed alongside his congressional colleagues and other notable people: MLK Jr. Rosa Parks. Nelson Mandela. President Clinton. President Obama. The photos show my young dad, with a full head of jet-black hair. They show my old dad, gray-haired and balding, the slightest paunch settled into his midsection, his once squared shoul-ders a bit rounder, his signature mustache as thick as ever.

Across the span of years captured in those pictures, my father's ingenuity reshaped entire arenas, whether policing and law enforcement or health care or human rights. If you asked Pop which of his legislative victories he prized the most, he would cite, in addition to the MLK holiday and Hate Crimes Prevention Act, his authorship of several other major laws. His Helping Families Save Their Homes Act aimed to counteract the 2007 through 2010 subprime mortgage crisis that hit Blacks and Latinos, including ones with higher incomes, especially hard. His Pigford Claims Remedy Act aimed to shield and retroactively compensate Black farmers who, for decade upon decade upon decade, have continued to be refused federal farm loans for which they qualified. His Innocence Protection Act increased the use of DNA evidence in challenging criminal prosecutions where the death penalty was being sought. The Alcohol Beverage Labeling Act warned of the potential health harms of liquor. The Motor Voter Act allowed persons to register to vote when they signed up for a driver's license.

There was Pop's Emmett Till Unsolved Civil Rights Crime Act; Help America Vote Act; Hate Crimes Statistics Act; Sexual Abuse Act; and other signature, solo initiatives.

The Jazz Preservation Act designated that genre of music an American art form. "His political activism on behalf of jazz had such an impact; it made him a hero in the jazz community," Kresge Foundation executive and former journalist W. Kim Heron told me of Pop, the former trumpeter who'd been in the marching band of the Northwestern High School. Mr. Heron had seen my father in the audience and backstage at major events. They included a special Detroit Symphony Orchestra concert featuring international jazz great Yusef Lateef, the woodwindist, a native Tennessean whose family moved to Detroit when he was five.

"Before your father, jazz was not much a part of academia. Jazz had no well-established, mainstream organizations. Opera had its organizational infrastructure. Jazz had attempts at that going back to the 1920s . . . but it had no permanent institutional structures. The artists primarily were Black and, certainly, race complicated things. But, also, jazz was a new music. On the timeline, it takes a while to have things to coalesce."

When Detroit's Societie of the Culturally Concerned hosted its Bluebird Reunions, Pop was there. He—the first recipient of the Grammy Awards' honor for legislators—was paying homage to the elders of jazz and the Bluebird Inn, a main force in the development of Detroit's bebop community in the 1950s. When President Carter, a fellow jazz lover, was in office, my father was instrumental in Carter's decision to host a jazz festival on the White House lawn. Dizzy Gillespie, Max Roach, Herbie Hancock, Sonny Rollins, and Dexter Gordon were among its headliners.

Pop seemed to like President Carter, the human being. Yet, he doubted Carter's acumen as leader of the purportedly most powerful country in the developed world. The *Washington Post*, in its obituary of Pop, noted his views on a couple of fellow Democrats who'd resided at 1600 Pennsylvania Avenue. "In 1979, he described President Jimmy Carter as a 'hopeless, demented, honest, well-intentioned nerd who will never get past his first administration.' Decades later, Mr. Conyers criticized Obama for making foreign policy too dependent on military muscle. His intention, Mr. Conyers said of Obama, was 'to make him a better president.'"

Obituaries by the *Washington Post*, *Wall Street Journal*, *New York Times*, and other news outlets, great and small, cited laws for which Pop was the sole author. But my father didn't always go it alone. He shepherded a number of measures that he cosponsored: The James Zadroga 9/11 Health and Compensation Act, establishing a health care fund and compensation claims program for first responders who were seriously sickened by toxic debris of the September 11 attacks on the Twin Towers. The bipartisan Second Chance Act to expand employment, education, housing, and other services for those released from state and federal prisons. The Voting Rights Act of 1965.

No less important were the things he helped deliver for Detroit. He stopped the shutdown of safety-net hospitals, blocked US imports of dangerous Asian carp, and secured funding for everything from anti-gang initiatives to protections for freshwater resources in the Great Lakes.

Producers of the 2015 movie *Concussion*, starring Will Smith, cribbed a C-SPAN clip of Pop's 2009 hearings on head injuries in the NFL. Pop, who had a real live cameo appearance in the film, shaped much of the world we exist in today.

Despite his feelings about head injuries, Pop didn't block me and my brother from playing football, although he'd rather we'd stayed off the field. When I was twelve, I needed a parent's signature to join the middle school football team. I asked Pop to sign the waiver enabling me to play. He curtly told me no, but added, "You can ask your mother." She, of course, obliged.

For me, what especially resonates and cements Pop's position as a forerunner are his protracted undertakings to reform systems that were glaringly insufficient and/or unfair. He confronted a criminal justice system that offers an unfair advantage to the monied, famous, and well-connected, while having too little mercy on poor people of every stripe and on people of color in almost every income bracket. My father was the first House member to draft legislation outlawing racial profiling by police and legislation automatically giving those released from federal prisons the right to vote. Throughout much of his tenure on Capitol Hill, Pop hosted town hall meetings on crime and justice in our hometown, but also hopscotched the country to parse the subject in other locales.

"The current price tag for fighting crime at the federal, state, and local level is $22 billion a year, five times more than was spent ten years ago when the crime rate was half the level of 1976," said my father, in his opening remarks at a San Francisco gathering in 1977. "This fiscal year, the federal government will spend directly only $11.8 billion on jobs and job training programs. This two-to-one ratio of spending on crime versus jobs is an important indication of where our priorities have been misplaced.

"The Subcommittee on Crime of the House of Representatives, which I chair, has been holding extensive hearings on the relationship between crime and unemployment. Several weeks ago, the acting director of the National Institute of Law Enforcement and Criminal Justice, the research arm of the Justice Department's Law Enforcement Assistance Administration, gave the subcommittee this startling piece of information: 'At the present time, we do not know whether unemployment and crime are causatively related, or merely correlates of economic, social, and psychological processes that impact on both. . . . We know very little about the manner in which unemployment and crime interact.'"

Nonsense! That was Pop's view. In the 1970s, speakers he invited to one of what he dubbed his "interrogatories" included researchers of what drove crime in San Francisco's Chinatown and other neighborhoods. They also included people who experienced the underbelly of urban life and who as a result found themselves behind bars. Pop gave them a platform to provide essential insights. He listened to them. He went on to say: "After eight years and more than $20 million expended on criminal justice research projects, that Law Enforcement Assistance Administration, or, for that matter, the Justice Department, is still unsure of social costs of unemployment and the social roots of crime. But what is a mystery to the professional crime-fighting establishment is rather clear to many citizens who have studied or lived with the problem."

In that decade and ensuing ones, Pop kept crime and justice at the forefront. He met key players in that arena on their own turf, conducting listening sessions with community people. At one planned hearing in Harlem in 1983, Shirley Roper burst into a room so overcrowded that, for safety reasons, Pop's House Judiciary Committee interrogatory had to be rescheduled. "They killed my son. Eight bullets. They killed my son!" Roper was screaming. Six weeks prior, three NYPD officers shot her child, Kenneth Thompson, alleging that he'd tried to attack them with a knife. Internal NYPD investigators ruled that the police justifiably defended themselves. Roper told the *Daily News* (New York) that she had no choice except to press her way into that packed hearing room: "When everyone started pushing in, so did I. And I said what I had to say because I'm hurting inside."

Especially when they appear to have lost all else, people had to have their say. In a country that has stripped Black people of so much, we more than deserve that. Pop clung to that fact. He tried to meet folks right where they were, at their very point of need. Likewise, he met in their respective municipalities and invited to Washington both some of the most divisive figures in law enforcement as well as some of the forward-looking police officials and brightest minds across the field of outside experts in that sector.

Pop also had a knack for surfacing issues that his congressional peers seemed to relegate to the back burner. He was the first House member to propose a Medicare for All Act. Also known as the United States National Health Care Act, which he introduced back in 2003, the proposal would have created a taxpayer-financed, government-run system similar to those in thirteen of the world's most developed nations, where good health outcomes outpace ours. That proposal revved up the long march toward what we now know as the Patient Protection and Affordable Care Act. Colloquially called Obamacare, it delivers health care coverage to people earning too much to qualify for Medicaid, the federally and state-funded coverage for the poorest of poor Americans, but too little to snag health insurance in the money-hungry private marketplace. Before

Obama, in 1943, three Democratic members of Congress (Senator Robert Wagner of New York, Senator James Murray of Montana, and Pop's fellow Michigander, Representative John Dingell Sr.) proposed legislation for a national health insurance program for all Americans. That 1943 proposal would have made such a health insurance program part of the Social Security system. Both President Franklin Delano Roosevelt and his successor, President Truman, initially supported the legislation. Truman buckled to protests from the American Medical Association, which opposed it.

Pop studied that history. He'd broken down the broad strokes and minute details of health disparities driven by income and race—research finds that some white doctors believe Black patients can withstand more pain and, thereby, refuse them needed pain medicine—and other factors that were codified in the landmark Kerner Commission Report of 1968. That analysis was prompted by Black citizens' historic 1967 uprisings against police and other American systems in Newark, New Jersey, then Detroit, then a chain reaction of other cities.

My father examined his predecessors' strategies around overhauling the health care system. He drew from them in drafting his own legislation for a system that might leave no one without health insurance or the medical services that insurance ensures. Pop knew he couldn't tackle health care all by himself. Dr. Herbert Smitherman Jr., an internist and public health researcher in Detroit, became one of my father's key allies. A health policy analyst on Pop's congressional staff had heard the doctor expounding on the merits of and arguments against the proposed bill during a trip back home to keep an ear to the ground on the concerns of Pop's constituents. "He said," Dr. Smitherman recalled of Pop's staffer approaching him, "'I want to introduce you to Representative John Conyers.' I and my wife, who is also a physician, had chosen Detroit purposefully when applying for our residency programs. We were looking for a community that had a large population of African Americans who we could serve. We looked at Atlanta, we looked at DC, we looked at LA. We went to Michigan.

"There seemed to be a lot of political power in Detroit, which had an African American mayor . . . and [Black congresswoman] Carolyn Cheeks Kilpatrick. And, of course, we knew who your father was. Detroit just seemed to be a power base for trying to solve what are really national problems. And Congressman Conyers was so much a part of that problem-solving."

Back in the 1980s, when the doctor arrived in his newly adopted city, 20 percent of Detroiters were uninsured. "You're talking about 200,000 people," said the physician, who has directed federally funded medical clinics for the poor and working class. "That's larger than the population of many small- to medium-size cities. And I'm seeing these patients in the emergency room, where we can't provide them appropriate care and we're sending them home with no plan of follow-up care. Because they don't have insurance, we're sending them out without appropriate medications, et cetera, or we can't give them a follow-up procedure. It became clear to me, at that time, that our present system wasn't going to work."

In their first meeting, arranged by Pop's health care policy staffer, Dr. Smitherman dissected for my father a slew of research about the merits of universal health care, even though the doctor wasn't, for practical reasons, quite sold on it. "Politically, I did not believe we could get it done. I didn't believe there were the votes—in any way, shape, or form—to move us toward a system where the insurance program was funded by the federal government, but also where the federal government also controlled the delivery system. Meaning that the government ran all the hospitals and the doctors and everything else as the European programs do, the United Kingdom's programs do."

So he suggested to Pop a less ambitious, incremental expansion might work. Maybe the age to qualify for Medicare might be lowered, capturing more older adults? Maybe the income ceiling for being eligible for Medicaid might be raised so that more working-poor people would get health care coverage? Dr. Smitherman, at Pop's request, testified before Congress, offering his potential remedies. Pop introduced the physician to President Obama, who named the doctor to a White House advisory committee. On the pressing issue of health care access, my father kept leaning in the direction he'd been heading. He was known for not backing down. He was willing to wait out critics—and there were plenty—who distorted his views and sometimes didn't even bother to read his legislation.

"People kept telling me that your dad, you know, was kind of a radical," said the doctor, a former president of the Michigan State Medical Society. "And they tried to say he was pushing socialized medicine, where the delivery system—that means all the doctors and hospitals—plus the insurance market is run by the government. But he was only talking about having the insurance part. And he absolutely was the most progressive congressional member on health care, just the most progressive health care zealot in the Congress. . . . He and I got into this whole big conversation, and that is what solidified our bond, that's what made us friends. We were kindred."

Pop had nudged President Obama to tap the Detroit doctor as the nation's surgeon general. The job went, instead, to Dr. Regina Benjamin, a MacArthur Foundation "Genius Grant" winner who'd founded a rural health clinic in her native Alabama. There, her brother had died of HIV, her dad of hypertension and diabetes, and her mom of lung cancer. She'd listed each of those illnesses in the broad category of preventable diseases Dr. Smitherman had seen too often in Detroit emergency rooms and the clinics he oversaw.

He didn't become the nation's top doc, which was fine with

him. Functioning as a kind of private health czar to my father for more than fifteen years elevated Dr. Smitherman's standing among Michigan health care executives and the lawmakers who decided how medical dollars get spent in Detroit and throughout Michigan.

"What's that saying? 'All politics are local.' Your dad knew that," the doctor told me. "And he wanted the best for people. Just because you got cancer or some chronic illness or had a heart attack or had a major accident and lost the use of your lower extremities . . . through no fault of your own . . . and, now, you're being penalized for it? Can't get care because you have no money? For a country this rich, that was just immoral. And that's where your dad was; that was his position."

A half century after that Kerner Commission analysis, Dr. Smitherman told me, the largely unchanged economics of many communities have meant that those health disparities he'd first witnessed in the emergency room remain entrenched. "The correlate still stands. The wealthier you are, the healthier you are," he said. "The poorer you are, the poorer your health status. This is true across the country, no matter what city, state, county. And it is true around the world."

My father knew that, among other characteristics, poverty, region, and skin color are determinants. They are determinants everywhere on the globe. Is it an accident that the darkest people are the poorest and most outcast? Everywhere? So I find myself repeating Pop's favorite mantra whenever I hear these stories about him from people who were on Pop's team, literally, figuratively, and philosophically: "It's all connected."

Over and over and over again, since I was a boy, I'd heard my father say that. When I was younger, I only half listened to those three words. I could not know their importance or impact. When I was younger and had not yet lived enough to see or conceive of connectivity, Pop's mantra seemed like an oversimplified catchphrase, especially coming from a man as learned and big-thinking as Pop. But, with his passing and in my going on without him and in my search to better know this person we put in the grave in 2019, I embrace these notions of connectedness. I see connectivity, beyond a shadow of a doubt. Consistently, Pop used the term "all" to characterize the domino effect of just about every action. Knowing that we are *all* connected somehow should force us to at least try to see one another as equals. Pop tried, for example, not just to demonize as religious fanatics and anarchists the members of the Branch Davidians who were involved in a fifty-one-day standoff with federal law enforcement officials on the outskirts of Waco, Texas, in 1993. My father tried to humanize them. He gave them their measure of respect. He treated them as the Americans that they are, worthy of a fair hearing and a place in this land of likenesses and dissimilarities, of hopes, of dreams realized and dreams dashed.

The Davidians were an apocalyptic cult, cloistered, living among themselves and waiting for Jesus Christ to return to Earth to fulfill what they deemed to be a biblical prophecy. Among other things, some men in that cult had taken teenage girls as wives. The standoff between armed members of the federal Bureau of Alcohol, Tobacco, and Firearms—it had been investigating cult leaders for illegal manufacturing and possessing firearms, grenades, and other deadly devices—and armed Davidians ended in an explosion and fire. Among the eighty-two Davidians who died during that siege near Waco, twenty-eight were children.

"Whatever abuse that happened needed to be prevented," Uncle Julian, a.k.a. attorney Julian Epstein, told me. Another of my surrogate uncles, he'd been chief counsel of the House Judiciary Committee when Pop was its chair. Pop oversaw the committee's investigation of what had gone awry at the Davidians' compound.

"At the same time," Uncle Julian explained, recalling what my father declared, "we have to have oversight to make sure there isn't unnecessary excessive force. And, so, when [the ATF] dropped the incendiary devices, your father's question was, 'Were there other means? Could you have starved them out? Were there other exigencies where you couldn't wait?' He saw his role as asking the tough questions: 'Before you use deadly force be 100 percent certain that's your best strategy.'"

My father had been temperate in his assessment of things and in the tone he set during those after-the-fact hearings. How do agents of the federal government greatly reduce the likelihood of a catastrophe like the one outside Waco? It's a relevant fact in an America where, among others, the Southern Poverty Law Center's Klanwatch project has been tracking a steady rise in anti-government, racial, religious, and other so-called fringe groups. (That tracks with the surge in a vicious, vengeful, conservative right wing in Europe and elsewhere in the world.) How do we stay vigilant, as a nation, against that threat?

Regarding the Davidians, Uncle Julian recalled, Pop "tempered his views, I think, a bit, during the course of those hearings. But he would always say, 'I am very pro–law enforcement, and I am for strong law enforcement, and I believe in law enforcement, and I believe law enforcement are our friends.' But he also would say, 'We need to make sure there are checks on the system so that we're not using excessive or deadly force when it's not necessary.'"

My father stayed on the quest for smart, strong policing that lived up to law enforcement's pledge to "protect and defend" the citizenry. With Black and Brown communities attacked from within by assorted crimes, including violent ones, Pop held law enforcement's feet to the fire. He also worked collaboratively with police, hearing them out about the challenges they face in the line of duty and asking how he might help them better perform their job.

"He'd say we need strong law enforcement; we also need to have smart law enforcement. He didn't see a conflict between smart and strong," Uncle Julian said. My father, he added, would have had a hard time, truly, with this unrealistic notion of defunding the police.

"He had good relationships with police and would meet with them all the time," Uncle Julian said. "He was pro-police but pro–responsible policing. He wanted to make sure we have the systems in place against excessive or unnecessary force—and that we policed in a thoughtful, progressive way, figuring out how to build cooperative relationships and how to purge the legacy of negative stuff. He was for positive reform, good training and recruitment, and diversifying police forces. He spent a lot of time with police organizations trying to build."

He was practical in that way. And was plain decent. It's easy to suggest that politicians are opportunists, mainly interested in having their egos stroked and their chances of reelection heightened. There was plenty of evidence of that. So far be it from me to suggest that my father had no ego. But his commitment to egalitarianism and humanity outweighed his self-importance. The ego took a back seat to legislating for what he believed was right and what his constituents said they preferred.

And Pop didn't just support Black freedoms; he supported the freedoms of all people. Decades before Palestine was on the radar for most Americans, Pop embraced the Palestinian cause. Behind California, Michigan has the nation's largest number of Arab Americans, including Palestinians. Metro Detroit is home to many of them. That proximity demanded his knowledge of and familiarity with Arab American communities. Pop's respect for their cultural and political story and the present-day struggles of a far-flung Arab diaspora allowed him to freely navigate those communities, to listen to the people in those communities. It let him see them as kindred, despite the tensions between Arab and Black Americans that can be glaringly obvious in Detroit and elsewhere in America. In our hometown, Black people like me who support Palestinian statehood have been made to feel unwelcomed—and aggressively so—when we venture into some Arab neighborhoods or patronize the region's plentiful number of Arab-owned establishments. Will that change for the better, and permanently, because of Black solidarity with Palestinians in the Middle East?

Pop's advocacy of the Palestinian cause wasn't merely a matter of political expediency; it was heartfelt advocacy for a people he counted as his neighbors.

Pop had mapped the changing boundaries of Palestine. He'd watched them go from being a sovereign nation to being dispossessed. He supported returning their land to them outright. Period. Six percent of Palestine's population was Jewish before the British in 1917 swiped Palestine from its Ottoman-Turk colonizers. European Jews' flight from Nazism made them, by 1948, 33 percent of Palestine's population. Now, more than 73 percent of the population is Jewish in Israel, whose government seized 78 percent of Palestine after winning 1967's Six-Day War. When misguided leaders of fundamentalist churches in Detroit and elsewhere across the country argue that Jews and Israel by divine edict are sacrosanct, they do so with an astonishing ignorance of history and a twisted interpretation of the Holy Land, the Promised Land described in the Bible. Never had that been more apparent than during Israel's boundless assault on the whole of Gaza—bombing schools, hospitals, homes, compounds where refugees from Gaza had taken shelter, caravans of international aid workers who were feeding them, et al.—as it responded to Hamas's murderous 2023 attack and taking of 251 Israeli hostages. Between the October 2023 start of the Israel-Hamas war and October 2024, roughly 41,600 Palestinians—ten times the number of Palestinian casualties during all prior Israel-Palestine conflict since 2008—and 1,700 Israelis had been killed. Though some argue that the data on fatalities are unreliable, news footage shows an irrefutably obliterated Gaza.

Like law enforcement's excessive use of force across the fifty United States, Israeli government–sponsored death and destruction went far beyond defending its sovereignty. It devolved into what I and so many call genocide. What was meant by "never again"? Does that cry of defiance and self-defense apply only to the embattled Jewish people who are immediately under attack? Or does it apply to every person who bleeds and hasn't a shield impenetrable enough to protect himself, herself, or their children? Yet, that Israeli government–ordered destruction has been the cause and flashpoint along a continuum of conflict in that region. Pop used to monitor the happenings there and had been profoundly saddened by them. He'd been in a minority on Capitol Hill, daring to speak against the Israeli government, with its bulwark of supporters in the United States, including political donors with deep pockets. Pop had cosponsored the 1978 "Palestinian Human Rights and Peace" conference at American University. Pop was one of nineteen congresspeople to sign Minnesota congresswoman Betty McCollum's 2015 letter to Secretary of State John Kerry. It implored the United States to demand that the Israeli government end its arrests, interrogation, physical abuse, and secret military detention of what the United Nations counted as thousands of Palestinian children.

Also in the summer of 2015, I had the pleasure of interning in the community outreach department of the Israeli Embassy in Washington. There I learned about Israel's mission in this country and its efforts to keep members of its US communities connected to their homeland. Those lessons enlarged my understanding of the Middle East and made me a forever friend of Israel. The internship came courtesy of Ambassador Ron Dermer, a US-born diplomat and political consultant who was meeting with Pop on Israeli issues. During one of those meetings, I walked into the office and introduced myself. Seeing an opportunity, I asked for an internship.

Despite considering myself an ally of Israel, I couldn't help feeling conflicted in the warring months about Israel's counteroffensive against Palestine—a counteroffensive that double-talking President Biden supported, while sending truckloads and planeloads of food, clothes, and other aid to bombed-out Palestinians. A good friend is candid about the folly he sees. Plus, I'm a Black man. The long-running subjugation of Palestinians mirrors the long-running racial assault against the Black diaspora wherever we may find ourselves in the world, including Africa. What principled man can ignore oppression? With equal vigor, he must condemn Islamophobia and anti-Semitism and the rest of a litany of perilous isms that destroy people and nations.

Neither Israel's right to thrive nor Palestine's right to be self-determining should cancel each other out. Neither goal is a zero-sum game. Real peace, real progress, real equality emerge out of recognition of our shared dignity, not unending recrimination.

Pop tended to take the long view. He recognized that, indeed, few degrees of distance separate one person from the other. Those were not lofty notions to Pop. They were not flimsy, ephemeral concepts. They formed the crux of my father's humanitarianism and his penchant for placing a clear and present danger in his crosshairs.

Three years before Washington lawmakers finally got around to banning US funding of neo-Nazi, white supremacist militias in Ukraine in 2018, my father had authored and won passage of an amendment prohibiting US tax dollars from being spent on that kind of evil. The Pentagon, however, expeditiously succeeded in having Pop's ban stripped from that fiscal year's spending. While Pop had vociferously opposed giving Uncle Sam's help to neofascist frontline troops in Ukraine, critics blasted Pop's amendment. Absurdly they charged that Pop's measure amounted to aiding and abetting Russian president Putin. By any means necessary, they argued, Ukraine had to stay independent and be weaponized against Putin and his encroaching armies.

Pop also supported a sovereign Ukraine. His wider, overarching concern, however, regarded suppressing a transnational surge in white supremacy and the havoc those neo-supremacists, unfettered, were causing and would continue to cause in these fifty United States and wherever else they were. He knew that US-born-and-bred Nazis were enlisting recruits all over the world. Denying American dollars to Ukrainian Azov Battalion, the white supremacist group Pop specifically named in his approved, then retracted amendment, was a no-brainer.

My father was not a pacifist. He had gone to war. But he didn't believe all wars were justified. He did argue that some things—whether one's territory, physical and emotional safety, family, or future—could be righteously defended. He defended the causes he believed in.

As I sat watching Uncle Bill's trembling hands during that more-than-five-hour homegoing celebration, in my mind's eye, oddly, I was rereading Pop's defense of that impeached president whom he considered a friend as independent counsel Kenneth Starr was steering the GOP's assault: "Thank you very much," said my father, then the ranking Democrat on the Judiciary Committee at the top of his opening remarks. "Mr. Chairman, my colleagues, and to the House itself: We stand poised on the edge of a constitutional cliff, staring into the void below into which we have jumped only twice before in our history. Some encourage us to take this fateful leap. But I fear that we are about to inflict irreparable damage on our nation if we do.

"This inquiry began with the tawdry, salacious, unnecessarily sexually graphic referral delivered to us by an occasionally obsessive counsel in September, with so much drama. And since that time, our proceedings in this committee have been marked by one partisan vote after another, beginning with the majority decision to release literally every shred of paper received from Mr. Starr onto the Internet. Although we have been able to reach accord on some matters, in too many respects this inquiry has been a textbook example of how not to run an impeachment inquiry. Time after time, we, the minority, have suffered the indignity of learning from the newspaper or television about important investigative or procedural decisions made by the majority. We learn about the decision to take depositions five minutes before the majority issues a press release to the world. One day, they decide to expand our investigation to campaign finance matters, and the next day we read that the subject is off the table. Just yesterday, even while the White House counsel was concluding his testimony, the majority released its articles of impeachment, articles so vague that they would be dismissed by most courts in the country.

"So much for fairness, so much for bipartisanship."

Every time I review those words, I fall more deeply in love with my father. I respect him that much more. I keep trying to find my place, yet again, in him. I do so as a full-grown man who stands on his own. Not everyone agrees with me that Pop made the difference in President Clinton's acquittal. "Johnny," Uncle Julian began, calling me the name Pop called me, "your dad played a very important role. But I wouldn't overstate it to say that anyone saved Clinton. Clinton had 70 percent public approval. And he had complete support in the Senate among Democrats. What I do think is that your dad helped muster a very, very important effort in the House to define the debate as Ken Starr being excessive, overreaching, engaging in prosecutorial abuse, and to show that the conduct in question was not impeachable. Your dad played a really, really critical, pivotal role. But I would not overstate it to say any member saved Clinton."

I've maintained the right to disagree with that take from, as I called him, Uncle J, who was on the Judiciary's staff during those impeachment hearings. To pivot is to turn around, to turn a thing around, and in this case, to fix it. The literal definition of pivotal is "of crucial importance in relation to the development or success of something." My father did that for Uncle Bill.

As a politician, my father was fierce. He was fire. No, actually, he was more than that. These days, we would say he was *him*. And a lot of folks who shortchange Pop don't recognize their subliminal bias, not even when they love and respect a Black man like my father.

Which isn't to suggest that Pop had no critics or that he was not justifiably criticized. Over the decades, our hometown's newsrooms chastised Pop for missing votes on the House floor. While some of that critique may be valid, the fuller story is that Pop's endeavors weren't strictly limited to what was occurring inside the Washington Beltway. He'd been dropping down in locales where he was needed all across the country, ever since he earned his law degree. Washington might have been his legislative ground zero, but the work driving his lawmaking was happening all over. When, for example, Muslim cleric Rabih Haddad was in pretrial detention in Chicago's Cook County Jail, Pop went to him to sort things out.

A Lebanese citizen who spent a couple of decades, off and on, in the United States, including in Michigan, Haddad had been accused of financing Al Qaeda through a charity for families he founded in the United States. But US authorities never formally charged Haddad with any of the crimes they'd set out to paint him with. Pop had said "set him free" from that Chicago jail and petitioned the court on his behalf, citing the lack of evidence. When Haddad was deported in 2003, leaving his family behind in Ann Arbor, that deportation happened because he'd overstayed his tourist visa. It had nothing to do with the terrorism that federal authorities falsified and never proved. The government was grabbing at straws and strong-arming, that's all.

Eulogizing my father, preacher-professor-author Michael Eric Dyson, a native Detroiter whom Pop highly regarded and deeply loved and mentored, reaffirmed what an exceptional human being Pop had been: "His life was situated by a divine arrangement to do what he did. He didn't just stumble upon this. . . .

"John Conyers represented a country that was not as good as his ideals and ambitions. But he kept on representing the country, despite the fact it didn't deserve a man as great as him. But he represented this country . . . when he stood against Nixon; that's why he was on his enemies list. John Conyers did not care. He stood against presidents and he criticized them even when they supported him—from LBJ down to Donald Trump. . . . He celebrated the first Black president, but he said, 'I'm sorry, sometimes, for having to defend your can—if you can't get in there and do what you got to do yourself.' John Conyers was unashamedly in defense of his country. . . . He represented his community."

In the gentlemanly, statesmanlike way that he'd conducted himself and orchestrated an all-consuming career, Rev. Dyson said, my father made music with his life and his politics. Music that redeemed, soothed, and corrected.

Pop and I shared music. We traded it back and forth. We critiqued it. We dissected a lyric, a note, the arc of a story in a song. I had hoped Frank Ocean, a friend of a friend in the music industry, would sing at Pop's funeral. That didn't happen. But after all was said and done on that day of Pop's last rites, after all the fanfare had died down and my mourning had begun to rise, I put Ocean's extended version of "Wither" in rotation.

For days, then weeks, and then occasionally, I'd listen to that song. I'd set it on repeat. I'd play it all night and all up and down the freeway, on my way to wherever. That's when I'd cry and still feel his presence the most. I'd be imagining my father and what he'd done. Which of his political victories were safe, secured? Which were under threat? How vigilant must we be, right now? Another old man, US senator Bernie Sanders, Pop's good colleague, leads the ongoing march toward a health care system that is less profit centered, more equalized, and leaves no one out. Even with all the progress that Obamacare engendered, 9.1 percent of Americans had no health insurance, according to the latest Census Bureau count. That amounted to a whopping thirty million people. Obamacare is not Pop's Medicare for All, which would have given every single American health care. Yet Obamacare could have been far more expansive had President Obama, alongside what then was a Democratic-controlled House and Senate, simply bulldozed the measure into law. Instead, he withdrew provision after provision from the plan, originally sponsored by US representative Charles Rangel of Harlem, in an attempt to appease Republicans. The GOP despised the first Black president. Except for one GOP abstention, every Senate Republican voted against Obamacare; one House Republican voted for it.

Obama's retreat baffled those who'd endorsed his presidential bid. After all, comprehensive health care reform was a major tenet of his campaign. Among those who chose Obama over his main opponent in the presidential primary, the better-known Hillary Clinton, were Pop and political lion Edward Kennedy. The Democratic senator from Massachusetts, ailing with cancer at the time, was the leading voice for sweeping health care reform in his congressional chamber.

As for Pop's lodestar plan for reparations to the descendants of enslaved Blacks, Democratic congressman Keith Ellison took up where Pop had left off. And when Ellison left Washington to become Minnesota's attorney general, he entrusted US representative Sheila Jackson Lee of Houston—though she died in July 2024—to carry it across the finish line. Who will carry the torch for that critical, unsettled issue and other issues my father put on the front burner that are unfinished and unwritten in the Library of Conyers?

With those simmering questions swirling in my mind, I've

returned, again and again, to the video of Pop's funeral, with its roster of forty people, preaching, singing, praying, trying to hold it together. I've taken an account of myself behind that pulpit podium at Greater Grace, my mustache like Pop's mustache, my pinstripes and cuffs a sartorial match to something that was in his wardrobe. Pop's self-declaring, self-defining words played that day, over the PA system, before I gave my tribute to him. My tribute followed phoned-in and emailed-in expressions of love and condolence from Quincy Jones, Harry Belafonte, and others too frail to be there in person. Others conveyed their gratitude, via letter or video: Debbie Allen. Doug E. Fresh. Then American Society of Composers, Authors and Publishers president Paul Williams. Then NAACP president Derrick Johnson. TransAfrica's Randall Robinson. Grammy winner Dionne Warwick; Pop's lawmaking ensured that she and others got the music industry royalties due to them. "He was," Ms. Warwick wrote, "a mentor to many, including me. He was a lover of music. But most, and above all, he loved *right*. . . . He was our champion, our tireless advocate."

"What we can do," Stevie Wonder said, from the pulpit where I also would stand, "is commit ourselves. . . . Don't talk about it, be about . . . heaven on earth."

Pop, in that mellifluous voice of his, said his piece, too. A still photograph of his face was flashing on a giant screen: "I do things when I want to. I'm working on my time clock. Not my parents', not yours, not the general consensus's—but on my own."

The day Pop died, our house had been flooded with people. They came in. They brought food, brought drink, hugs, kisses, reminiscences. They cried and wiped away tears. They laughed. A family friend who'd worked for my father slipped me a bottle of Xanax.

"You're going to need that," she said. She was correct.

I wrote my few words about my father at five a.m., six hours before the start of Pop's homegoing service. As I typed my heartbreak into my iPhone, I was punch-drunk with exhaustion. My homie Terrence, in from Cali, was sleeping in my bed; Pop taught me to treat the guest as a guest, no matter what. Eventually, I nodded out here and there on the couch, nervous. Had we overlooked a detail regarding Pop's funeral?

When it was my turn at the mic, something kicked in, something so outside of me, yet so inside of me. Adrenaline? Grief in hyperdrive? A son's unadulterated sorrow? Pop, telling me everything would be all right?

"To accomplish goals, you need patience," I began, finally at the mic, responding to a call and command from my father, his body absent but his face still beaming off that big screen at Greater Grace Temple. "The Martin Luther King holiday legislation took fifteen years to become law. That took patience and resilience. My father introduced H.R.676, what we now know as Medicare for All, in 2003; and H.R.40, the Commission to Study and Develop Reparations Proposals for African Americans Act, in 1989. Those two pieces of legislation are only now gaining media attention and traction.

"You have to be patient, trust in your purpose, and stay the course. Stay the course, be resilient, even if it takes fifty-three years . . . and you never see the fruits your tree may bear. . . . Everyone breathing in this sanctuary is someone's future."

As I spoke, my emotions forced me to pause. I tried to catch my breath, rein in my tears, and, at the same time, let them flow.

CHAPTER 9

GLORY IN THE PASTURE

By the time he retired from Congress in December 2017, my father was taking a cocktail of medicines. Seven pills every twenty-four hours: One for hypertension. One to stem memory lapses that sometimes precede all-out dementia. One big whopper of a pill put me on high alert. I traced it each time it crossed Pop's slightly quivering old-man lips, plodded roughly down his throat and past his protruding Adam's apple. I didn't want Pop to choke. My solitary wish was for his ease. Now that he was safely back in Detroit, under the watchful care of those who loved him most, he could rest, maybe. His decades-long, consuming, and nearly nonstop life as a lawmaker was over.

His return to family and the familiarity of his beloved Detroit was a good thing. During the last several of his fifty-three years in Washington, Pop's health had been declining in ways too obvious to ignore.

"There were times that he was manic, and he had us sorting his congressional mail, not by issue area, but by the size or the type of the paper—glossy versus newsprint versus eight and a half by eleven versus legal." Jared Hautamaki, a lawyer who'd been a legislative assistant and campaign adviser to Pop, loosely used the term "manic"—my father was never diagnosed with a mental illness—as he painted a picture of my father commanding his staff to do precisely what he'd told them to do. No questions asked. Pop wasn't budging; they'd sort the mail his way or else. His staff hushed up and complied. They wanted the momentary misery to pass. They wanted Pop, offended and agitated by their initial pushback against his mail-sorting instructions, to calm down. They wanted the even-keeled, patient, measured, kind gentleman they knew to morph back into his other, better self. Seeing the boss they respected and honored in a state of confusion hurt like hell.

As best Jared could recall, Pop's episode inside 2426 Rayburn House Office Building happened during the summer of 2003. Pop would have been seventy-four, which was relatively young for someone who lived to be ninety. I've no expertise in the health and well-being of elderly people, but I do wonder what factors might have put Pop in such a weird space. What had thrown him so off-kilter? Was it his medications, dehydration, or sheer, unrelenting exhaustion?

Jared's retelling of Pop acting outside of his usual character, incoherently, brought home the reality: Pop was just a man. Even men as mighty as my father, at some point, in some way, must surrender. They have to hang up their boots. Pop knew that but fought against it. "My work here is not complete," he'd said.

Pop was forced to retire from Congress after a longtime staffer made what were unproven, unadjudicated—and, in my mind, egregious—allegations of sexual harassment against him. At his age, and with his health declining, it wasn't a fight he could take on. Without his hand being forced, I imagine that my father might very well have become one of the hundreds who died while still serving as an elected official on Capitol Hill. But had he done that, I would not have gotten those last years with him, doing our father-to-son thing, strengthening our bond.

"He was a workaholic to the extreme. Because that's what he

knew; that was his life," said Yolanda Lipsey, who'd been the last director of Pop's district office in Detroit. "I'd say, 'Congressman, you don't have to be everywhere all of the time. We can sit this one out. You've already been to ten other places today. Just get some rest.' Every blue moon he would do that. But most of the time, 'No.' He'd grab a catnap in the car occasionally."

Jonathan Eig's biography of MLK devotes page after page to Dr. King's unrelenting, restless commitment to the cause he was called to. He allowed himself only a few hours of nightly sleep. The stress and exhaustion must have worsened what historians suggest was depression. Though he never was diagnosed with mental illness, MLK had twice attempted suicide as an adolescent. Dr. King's work willed him forward. Work, singularly, also energized my father. How did Pop function as he did for so long and, for much of that time, with sustained vigor?

"He was facing those health challenges, and he worked through them. He'd say, 'I'll be fine.' But you get to a certain point where, if your body needs rest but doesn't get it, your body's going to start shutting down. Those were the only times when he rested. Other than that, the man liked to keep going, going, going. He was not the type of person to take time off. Though there were moments where he would stop and do things with his wife or with his kids, he was not a person that would go have a vacation with the family. Seven days a week, it was all about work, work, work with him."

Whenever I'd ask Pop to consider scheduling an extended vacation, a real vacation, he gave the same dispassionate response: "Where would I go?"

Some might read his answer as sobering, sad even. But it was far from that. Some people work to live; some live to work. I learned that by watching my father and studying other iconic Black men. Celtics legend and Presidential Medal of Freedom recipient

William "Bill" Russell, born five years after Pop, identified more as a father and citizen of the nation whose injustices shared his activism than as an eleven-time NBA champion. Basketball was just his day job. When the Mississippi native died in 2022, his family posted this on social media: "But for all the winning, Bill's understanding of the struggle is what illuminated his life. From boycotting a 1961 exhibition game to unmask too-long-tolerated discrimination to leading Mississippi's first integrated basketball camp in the combustible wake of Medgar [Evers's] assassination . . . Bill called out injustice with an unforgiving candor."

Mr. Russell and my father were cut from the same proverbial cloth.

When Pop retired, he did so in part on the advice and warnings from his doctor. My father would have been at a heightened risk of blood clotting, heart attack, and stroke had he continued flying between DC and Detroit or to other locations.

Stepping down also had much to do with allegations of sexual harassment from his congressional staffers, including the one my mother was adamant that he not hire—and with whom, I and others are convinced, he had a consensual relationship involving whatever degree of sexual involvement Pop was capable of or desired at his age. He'd wanted the case to be tried in court. But his Detroit-based attorney, Arnold Reed, a Harvard Law adjunct professor, and other close confidants advised against pushing for a trial by a judge and jury of his peers. Pop by then was way less nimble on his feet. His recall of the facts was no longer instantaneous. He had less capacity to be eloquent, trenchant, and on-point whenever or wherever he'd assembled himself in front of an audience.

"The early stages of dementia were setting in," recollected Ms. Lipsey, one of those who urged Pop to retire. "In those moments when he couldn't remember stuff, when he couldn't draw from his memory, I would be whispering in his ear or writing notes and passing them to him. He liked having things down on paper. Things were changing, people were coming and going.

"For instance, if we were at an event and some people were about to approach him, elected officials or even just some common, everyday folks that I know and he knew, I would turn toward his ear, where it wasn't noticeable, and I would say, 'Here comes so-and-so, here comes Nancy Pelosi and her husband,' though, of course, he completely remembered Nancy. But there are others that he couldn't remember. So I just whispered, sometimes even when he was in the middle of talking to someone.

"And if I'd see how the conversation was going between him and somebody, and he couldn't remember the name or whatever, I was right there. 'Excuse me one second, Congressman. You've got this call coming up.' And I'd lower my voice, get close: 'That's so-and-so.'

"When you are the assistant to a congressman, no one knows when he's being briefed on something, right? That's how I was able to keep it under disguise. The way I helped him to remember things, nobody was the wiser. I was able to give him contextual clues because not remembering would frustrate him sometimes. He'd get in the car and say to himself, 'Okay, John. Get it together.' And I'd say, 'Don't do that to yourself. You can't help not remembering.'"

That Pop needed her intervention, added Ms. Lipsey, "broke my heart. Because I watched the progression of his health challenges. I saw his frustration."

She and Pop were kindred, Ms. Lipsey said. They kept each other grounded. She cherished his mentorship and he her straight talk. She adjusted her Detroit schedule to work more frequently out of the Washington office, where she'd worked full-time for several years so she could be more available to my father. "As far as I was concerned, I was his security blanket. I needed to be there."

I'm glad Pop had a few people on his side as he wrestled with whether to step down from Congress after those two former staffers accused him publicly of improperly touching, sexually propositioning, and otherwise subjecting them to sexual harassment; and a third, a former attorney for the House Judiciary Committee, claimed he bullied and yelled at her in public about the quality of her work as he saw it.

"There was a consensus that there should be some time for due process or for John to make a determination, with his family, about what he thought the appropriate thing to do was," Congressman Cedric Richmond, a Louisiana Democrat, said initially of Pop's dilemma. At the time, he chaired the Congressional Black Caucus.

Even so, another Caucus member, US representative James Clyburn, a Black man and Democrat from South Carolina, stood full-throated alongside then Speaker of the House Pelosi, the California Democrat, as they called for Pop to resign. It was an about-face from, as quoted in the *New York Times*, Congressman Clyburn asking whether the allegations "have any real substance. You can't jump to conclusions with these types of things. For all I know, all of this could be made up." Mr. Clyburn held sway as one of the oldest members of the Congressional Black Caucus. He's been referred to as a kingmaker, mainly for how his 2020 endorsement of Joe Biden is believed to have helped Biden, with 51.3 percent of the popular vote, unseat President Trump, the pick on 46.8 percent of ballots cast.

Pop's stepping aside would free up the chairmanship of the House Judiciary Committee, which oversees everything from impeachment hearings to nominations to the federal bench to how federal tax dollars get spent locally. Congressman Jerry Nadler, the New York Democrat in line to succeed Pop as the House Judiciary Committee's ranking member, issued a press release that besmirched the legal principle of "innocent until proven guilty." It put the cart before the horse: "The allegations against Ranking

Member Conyers are extremely serious and deeply troubling. Obviously, these allegations must be investigated promptly by the Ethics Committee."

Nadler, Clyburn, Pelosi, and their kind wanted to make room for a replacement of Pop who was younger, more agile, and less prone to falling asleep during legislative hearings and debate. As much as that, they thought his resignation would quell protests from the #MeToo movement, which was rightly calling out transgressors in C-suites in Hollywood, news networks, and other high places. More than halfway through the 115th Congress, Pop's retirement counted as the first of seven departures by elected officials accused of sexual misconduct.

Steadfastly, Pop maintained his innocence. Attorney Reed vociferously backed my father, getting into near-shouting matches with some news reporters who appeared to take the women's accusations as gospel truth. I was ambivalent about Mr. Reed's approach—my father's fifteen years as his client showed Pop's faith in Mr. Reed's counsel—and I tried in my own way to do the softening I thought necessary. "Women are to be believed," I told news reporters, when they stuck a mic in my face. My position probably surprised some people, I'm sure. Adoring sons, quite naturally, would be biased in favor of their fathers. But if Pop was in the wrong, I'd not stand by the wrongdoing. If he fucked up, well, he just fucked up. I'd not always held Pop in high regard. Because I'd been an angst-ridden boy with a father who was largely absentee, I was able to keep some distance. I could be objective about Pop. I could speak in defense of women who've been harmed by men.

But Mr. Reed was the face of Pop's defense. To balance what was one-sided coverage of Pop, sometimes the attorney would show up at the house on Seven Mile, where reporters had camped out. That's how he tried to rechannel the narrative.

On one of those talk shows designed more to let the host play provocateur than to provide robust, balanced, explanatory news coverage, MSNBC's Stephanie Ruhle opened with a presumption that Pop was guilty. Then she tried to talk over Pop's lawyer, to shout him down, and, I imagine, to provoke him. She heaved a sigh—*huuuuhhhhh*—into her mic at the top of the interview. The sigh was her overly dramatic opening. Shamedly, she proceeded to interrogate and interrupt Mr. Reed, who, in addition to my father, has represented everyone from Aretha "Queen of Soul" Franklin to survivors of domestic violence to the two mothers of small children who died in a Detroit house fire in a neighborhood where the fire hydrants had been disconnected from their water source.

"Is it your client's contention that all the misconduct allegations are false and that the women out there are simply making it up?" Ruhle said, straight out of the blocks.

"Stephanie, the bottom line is—" Reed said, before Ruhle cut him off: "Can you just answer that question, sir?"

"The bottom line," continued Reed, "is Congressman Conyers has categorically denied any conduct that remotely resembles sexual harassment. I mean, it makes great cannon fodder for programs like this and other programs that I've been on to say, quote, unquote, 'all these women.' But what's not being reported is there are affidavits that are blacked out, affidavits that are not even notarized. There's a claim by one individual who says that she was harassed during a job interview, yet she's breaking down the door to get a job again. Great cannon fodder. But when you say 'all these women,' who are you talking about specifically?"

Ruhle weighed in again: "I want to play part of a statement from Lisa Bloom, who represents the first accuser. And she said, quote, 'We call upon Mr. Conyers and the Office of Compliance to release my client from her confidentiality agreement, so that she may have a voice to tell her own story. Basic fairness and decency dictate that if Mr. Conyers can speak publicly about the matter, the woman should be free to do so as well.' So that, to me, would make a lot of sense. I would think Congressman Conyers would want that. Let's get all of this information."

> **Reed:** I would think, Stephanie, and all due respect, that this individual . . . would have had legal counsel before this alleged agreement was signed. So I would think—going back to when this agreement was signed—that would have been thought about . . . "I'm going to take this matter to trial."

> **Ruhle:** If this woman was harassed—

"Allegedly harassed," Reed interjected. ". . . In fairness, let's get the facts straight."

> **Ruhle:** All right. Then, would you and Congressman Conyers support releasing her from the NDA, letting all this information out in the open?

> **Reed:** What I would support is John Conyers continuing to do the right thing for himself, for the public and the constituents that he represents. Congressman Conyers has indicated from day one that he is not guilty of these allegations. A number of individuals I've spoken to have said that they've been in that office twenty, thirty years; these allegations did not happen. What I would support is individuals who say that they have been harassed when some type of agreement is put in front of you . . . don't sign it. Go to trial. . . . If you say you're harassed, you want your day in court. That's how it works. . . . He has a right to due process. He has a right to see this thing through, and he has a right to defend himself.

Ruhle: He absolutely does. A lot of women have laughed on the outside and they've cried on the inside. Arnold, thank you so much for joining me today.

Her closing lines were a non sequitur. They didn't genuinely attempt to uncover the truth or examine the accusations against Pop. They reflected Ruhle's predetermined conclusion and her failure to have an actual discussion with some semblance of a fair inquiry.

Like most reasonable people, I recognize the seriousness of sexual misconduct. I would give no one, including Pop, a pass if they committed that crime. But no one can convince me that what my father did was criminal.

Nor did I understand the double standard of Pop's treatment by his House colleagues.

"Nancy Pelosi had not asked Al Franken to resign," Mr. Reed noted of the comic-turned-US-senator from Minnesota. Also facing allegations of sexual misconduct—one well-publicized photo showed Franken's hand grabbing a woman's breast—he came under fire around the same time as Pop. As other high-ranking Democrats kicked off calls for Franken to resign in November 2017, Speaker Pelosi was mute. Franken resigned in January 2018.

"To hell with Nancy Pelosi!" Mr. Reed once exclaimed, on camera, as he was fending off those allegations against my father.

"One woman claimed that John fondled her in church and got in the car and was driving seventy or eighty miles an hour on the freeway and put his hand between her legs while on the freeway. Anybody who knows your father knows he can't drive, let alone do all that on the freeway," Mr. Reed told me.

After hurling those false charges, the same woman begged Pop to add her daughter and her niece to his congressional office's payroll. To echo Pop's attorney, "If you are in such a threatening and volatile environment, why do you want to bring your daughter and niece into it?"

Plus Pop had previously chastised that same accuser for pocketing funds. These funds were reserved for securing food and other essentials for poor people—charitable duties she'd been assigned. This community work was particularly important to my father. Several witnesses had lined up to offer that and other testimony had the case gone to court.

Another accuser alleged that my father made three unsolicited sexual gestures toward her during the eight years she was on Pop's staff. Despite that, she took a job as a nanny for me and Carl, Mr. Reed said. "If you're sexually harassed," he began, issuing another challenge to Ms. Ruhle of MSNBC, "why do you move into someone's house? . . . She's got credibility issues." This person's accusations, in particular, shocked me when I learned of them years after she made them. The accuser had often tried to arrange playdates between me and her grandson, who was close to my age. During a brief period, she'd occasionally watched my brother and me when my father left for one of his events and my mother hadn't yet returned home. It was casual and familial, not a formal nanny role.

Part of me, nevertheless, can't help feeling like Pop messed up. There's no getting around that. Pop loved women, and plenty of women loved him. Perhaps that's part of the reason he married so late in life. I'm willing to bet a boatload of money that he had his own "Let me alone, Becky" moment. I believe those were consensual. I believe those indulgences are a key reason why my parents defaulted to sleeping in separate bedrooms in the house on Seven Mile. Those extracurriculars, I do believe, are why my mother filed for divorce in 2015, although, in the end, she didn't have the conviction to sever herself from Pop or the Conyers name. Still Pop's

Washington life didn't always sit well with my mom. For one, she felt my father could have done more to screen the people surrounding him. As an employer, my father had a reputation for bringing onto his payroll individuals he suspected needed a little help and for bringing on individuals for reasons that mystified members of our family and his staff.

"They didn't have the skill or the mindset," Ms. Lipsey told me.

"At one point," Jared Hautamaki reminded me, "he hired a homeless guy to be the driver in Detroit to try and give him a hand, to try and give him a step up. Two or three weeks later the guy disappeared with the car."

Among the misfits Pop added to his staff was one of his accusers. That was the view of Ms. Lipsey and others ready to testify in court on my father's behalf had those allegations ever been adjudicated.

"The congressman was on the way home one weekend," said Ms. Lipsey. "The staff was sitting around in the reception area, laughing, talking. I was just listening, letting them have a little downtime. I heard one of [his accusers] say what it takes to get him sexually aroused, something like rubbing on his thigh or holding his hand. She was naming different things.

"And I'm thinking to myself, 'How would you know that?' I never said anything to her, I just kept it as a tool in my toolbox. Later, I'd heard rumors—part of that came from your mother, and I don't know if it was speculation or something she could prove— that that particular staffer had gotten a substantial pay increase. And she was like, 'I think she's sucking my husband's dick to get a raise.'"

One of his accusers had complained that she walked into Pop's office to find him in his underwear. "But," Jared told me, "he changed clothes in the office all the time, as he was moving from one event to the next. All of us, men and women, saw John Conyers

Jr. in his underwear. We didn't think anything of it." He's not lying. Shit, I changed in that same office countless times.

Pop's staff, nevertheless, was not blind to Pop's inclinations or his infidelities. He'd had a fixation on an actress, Jared told me. When Pop asked that a $20,000 check be cut to the actress to cover a trip she wanted to make to DC, with her personal makeup artist in tow, Chief of Staff Greg Moore hit the roof. He wasn't having it. Pop backed down. I still have that photo of her, with Carl in her arms and me beside her. I was maybe ten or eleven years old.

One of her unwitting duties, Ms. Lipsey told me, was to try and keep that part of Pop in check. "I was like, 'Okay. Look, you put me in a situation where your wife is going to ask me questions? I won't lie for you.

"Sometimes he would chuckle, depending on how I said it. Other times he would just look at me like he wanted to push me down the stairs. He wasn't beyond wanting female companionship at times, even if it was just conversation.

"He would try to hide certain things from me. For instance, if I was supposed to go with him somewhere, he would tell me, 'Oh, Miss Lipsey, listen. You can just have the night off. I'm going to have so-and-so take me there.' And when I caught on to that, I would tell him, 'Oh, you not slick, not at all. And I'm gone mess up your game.' So I'd cock-block."

Hearing those aspects of my father's behavior wasn't difficult; I was listening to a cautionary tale. I don't want to make the same mistakes. To paraphrase an oft-translated quote from Otto von Bismarck, "A fool learns only from his own mistakes; a wise man learns from the mistakes of others."

And it is what it is, as they say. I, especially now, try to see Pop in his entirety, the truth of him. I regret what, perhaps, he also regretted. Forever, maybe, I will grieve his unplanned departure from Washington and the factors driving it. I knew Pop should have come home long before those allegations could taint the body of legislative work that remains vital, significant, and transformative for his people and his nation.

When he formally announced he was leaving Congress, Pop telephoned his decision into Detroit's popular *Mildred Gaddis Show*.

"We're pleased to be here with you," attorney Reed began that morning. "It is important that the public know that the congressman felt it was necessary to address the individuals that elected him. . . . So, without further ado, Mildred, with me is the Dean of the House."

"Top of the morning, Mildred," Pop began, his voice noticeably weaker.

"Congressman," Ms. Gaddis began, "how have these allegations impacted you and your family and your legacy?"

"We take these in stride," Pop responded. "This goes with the issue of politics and the game of politics which we're in. We take what happens, we deal with . . . We keep going to try to make as much as we can of this tremendous opportunity that's been given to me for so long. And I'm glad to let you know my family is doing well. My wife and two boys are doing great. My brother Nate is here pitching in in a very important way. My family and health are excellent."

Rattling off a short list of Pop's many accomplishments, and highlighting Pop's pending reparations bill, Ms. Gaddis reiterated the big question, the one that haunts me still: "Do you think these allegations will impact that legacy?"

"Oh, absolutely not," my father said. "My legacy can't be compromised or diminished, in any way, by what we're going through now. This too shall pass. And I want you to know that my legacy will continue through my children."

After the broadcast, Ms. Gaddis told the journalists from near and far who'd packed her studio to hear what Pop had to say, "His legacy is not going to be tainted at all. The work that he did was so impactful that you don't forget those kinds of things. Of course, it will be a story that we'll be talking about a long time. . . . Let me just tell you, people in the Detroit area love John Conyers."

Whatever the future held for the Conyerses' legacy, Ms. Lipsey had said of my father's being forced out of office, "It was like a death. When someone experiences a death and you don't know what to say, you just try to give your condolence. He was like, 'How could they do this to me? Why would they say those things to me?' He just couldn't grasp the fact that people were saying these things about him."

I cannot imagine what Pop felt, viscerally, on the day that he, his attorney, and my mother, for the last time, exited the glass doors below those mammoth columns fronting the Rayburn Building. A taxi ferried them up Independence Avenue to an airplane bound for Detroit. Rayburn's construction had been completed in 1965, the year Pop was sworn to what, for him and his kind, was God-ordained ministry in Congress during an urgent, needing time. How would a man for whom Washington felt like home adjust to so violent a pivot? The US House of Representatives had been my father's dwelling place, my father's house, if you will. It was his refuge and incubator. It stands to reason that his departure from Washington broke many hearts, mine included. I'm sure it broke Pop's heart, too, though outwardly he tried, at first, not to project pain.

The hurt erupted, nevertheless. Shortly after Pop had been banished from DC, he wound up in the hospital for three days. I was afraid he would die. And I did not want him to go out like that. Abruptly, somehow unrequited, without a last say about himself or a choice in how to close out his final chapter. Though overdue, that retirement was not on his terms. It came, as talk-show host Gaddis noted, as Congress had spent $17 million to settle congressional staffers' allegations of racial and other types of discrimination and accusations of sexual misconduct by various members of Congress. The federal Office of Compliance did not disclose the names of all the alleged accusers.

Pop did rebound from that sudden, stress-related hospitalization, triggered by his retirement. His restoration was a gift. It bought him more time. It gave me more time with him. It let the Detroiters who loved him offer a proper goodbye before Pop transitioned to the other side.

After Pop's scary stay in the hospital—he'd announced his retirement from his hospital bed—Pop returned to an awareness of himself and a full knowledge that he was still among the living. He settled into that.

He was no longer a congressman, by official title, but he still was himself. He pored over news headlines. He was discussing reparations and other unresolved issues regarding Black people but also marginalized others. He still was taking calls and meetings from whosoever.

There were days when, wizened and raspy, he asked, "What time are we leaving for the office?" He had to be reminded that the office-going had ended. His offices had been shut down and emptied out. African artwork on loan to Pop was returned to the Smithsonian. Shipped to the house on Seven Mile Road from the Rayburn Building was a painting of Pop, my brother, and me. The record player, vinyl LPs, books, upright bass, congas, and djembe drums, the fridge that chilled his cartons upon cartons of milk, and Pop's files, all of his congressional things, were packed into a shipping crate bound for Motown.

In lieu of the familiarities and comforts of his Washington life, we shared the intimacies of my home-cooked meals. There was me, at the kitchen countertop, carving a brisket that I'd just taken off the grill. Pop, in his Fruit of the Loom briefs, T-shirt, and bathrobe, sat on a stool next to me, waiting for me to slide a plate of food over to him. Carl was there waiting, too. We feasted, also, on Pop's other favorites: a pepperoni, mushroom, and onion pizza from Gregg's, fried catfish, and pan-seared salmon. Whatever he had a taste for was my favorite thing to prepare. The main course was the conversation but also the silences connecting us. Carl and I settled into them and the tranquility of my father, older and slower, his shoulders rounder and less ramrod straight. He was walking his last mile. We relished the moments.

Also, during Pop's last two years on this side of Creation, he and I tooled around the Motor City, the place that launched and loved him. With me at the steering wheel and Pop in the passenger seat, we hit his usual spots. There was dry cleaning to be picked up at Sunrise Cleaners. Corned beef sandwiches from Lou's for lunch, or a bambino from Gregg's on Livernois. On those jaunts, Pop took time out for just about everyone who recognized him and who wanted to shake his hand, say thank you, recall some miracle he made happen for them, or ask to snap a selfie with him in the foreground.

Pop chopped it up with whoever wanted to be heard and to hear, often about the same issues that still occupied Pop.

All the while, I lay back. Those reciprocal tributes and thanksgivings, Pop to his people and the people to Pop, needed to be.

And Pop needed to speak his own last words. "We're here to strengthen the bonds between us as relatives, as friends, as young people, and as those who are trying to . . . make this a better city, a better country, a better world." That was my father, five months or so before he died, saying grace over a community feast celebrating his last Mother's Day with his "darling wife," as he called my mother—to whom he remained devoted, somehow, despite their rocky road of a marriage—and celebrating the rest of us.

I keep several of Pop's out-loud prayers on my cell phone. When I need to know he is not far off, I listen to them. The living and the dead are only thinly separated, if, in fact, we are separated at all.

CHAPTER 10

BAPTIZED BY FIRE

The first Black rebellion on record in Detroit took place in 1833. History books, inked by Caucasians with a white-knuckled grip on their version of events, even today refer to what happened as the Blackburn riots. They jumped off on June 17 of that year, a day after escaped enslaved Rutha Blackburn's friends, Tabitha Lightfoot and Caroline French, disguised and smuggled Mrs. Blackburn out of a Detroit jail where she and her husband, Thornton Blackburn, were being detained. Fettered by white men who got paid for recapturing Blacks who'd found the strength and fortune to wrestle themselves free, momentarily, from their enslavers, the couple had been arrested under the first version of the federal Fugitive Slave Act, passed in 1793. They were slated for return to captivity on a Kentucky plantation, below the Mason–Dixon Line separating Confederate territory from Union states such as Michigan. It should be noted that slavery was also the law of the land in the Union too, but the North outlawed that form of tyranny sooner than the South did—even once outlawed, the Fugitive Slave Act protected Southern-owned property (*read: slaves*) even if it should somehow find itself up north (*read: escape*). Crossing the Mason–Dixon didn't mean you were safe.

In February of 1793, forty-eight members of Congress voted for, seven voted against, and fourteen abstained from voting for the villainous law. President George Washington, slave owner in chief during his two terms in the White House, rubber-stamped the measure. It emanated from a debate over whether a free Black man who'd been kidnapped from his home in Pennsylvania and pressed into slavery in Virginia would have his freedom restored. John Davis, the illegally abducted Black man at the center of the case, died enslaved. His three kidnappers got away with their crime, though Pennsylvania's governor at the time sought their extradition to stand trial in his state.

Four decades later, in Detroit, a stop on the Underground Railroad, Black people and a handful of white people raised a public outcry outside the city jail on June 18, 1833. "Release Mr. Blackburn," demanded those protesters, estimated to number between forty and four hundred.

Parading Thornton Blackburn in front of his supporters, Sheriff John M. Wilson tried to get the crowd to ease off. In the meantime, someone slipped Blackburn a pistol. Threatening to shoot, he pointed the gun at the sheriff, and the sheriff tried to grab it. The two men tussled over the weapon. And the protesters—white historians labeled them a mob—gave the sheriff and his jailers what they had coming, what they deserved. The protesters fought back. At the hands of an undetermined person, the sheriff was killed.

The pandemonium paved Thornton Blackburn's path to a boat waiting on the Detroit River. He, his wife, and some of their defenders fled to Canada, whose nearest city, Windsor, sits south of Detroit across the river. Standing on Detroit's shore, you can see it. Three decades before Lincoln's Emancipation Proclamation in the United States, Canada's Slavery Abolition Act of 1833 ended two hundred years of chattel slavery by our neighbors to the north, eventually freeing more than 800,000 enslaved in Canada.

In 1850, white enslavers in the US South and their sympathizers insisted upon and won an even more restrictive codification of the Fugitive Slave Law, whose first prosecution was against the Blackburns. So, long after the Blackburns were dead and buried on the other side of a shared border, white oppression against Black Detroiters was unceasing.

Whenever people—of any creed or color, anywhere on earth—are pressed down, hemmed in, locked out, trampled upon, or left to wither and scorch on the vine, it doesn't take much to fuel their fires. Those people may turn inward. They may wage an internecine, implosive, intra-tribal civil war. Or they may be more outwardly demonstrative, exploding for all the world to see.

That's what happened ninety years after Detroit's first recorded riot. Beyond exasperated and refusing to put up with Detroit-style discrimination, Black Detroiters, in yet another extraordinary effort, took to the streets in the summer of 1943. The backdrop to those two days in June was this: Black people could get a job while factories and other workplaces were in overdrive during World War II's military buildup, but they had very little decent housing to choose from. They couldn't marshal, on their own, what it took to access all the benefits of full citizenship in America.

Most of the roughly 200,000 Black Detroiters resided in the sixty square blocks of largely commercial Paradise Valley and its adjacent Black Bottom community, where Pop was born and where families piled into small quarters, stacking themselves on top of each other. When city officials attempted to construct housing for Black residents in a mostly white neighborhood abutting the predominantly Black Conant Gardens, more than a thousand white individuals pitched and lit a Ku Klux Klan cross on the site of the new housing. Some brandished guns as they furiously protested Black newcomers and chastised elected officials' unmitigated gall to force the races to commingle. Whites resorted to work stoppages, irate about working alongside Black factory employees or, heaven forbid, being bossed by newly promoted Black managers who, frankly, were few and far between.

Dueling false rumors prompted those two days of racially motivated brawling in 1943: Whites had, allegedly, thrown a Black woman and her baby off the Belle Isle Bridge into the Detroit River. From Forest Social Club in Paradise Valley, upset and angry Black people poured out onto the streets as they got wind of that pretend crime. From the intersection of Forest and Hastings Streets, as they attracted more Black protesters and gained steam, they destroyed white-owned businesses. Randomly, they assaulted white individuals who, for discontented and disinherited Black people, were a proxy for all white people. Dr. Joseph DeHoratiis, a white physician, was beaten to death while making a house call in Paradise Valley.

Fueled by a different fast-moving fiction—Black men, supposedly, had raped a white woman near the same bridge—white people retaliated. In the hours before dawn, they severely beat Black men exiting the Roxy Theatre on Woodward Avenue. They upended Black-owned vehicles and set them afire. They rampaged into Black neighborhoods. Police officers stood by, watched, and let the destruction go on uninterrupted.

On the morning of day two, with Black leaders begging him to summon the Michigan National Guard, Detroit's mayor Edward Jeffries, a Democrat, sought help from Harry Kelly, Michigan's Republican governor. The governor obliged. Rolling into the Motor City in jeeps and armored tanks, their automatic weapons at the ready, 3,500 troops cleared the streets. When it was over, the Black dead numbered twenty-five, seventeen of them by police violence. None of the nine whites who died were felled by police. The injured numbered 675. Damage to property, mainly in Paradise Valley but also in Black Bottom, amounted to $2 million, the equivalent of about $36 million today.

The governor's office touted its August 1943 assessment of what caused hell to break loose as it did on June 20 and June 21 as a fact-finding mission. It contained zero mention of the systemic economic, social, and racial inequities igniting the firestorm.

Twenty-four years later, in the wee hours of Sunday, July 23, 1967, as Detroit, yet again, was burning with a Black rebellion, Pop stood on the roof of a car parked alongside an angry Black crowd on Twelfth Street. He could see smoke billowing off in the distance. Firefighters couldn't extinguish the blazes fast enough. Pop's sleeves were rolled up above the top of his biceps. Bellowing into a megaphone, he said something to the effect that his fellow Black Detroiters should go home. Instead, for five searing days and nights, they stayed in the streets for what was one of the bloodiest Black rebellions in US history. It was exceeded only by Californians' 1992 rebellion against a suburban jury's acquittal of four LAPD officers caught on camera bludgeoning Rodney King, a Black man, for a long, long fifteen minutes. King was left with permanent brain damage.

There were 7,200 arrests in Detroit in 1967. Almost 1,200 people were injured. Four hundred buildings were destroyed. Thirty-three Black people and ten white people were killed during those five days. Police and National Guardsmen shot dead twenty-nine of those individuals, according to the *Detroit Free Press*. "A majority of the riot victims need not have died," the *Detroit Free Press* wrote in September 1967. "Their deaths could have been—and should have been—prevented."

What particularly struck Pop and stayed with him forever was the sight of those police officers patrolling Black Detroit: "Here were all these policemen dressed in black with helmets, weapons. And then they had bayonets on their rifles. A platoon of them were standing at the top of Twelfth Street. It was so provocative. Everybody would come by and say that 'See that. They're getting ready to attack us.' . . . I'm looking at people I knew. These were my constituents. These were people I knew and who knew me. They were angry, so angry."

During a 1988 interview with Rise Up Detroit, my father kept reflecting: "The night that it started . . . we were hoping it could still be turned off. We were saying, 'Well, you know, if everybody would go home and go to sleep and we clear the streets . . .'

"Police had raided this after-hours place, which had thought that they were paying money to the police for protection, and they ended up having these women thrown down the steps. And this is what really angered the crowd. The police captain on duty was not there that night and this lieutenant decided they were going to raid this place. Just something as unforeseen, unpremeditated as this could kick it off. That's how it started, that was the genesis. . . . It was just shock and outrage that this kind of violent police action could be brought to this after-hours place.

"When we got out there, there was a hope that maybe we could head it off right now and everybody would calm down and cool out and things would become stabilized. But that was not to be the case."

Detroiters were fed up; they were not having it. They would not retreat. They would not cower indoors. The celebrants at the party police raided around 3:30 a.m. on July 27 were two Black veterans recently returned from the terrors of the Vietnam War, where in 1965, Blacks comprised 31 percent of combat battalions and 24 percent of army casualties. With Blacks accounting for just 12 percent of the US population, Dr. King remarked that those soldiers were waging a Black man's fight in a white man's war. It was a fitting metaphor. It encapsulated the contradictions of living while Black in this country, of being the mule bearing someone else's load.

Flagrant injustice and the capricious brutalizing of Black people by white Detroit police officers made it hard to stomach what

Pop was saying about staying calm. So the protesters shouted down my father, who was in the first year of his second two-year term. His constituents' back talk to him was so adamant, so vehement, so boisterous that he was ushered off the top of that vehicle and whisked away. Pop's colleagues didn't want him singed in the searing heat of the moment. It was a powder keg moment, with President Johnson sending in the US Army's 82nd Division and 101st Airborne Division, and Michigan governor George Romney dispatching the state's Army National Guard. Things could have gone any which way.

On Pop's efforts to quell the crowd on night one of the 1967 rebellion, Jamon Jordan, who became the City of Detroit's first-ever official historian in 2021, told me, "Some of them began throwing rocks at him."

Georgia-born Arthur Johnson, who was with my father that night, is among the countless, mostly unsung heroes of the Civil Rights Movement. He and MLK were Morehouse classmates. Johnson had led the NAACP nationally and in Detroit. Before he died in 2011, when he was eighty-five, he'd been the first Black assistant superintendent of Detroit's public schools; and, as a board member of Detroit Symphony Orchestra, he founded its Classical Roots youth musician development project. Jordan joked that Johnson loved his car too much to have it nicked and scraped by Blacks chucking rocks at Pop. And I don't doubt that. But I imagine he also was aware of what can happen when Blacks, unremittingly wronged by white systems, unleash the wrath they've kept pent up. That released pressure can be contained about as much as a toddler can control a fire hose.

Pop knew he was vulnerable too, even as he, via megaphone, urged protesters to quiet themselves. He also knew that being in harm's way came with the job. He understood what had riled up the constituents whom he saw, above all, as his neighbors. Every one of us, Pop reminded me more times than I can remember, is supposed to be our neighbors' keeper.

Regarding the many who were arrested, Pop explained to a TV newsman, just hours after the military snuffed out the rebellion, what was up: "I've described them as the economic have-nots in our community who have risen to the surface. . . . They're the people who could see that they had nothing more to lose than they had to gain, and this spread. My shock is that there are many more of these people than I thought.

"This element was added to by, of course, casual looters who could not be described as economic have-nots. Then, of course, we add to that our Black nationalist element who, to me, perhaps, formed the hard-core resistance of the sniper activity. . . . Ironically, the original snipers arrested by the police were white."

The rebellion was too complex to be summed up as a mere race riot. The rebellion was unavoidable, my father emphatically informed the TV interviewer. Take 250 years of slavery and overlay that with 102 years of "second-to-tenth-class citizenship, according to where you live," Pop said, ". . . you begin building up this kind of resentment, this kind of humiliation . . . this loss of dignity, this recognition of powerlessness."

Twenty years later, as questions of what set off the riots kept coming at him, Pop echoed what he'd already said. He restated the defining characteristics behind the riot: "What the government termed as urban renewal was Black removal in the 1960s. White flight was soaring ever higher. Businesses were fleeing Black Detroit: The segregated patterns—housing, residentially, job-wise—were really very, very tight. There were no affirmative action programs. You must remember that we didn't even have a national civil rights law at this time. All of it was creating a buildup of tensions that were going to ultimately lead to an explosion. And the mayor himself was powerless to deal with it, just from a municipal point of view. [The problems] were far more intractable than that. . . .

"There was a nascent Black Power movement developing that was rebellious to both Black and white leadership, that was making it clear that 'this is not going to go on.' It had its own leaders. It was really calling for a confrontational, if not physical, reaction to this segregation that was steeped in every part of life for a Black citizen in Detroit."

It was hardly just the raid on an unlicensed after-hours joint— known by police as a "blind pig" for selling illicit alcohol—that set things off, Jamon Jordan, the city historian, told me. It was that *plus* everything else.

Especially fanning the flames was the protracted displacement of Black people from the city their forebears flocked to during the Great Migration from the South. They'd come searching for their proverbial pot of gold, the historian said, explaining that past and its connection to present-day realities: Responding to the notorious 1943 racial conflicts sparked by false rumors and real-life inequalities—state and local leaders blamed Blacks for the race-based combat—Mayor Jeffries in 1944 proposed what he called the Detroit City Plan. It blueprinted the wholesale destruction of Black Bottom. In 1946, the City Council approved the plan but put it on hold; there weren't enough funds in city coffers to carry it out. In the interim, they tore down a few structures.

Their go-ahead to obliterate Black Bottom and Paradise Valley came in 1949 when President Truman signed into law the Housing Act. "Cities lobbied for this. Cities complained that the United States government is rebuilding Europe under the Marshall Plan," Jordan told me, "but they're not doing anything for the cities. And the cities are still hurt from the Great Depression and from World War II. The cities are crying out for help.

"Truman's Fair Deal plan included massive money for cities to destroy old structures. They called it slum clearance. . . . Overwhelmingly, but not totally, Black neighborhoods were targeted for this."

As the federal government funded the destruction of old neighborhoods in Detroit and other locales, it offered money for new structures for low-income and working-class people on sites where their prior homes had been razed. Who knows whether Jeffries would have accepted money for affordably priced housing developments, targeting families displaced when Black Bottom was erased. He was no longer in office by 1950, when Albert Cobo, a former corporate salesman who had won successive elections as the City of Detroit's Republican treasurer, became mayor. He successfully campaigned on the promise to prevent a "Negro invasion" of white Detroit neighborhoods and to block public housing. He was a lying, mythmaking race baiter. "There is no reason," he openly complained, "why some Detroiters have to 'carry' others who are well able to pay their own way."

"Cobo," the city historian said, "refused any federal funds to rebuild for low income and working-class people. He took the money to destroy Black Bottom, but he refused any funds to rebuild it for that same group of people to come back. He only accepted private development, private dollars. And we got Lafayette Park, which, of course, was built for upper-class, upper-middle-class, wealthy people."

Cobo got his name plastered on Detroit's main convention center (though the facility was stripped of that name in 2019). The tired and poor of Black Bottom, who mainly were tenants, got an eviction notice. The community's relative handful of homeowners got paid something to move away, but much less than what their property was worth. Whoever was left out of those two unfair provisions got their property taken by eminent domain.

Those who were forced to relocate had few options inside Detroit. Some headed back to the South. Some got an address in Inkster (which became predominantly Black), Pontiac, or other Michigan cities. Some went to neighborhoods with just enough Black people to lessen their risks of being discriminated against. Some went to the old West Side, some to the North End. Many settled in the largely commercial, densely populated Twelfth Street corridor, ground zero of the 1967 rebellion. In a 1968 analysis, "Official Interpretations of Racial Riots," Columbia University sociologist Allan Silver wrote, "America has had an affinity for collective violence—the violence of vigilante groups, lynch mobs, strikers, strike-breakers, and private police. Unlike the violence of daily life, unorganized crime or juvenile delinquents, collective violence expresses the values and interests of groups which must be taken into account by reason of their power, size, or strategic location. To describe America as prone to collective violence is to say that significant conflicts among groups contending for political, economic, and social goals have often been expressed in joint acts of attack on life and property."

For his analysis, Silver had drawn from, among other research, that of three Black men—Howard University sociologist E. Franklin Frazier, labor unionist and civil rights activist A. Philip Randolph, and poet Countee Cullen—who New York City mayor Fiorello LaGuardia commissioned to explore the root causes of the so-called Harlem riot of 1935. The trio pointed to the mortifying condition of Harlem's schools as indicative of what existed throughout that Upper Manhattan neighborhood. The analysts wrote,

Let us take a look at, perhaps, the worst of these schools, P. S. 89, at the corner of 135th Street and Lenox Avenue, which was built in 1889 and had an addition made to it in 1895. This school contains in an extreme degree all the bad features of the

schools of Harlem. First of all, within a radius of two blocks
of this school, there are eighteen beer gardens, six liquor sa-
loons, four moving picture houses and two hotels alleged to
be disreputable, besides one solid block of rooming houses
which are known to be the center of vice and the hide-outs of
vendors of narcotics and other criminals. If one attempts to
enter the building, one must be careful to step or walk around
unemployed men seated on the steps of the entrance. After
entering the school building, an offensive odor greets one as he
passes up the stairs leading to the principal's office . . . [where
there] was a pile of old shoes strung across the floor and a pile
of old clothes stacked in one corner. . . . At the time the visit
was made to this school, ten of the forty-five rooms were out
of use because of a recent fire.

Learning still was expected to take place in those awful schools
in Harlem, where a famous 1935 rebellion happened after a white
dime-store owner summoned police on a sixteen-year-old Black boy
who'd stolen a penknife. Twenty-nine years later, the 1964 Harlem
riot jumped off after an off-duty police officer shot and killed a
fifteen-year-old Black boy. How can there be no response to such
violence that, if not state-sanctioned, was tacitly condoned by the
state?

In the face of such barbarity, Black people, to me, have been
less adept and less quick than many other ethnic groups to circle
the wagons when members of the Black community unjustly come
under attack. And of late, we've had several staggering examples of
how, as we say, all skin folks ain't kinfolks. It's fine—I guess—that
conservatism is the preferred politics of US Supreme Court Justice
Clarence Thomas, US senator Tim Scott, and US representative
Byron Donalds, Black men who seem to hate Black people but distinctly love Donald Trump. Scott's fealty to Trump, who's aligned

with racist neo-Nazis and the KKK, makes me wonder if we'll ever get free. So does Donalds's declaration that Black people were better off under Jim Crow—which ended in 1965 with a "yea" vote from my father and 362 other of Congress's 435 members.

Justice Thomas is a hypocrite; he was admitted to Yale University under affirmative action. We can diverge on political philosophy. But it is not okay to sacrifice the entire group by denying that racism exists and that we've made enough progress to safely lay down our battle-axes.

What's at the root of such internalized, misplaced racism against other Black people? Is it guilt over having benefited from those protections? Shame? Failure to reconcile the fact that, though you were fully qualified for the job, you'd never have gotten a seat at their table, never have gotten a hearing from them in the first place, were it not for those protections?

Or is it the fear of a perpetual white gaze that sizes up a Black man as inherently ill-suited and unqualified?

Black Americans' ongoing eruptions don't emerge out of nowhere. They happen when fault lines reach a certain pressure point and friction, rock-hard resentments scraping against each other. The eruptions have been emblematic. The circumstances driving them remain pervasive. The names of the cities that erupt have become almost interchangeable, an Anywhere USA when it comes to the conditions in the housing, health care, education, employment—you name it—of Black neighborhoods that are embattled.

In Detroit, the city and state governments singularly faulted Blacks for 1967's chaos. What kept my father activated, in part, were the deflections, abdications, and refusals to examine the government's role, the role of corporations, and the role of some everyday white people in fomenting an uprising. White blame-shifting kept Pop alert and paying attention. It prompted Pop in 1967 to propose a $30 billion fund for those who'd been systematically oppressed, dispossessed, disenfranchised, and discriminated against by various means.

White neglect and unaccountability helped sow the seeds of what would become Pop's reparations bill. It sprang, in part, from the work of longtime Detroit activist Raymond "Reparations Ray" Jenkins, a real estate agent. Mr. Jenkins proposed in 1967 that every descendant of African Americans get $1 million in "slave labor annuity pay." Later, he suggested creating a $40 billion trust fund for free scholarships to Black college students.

In 1964, Mr. Jenkins hosted, in his home, a congressional campaign fundraiser for my father. Ricardo "Rico" Jenkins, Reparations Ray's son, was there. "The house was packed," former Detroit Police Officer Jenkins told me. "Mr. Conyers was a very suave, debonair man. I wasn't that interested in what was going on—I was just ten years old—but I could tell he was holding the room with his conversation."

Eighteen years later, Pop brought the elder Mr. Jenkins onstage to salute and properly credit the eighty-one-year-old during a historic rally for reparations in Washington as the reparations cause was gaining momentum, despite how uphill that battle remains. "Reparations Ray Jenkins! This is the man that did it. He hung in during the lean years, when we couldn't get thousands upon thousands out," my father exclaimed. "When he couldn't get an audience with anybody, he kept on keeping on."

My father held Mr. Jenkins's hand in his, lifting their joint grasp heavenward in triumph, hoping and trusting for what likely is a far-off victory, if, at all, we are victors in this.

His father's initially solo fight for reparations extracted something from him. It cost him, Jenkins added, "a lot of ridicule. I was a kid, going to meetings with my dad. He'd get up and say what he believed. And they laughed at him so much that I didn't want to go back with him anymore. And these were Black people I'm talking about. . . . But my dad didn't care what people thought or whether you agreed with him or what the odds were against him.

"But my dad is getting a little bit of his flowers now. . . . And your father helped my dad, when he was screaming and clawing, by taking the reparations issue to a national level. If it wasn't for Congressman Conyers, we would not be seeing a light at the end of the tunnel on this."

From their respective places, Pop and Reparations Ray, eyewitnesses to their burning, Black city, were doing their part.

Their city, my city, our city—named by a French interloper on Indigenous people's land—had transported travelers across lines dividing enslavement from something that felt and looked a little more like freedom. For even Detroit had its slavers. According to one historian's count, which is based on incomplete records and likely underreported data, 127 enslaved Blacks and 523 enslaved Native Americans lived in Detroit during the 1700s and early 1800s.

Section 3 of 1793's Fugitive Slave Act, which almost ensnared self-emancipated Thornton and Rutha Blackburn, plainly lays out its evil intent:

> And be it also enacted, That when a person held to labor in any of the United States, or in either of the Territories on the Northwest or South of the river Ohio, under the laws thereof, shall escape into any other part of the said States or Territory, the person to whom such labor or service may be due, his agent or attorney, is hereby empowered to seize or arrest such fugitive from labor, and to take him or her before any Judge of the Circuit or District Courts of the United States, residing or being within the State, or before any magistrate of a county, city, or town corporate, wherein such seizure or arrest shall be made, and upon proof to the satisfaction of such Judge or magistrate, either by oral testimony or affidavit taken before

and certified by a magistrate of any such State or Territory, that the person so seized or arrested, doth, under the laws of the State or Territory from which he or she fled, owe service or labor to the person claiming him or her, it shall be the duty of such Judge or magistrate to give a certificate thereof to such claimant, his agent, or attorney, which shall be sufficient warrant for removing the said fugitive from labor to the State or Territory from which he or she fled.

How many continue to recognize race as America's great, haunting, unresolved dilemma? Must that be our reality? Still?

Thomas Mifflin, the Pennsylvania governor in 1793, was doing the right thing when he asked the nation's first president to help ensure that criminals who'd kidnapped a free Black man and jolted him into Virginia slavery got their just due in court. But George Washington turned a deaf ear to that request. Mifflin was one kind of white man; Washington was another. Mifflin was striving toward morality, whether or not, given the times, he saw a Black man as his equal. Washington was an enemy of morality, standing squarely on the opposite side of it. That the governor's extradition efforts got no traction is symptomatic of an American sickness. From 1776 onward, whenever folks of good moral character upheld ideals of equal justice for all and of the innate truth that no human is inherently superior to another human, those efforts got nixed by folks who were more powerful and persuasive. During World War II, the influential *Chicago Tribune, Daily News* (New York), infamous US senator Joseph McCarthy, and other institutions and individuals in the America First movement—that era's version of Make America Great Again—defended German Nazis. They also shielded American Nazis hell-bent on overthrowing the US government. If that white-against-white-against-white treachery was allowed to flourish, what chance was there for those distinguished and subjugated based on the hue of their darker skin and the kink of their hair? Though Trump incited the January 6 insurrections, the US Supreme Court gave him and his maddening MAGA cult a pass. What Black person could ever, ever, ever be granted such a dispensation?

Back when the Blackburns snatched their freedom from an enslaver's hands, white Detroiters were enraged by the methods of protesting, rebelling, freedom-fighting Black people and their white supporters. The enraged white people were defenders of the slain white sheriff who'd immorally detained a Black couple. On June 18, 1863, after the Blackburns were ferried by boat into Canada, angry white Detroiters set fires that burned down forty buildings. In a free-for-all of violence, whites attacked Black men, women, and children on the streets. Twenty-nine people, including some whites, would be arrested for unlawful assembly. But only Blacks, eleven of them, were found guilty of the crime during hearings on June 21 and June 22. Competing protests continued into July, with marchers assembling outside Detroit's jail, demanding that protesters who'd not been charged with a crime be released. The jail was set ablaze. Though that fire was extinguished, one set at the stables next door burned those stalls down. Troops from Fort Gratiot arrived on July 30, ordered there by the US secretary of war.

The rioting ended. But the assaults on Black people continued.

The Detroit City Council and the city's mayor started requiring Black people to carry lighted lanterns at night, making them more visible to white police, vigilantes, and others. A nine o'clock nightly curfew was imposed against Blacks. Night watchmen patrolled the Detroit River. Canadian boats coming through or docking in Detroit had to be searched by Detroit authorities. As a penance to undo damages done during the riots, those who were jailed had to repair the streets.

Perhaps of greatest consequence was the rule requiring that any Black who did not register with the county clerk and pay a bond of $500, proving they were a free person, be banished from Detroit. It was an onerous provision. In today's dollars, that bond would amount to more than $12,400. Unable to come up with that kind of cash, masses of Black Detroiters moved to Canada.

My father knew and forever studied the critical parts of our migrations and exoduses and struggles to find a home that really is ours. He knew how pendulums do swing. He watched, sometimes in disgust, our warring against each other. He watched our *othering* of one another—often for the simple sake of aggrandizing ourselves—and the dangerously wrong actions that are the spillover of being self-interested.

In relative terms, given that he would eventually spend fifty-three years in Congress, Pop was a fledgling politician when parts of Detroit went up in flames in 1967. Fires, in nature, often occur spontaneously, organically, divinely. Out of the ashes—whenever we let nature follow its rightful course—something lush sprouts anew in the very same spot.

Amid the disorder of a Black rebellion in 1967 Detroit, my father, an eyewitness, looked for ways to control a firestorm and, in its aftermath, tend to freshly fertile ground and the regrowth it might yield.

CHAPTER 11

"DETROIT VS. EVERYBODY"

When members of the national news media got wind of a cultural and economic resurgence happening in parts of Detroit, they parachuted in to tell the story, but only a certain version of it. Often, they trained their sights on places such as Shinola, which started out manufacturing and selling handmade wrist and pocket watches with price tags that have a comma on them. Since the luxury brand's 2011 arrival in Detroit—its parent company is a Texas-based private equity firm owned by a founder of Fossil watches—Shinola's reach has spread far and wide. There are expensive Shinola leather goods, home goods, bicycles, sunglasses, pet beds, pet collars, and leashes. They've even ventured into making record players and speakers.

"Detroit's living room" is how the company describes its eight-story, 129-room, boutique hotel in downtown's historic Woodward retail district; it made *Travel + Leisure* magazine's reader-curated "World's Best Hotels" list in 2023. A year after that accolade, in early 2024, a twenty-seven-year-old Black man with a consistent track record in jobs at the front desk and elsewhere in hotels filed a lawsuit against Shinola, alleging that its HR department refused him a job interview until he swapped out his actual last name, Jackson, for a fake one, Jebrowski, on what were identical resumes. The plaintiff credits the fabricated, white-sounding name for, after four months of trying, getting him the interview. He mentioned to the interviewer the rigamarole he'd been subjected to, calling the way he'd been jostled racially motivated and criminal. Promptly, Shinola, whose website shows a diversity of employees at work, dropped him from the pool of contenders hoping to join its payroll.

Name bias is a material fact. The National Bureau of Economic Research provided proof of that in its 2022 working paper "Systemic Discrimination Among Large US Employers," an analysis involving 83,000 fictitious applications. The lawyer for Dwight Jackson, the Black worker Shinola Hotel rejected, put it this way: "To be denied a job in 2024 in your hometown, for the color of your skin, goes beyond dollars and cents. It goes into the psyche of a person."

For all of its Motown boosterism and bragging about creating opportunity in Detroit—and Shinola has brought hundreds of jobs—the brand raised the Federal Trade Commission's ire for falsely claiming its timepieces were built in Detroit. In truth, 30 percent of the moving parts in Shinola watches were the product of Asian manufacturing, and 70 percent were Swiss, according to several news reports. The FTC ordered Shinola to overhaul its marketing, dropping the "Made in America" tag. That's the thing about a popular resurgence. Sometimes, it is more fiction than fact. In whole or in part, it can be smoke and mirrors. It's bound to exclude a whole lot of somebodies and to obfuscate elements of reality.

At least partly, that's the case for Detroit, where an array of Black entrepreneurs, big and small, often native-born, had been opening businesses, keeping them afloat, and hiring Detroiters, before and after the city was resurfacing from an embarrassing, painful filing for Chapter 9 bankruptcy relief and reorganization in 2013. In US history, Detroit is the largest city to declare bankruptcy; its untenable indebtedness was listed at roughly $20 billion. By comparison, two years prior, a bankruptcy filing by Jefferson County, Alabama—home to Birmingham, where Blacks accounted for roughly 68 percent of the population, is its county seat—listed $4 billion in debt. Jefferson County had 658,000 people and Detroit had 700,000 people, respectively, when each filed for protection under the bankruptcy laws. We've been trying to outrun that rabid dog of a story ever since. A cross section of Detroiters, not just those with Shinola's deep pockets, has been trying to shine a light on what many of us have been doing to bring about our city's renaissance.

"The media just went with where it seemed like the money was. The people who came in with the big money, that's who got the camera," Tommey Walker Jr., founder of the now-famous Detroit-VS-Everybody brand, told me.

He was describing what both of us see as the half-told story of a Detroit resurgence that centers on uber-monied people like billionaire Dan Gilbert. Born in Detroit and raised in suburban Southfield, Gilbert had been "single-handedly bankrolling Detroit's revival," *Forbes* magazine opined a few years back. He's the majority owner of the NBA's Cleveland Cavaliers and Rocket Mortgage, which, by a recent tally, was the nation's second-largest home mortgage lender and founder of, or investor in, dozens of other small companies, including some start-ups. Gilbert's plentiful real estate holdings in downtown Detroit have prompted some to call the commercial district Gilbertville. Depending on who's throwing around the term, it's an insult or a compliment. It could be said that Gilbert's investments—he's also put a big chunk of change into Shinola—are capitalism gone wild. It verges on being a monopoly. I don't knock the capitalist, since I'm unabashedly capitalistic myself. But my father's socialist moorings are also my compass. They are a hedge against the soul-sapping selfishness that seems at risk of making oodles of cash and letting all that money go to your head.

In Detroit and worldwide, Pop would say, wealth should be far less concentrated. It should be evenly distributed to prevent anyone from going without the resources needed to pay for a person's basic, everyday essentials. No willing worker should be jobless, underpaid, exploited, or left on the economic fringe. No person whose physical or mental disability or neurodivergence lessens the probability of holding down a job altogether should be left without a sustainable, decent safety net of services and income.

Tommey and I have been acquainted since I was in high school and he was in college, before he trademarked his slogan. Ubiquitous in Michigan, it's been made available for licensing to other locales feeling as if they also need to cheer and champion themselves within and outside their borders.

Tommey's business savvy has been effective. The expanding brand has partnered with a long list of brands, professional sports teams, colleges, and clothing companies for collaborations and collections. Famed fashion house Gucci is among them. Detroit-VS-Everybody coffee mugs, T-shirts, hoodies, baseball caps, crossbody bags, and other products bear the proud, provocative, confrontational mantra. Tommey told me he came up with it as a refutation. It was his protracted, if moneymaking, means of pushing back on other folks' images and stories of Detroit. That Detroit was stuck in a time warp. It was based on the misperceptions of people who did not hail from the Motor City and often had never stepped foot inside our city limits.

Like me, Tommey was born into the millennial generation. We were barely men when Michigan's rising political star, Kwame Malik Kilpatrick, after six years as Detroit's 72nd mayor—and the third of five, consecutively, who were Black—got caught with his hand in the cookie jar. In a truth-is-stranger-than-fiction sort of way.

For those who weren't present during that time and place, the abridged series of events goes like this: Kilpatrick hosted exuberant—and that may be an understatement—parties at the taxpayer-funded, built-in-1928, riverside Manoogian Mansion, the official residence of Detroit's mayor. According to those with first-hand knowledge, buddy was wild. His penchant for partying was so well-known and documented that, in 2002, police in Washington, DC, refused to provide the Detroit mayor with protection custom-ary for local and state elected leaders conducting official business in the Capitol. The family of exotic dancer Tamara "Strawberry" Greene, who was hired to perform during a rumored 2003 party at Manoogian Mansion, filed an unsuccessful lawsuit, alleging that the violent death of the twenty-seven-year-old mother of three was a deliberate hit. They said she had pulled her car curbside to drop off her boyfriend when a man in a white Chevrolet Blazer pulled up nearby and started shooting. Law enforcement officials never implicated Kilpatrick in the murder. But the unofficial word on the street in Detroit was that he must have had something to do with it. In a 2024 true-crime podcast, Greene's daughter, who was seven at the time of her mom's murder, insisted that the mayor and the stripper had an affair.

However unproven those allegations, Kilpatrick was culpable elsewhere. In 2008, when he was thirty-eight years old, he pleaded guilty to two felony counts of perjury and obstruction of justice and resigned. He'd lied during a police whistleblower trial. Kym Worthy, the first Black woman elected chief prosecutor of Wayne County, where Detroit is the county seat, handled the case and ordered Kilpatrick to pay the City of Detroit $1 million in resti-tution. In 2013, for his chicanery in handling city contracts and other aspects of city business and business he'd been involved in as a state legislator, Kilpatrick was convicted on twenty-four federal counts of wire fraud, racketeering, extortion, and bribery. He was sentenced to twenty-eight years in federal prison. Eventually, he admitted to lying.

The Kilpatrick era highlighted a deeply divided Metro Detroit region. Before he was convicted, his detractors and opponents stood outside the courthouse hurling their points of view at each other. For years, Kilpatrick's supporters petitioned the White House on his behalf. President Obama took a pass on granting clemency. But President Trump, himself now a felon, pardoned Kilpatrick after he'd served eight of the twenty-eight years of his federal sentence.

"It has been made to appear," read Trump's January 2021 order, "that the ends of justice do not require Kwame Malik Kilpatrick to remain confined until his currently projected release date of Jan. 18, 2037, and the safety of the community will not be compromised if he is released."

Trump let stand a requirement for Kilpatrick to make restitution payments totaling more than $4.8 million—the figure was later reduced to roughly $1.5 million—for his lavish living and other malfeasance at taxpayers' expense. Trump also left intact a requirement for Kilpatrick to be under parole supervision for three years after he left the low-security federal prison in Oakdale, Louisiana, where he'd been incarcerated. In 2024, trying to keep his assets from being seized, Kilpatrick insisted that he did not owe the government a remaining $824,774. Kilpatrick's lawyers also sought to move the issue to a federal court in Georgia, where the former mayor relocated after his sentence was commuted but his conviction left on the books.

Full of bluster and seemingly lacking as much as an ounce of contrition, Kilpatrick, with his wife standing beside him at the mic soon after his release from prison, said several things an errant politician like him would be prone to spitting out. He was, in the eyes of many, full of pomp, hubris, and indignation. A comeback was in his future, said Kilpatrick, now an ordained minister and chief administrative officer for motivational ministries at JustLeadershipUSA, a New York City–based nonprofit policy organization run by and for formerly incarcerated people. But one line—whether or not Kilpatrick deserved to put it forth—rang true for so many in my hometown: "We fall, but this city always gets up."

My old friend Tommey would agree with that part.

"As a son of Detroit, I created the Detroit-VS-Everybody brand to shine a light on this resurgence of creative energy that was going on, like, at least five to ten years before it got any media attention. That was my main concern as a designer," said Tommey, who has worked with Interscope, Def Jam, and Jive recording labels. "In my travels, I'd be approached and asked, 'Where are you from?' There was this negative stigma around Detroit, about our history, and it wasn't even all of our history. What people thought wasn't even current. And the negativity seemed to be on purpose."

As he talked to me about the local genesis of his now international brand, I couldn't help feeling incredibly proud of Tommey. Local creatives, especially from my generation, admired and looked to him for artistic direction. He'd figured out how to succeed in Detroit, without leaving and without lying. He deserved credit for inventing a mantra that united many Detroiters right around the time the feds sent former mayor Kilpatrick to prison and our city declared itself bankrupt. Tommey, among others, had a clear and better vision of Detroit as it was coming to terms with and repairing itself. His vision included all of us, not just the fat cats.

Early in his branding of Detroit-VS-Everybody, Tommey passed rap superstar Eminem at LAX. The two Detroit natives saluted each other, almost reflexively. Even when we have only a passing knowledge of each other, countless Detroiters feel bound by our common culture and conviction, and our city's challenges. Like me, those two men can't help but love Detroit.

Eminem would agree with me that Detroit battles an Everybody who, by turns, is mythic and real. So the fight against that demon is fought by tangible and symbolic means. Eminem is one of many known for sporting Detroit's hugely recognizable "D," a logo in Old English typeface, whether on caps, hats, bumper stickers, or uniforms of our hometown baseball team, the Tigers. Even among Detroiters who are strangers, there's often an instantaneous bond when we see each other donning that D, no matter where our paths cross. Outsiders might deride or respect that D; or they might have no opinion at all about the way we boast. Either way, tried-and-true Detroiters do stand on who we are.

After that chance encounter at LAX, Tommey, back to his hotel room, watched yet another TV news story about our evermore-disgraced former mayor. "I guess it had to be told. It was a story to tell," Tommey told me. "For me, it also meant Detroit, in the grand scheme of things, is still important. . . . People who have roots in Detroit are still significant. If you're not with us, you're against us. That's our battle cry."

We were Detroiters when Berry Gordy created a distinctly new brand of soul music. We were Detroiters when Eddie Murphy played native son Axel Foley on the big screen and went to Beverly Hills. We were Detroiters when Malcolm X, then a hood, was known as Red. We were Detroiters when the Lions went 0–16 (and when they were a fourth down play call away from the Super Bowl). We were Detroiters when Pop passed legislation to make jazz an American treasure, and when MomCon went to jail. "It's all connected," to quote Pop. We are all connected, for better or worse, through the lows and the highs.

Black success is not new to Detroit, which has an ample supply and history of pedigreed professionals, taxpaying entrepreneurs (and employers), legends and leaders of entertainment and the sciences, and highly skilled tradespeople, including those in the unionized auto industry. They comprise Detroit's middle, upper, and ultra-upper classes. They reside, still, in enclaves such as Palmer Woods, with its homes valued in the millions and its winding, tree-canopied streets. Many a Democratic Party donor has, over the years, packed into political power broker Virgie Rollins's home, whether the party was fundraising for my father or any of several would-be US mayors, senators, congressional servants, and presidents.

"Detroit—Black Detroit—has been a major player in Michigan. And our influence has shaped national politics. All kinds of people, including presidents, recognized that and came through here as a result," Rollins, a former chair of the Democratic National Committee's Black Caucus, told me. "Congressman Conyers was a national player. People just wanted to be in the room with him. They wanted to be in Detroit, with him and the rest of us."

Rollins joined the Black Panthers around 1967. The walls of her home are plastered with art by the famed painter Jacob Lawrence, photographer Gordon Parks, and others whose artistry doubled as their activism. Alongside those works are photos of the faces of notable Democratic players, community activists, and others who supported my father; Detroit's first Black mayor, Coleman Young; and the causes that a Black political class would embrace during the fiery 1960s. Also in those photos were US senator Bernie Sanders, my father's friend in politics and in life; Michelle Obama; Bill and Hillary Clinton; a campaigning President Obama addressing an audience on Rollins's front lawn; and boxer Muhammad Ali, the activist who told the US government he had nary a grievance against Vietnamese people and would not be drafted into what would become a war spanning nineteen years, five months, four weeks, and one day in that foreign land.

Palmer Woods is bounded by Woodward Avenue on the east, curving Strathcona Drive on the north and west, and by Seven Mile on the south. Our Seven Mile home is just across from Palmer Woods. Before it became, as it currently is, almost 80 percent Black, its earliest inhabitants were Alfred Fisher and William Fisher, co-owners of the Fisher Body Company, a major Motor

City player. William's Palmer Woods home was a mammoth 35,000 square feet, though the 300 homes of the niche neighborhood included ones as small as 2,000 square feet.

Former Michigan governor George Romney, who'd been chairman and CEO of American Motors, lived in Palmer Woods. His son, who then US senator Barack Obama beat with a thin 51.1 percent of the presidential vote in 2012, was born in Detroit. But Mitt Romney grew up in the affluent Bloomfield Hills suburb, where his parents relocated their family. Former presidential hopeful Romney attended Cranbrook, the same private school where my parents would enroll me and my brother. Cranbrook Schools sits on 319 acres in Bloomfield Hills.

The Romneys opted to move outside the city limits in 1953 when white departures were an outgoing trickle compared to the flood that would follow. During the two years after the 1967 rebellion, an estimated 150,000 whites quite literally fled Detroit to surrounding suburbs and farther reaches. Eventually, Black people would be counted in that exodus, too. Between 2000 and 2020, Detroit lost about 295,000 Black residents, amounting to 37.4 percent of its Black population. No other US city had lost more Black residents during that period. Between 2000 and 2010, more than 44,000 whites left Detroit. But, since then, during the same period, their numbers grew by 5,100. There also was growth among the city's Latino and Asian populations.

A slew of Detroit-born Blacks who traded city taxes for addresses in Southfield, Dearborn, Livonia, Wyandotte, Romulus, Novi, and any other of my hometown's more than eighty suburbs, nevertheless, are apt to tell a stranger they remain ride-or-die Detroiters.

Blacks fled the city, said Bert Johnson, a former Michigan state senator, Pop's final campaign manager, and one of his trusted confidants, for many of the same reasons whites did. "The first is probably economics. It costs a lot to be in Detroit along a number of fronts. Insurance is high; property values are lower than what they should be. They've been depressed over the years by policy and by a bunch of stuff that has happened in the banking sector.

"There's just the reality that crime was high and out of control and wasn't being reined in quickly enough. Where women and men don't feel safe, they don't stay. There's also the reality of very poor educational outcomes and options for people. And there are other locales that have been, frankly, more inviting to people. Atlanta swung their doors open and said, 'Hey, if you're Black and you're upwardly mobile in your business, and you're this, you're that, come here.' I know a bunch of people who left the state looking for safer, better, sunny shores."

It is ironic and, perhaps, poetic that a city so populated by descendants of Black people who'd fled the Jim Crow South would confront a reversal of the Great Migration, to the north and west, of Black people from my maternal grandparents' generation. But if Atlanta, given its state's slaveholding past, can write a new narrative regarding what it affords Black culture and Black economics, I'm hopeful about Detroit's next chapters.

Among other necessary corrections, said Johnson, who grew up in the famed Dexter Linwood area where the '67 rebellion took place, is the dismal state of public schools. They've also compelled many families, Black, white, and others, to exit Detroit. "There's been a deliberate attempt to demean and to punish the Detroit school district," he said. "It's been a thirty-year effort to disenfranchise the citizens of Detroit by messing over their school system. The state legislature has passed laws to do just that, to put emergency managers in to oversee the district, to bankrupt the district functionally and literally, to strap the district with certain policies that, at the state level, people knew weren't going to work. This undermining has been strategic."

Some will counter Johnson's assertions. They will contend that

Detroit schools needed an outsider's intervention. During Governor Richard Snyder's two terms in office, which started in 2011, his administration called Detroit the nation's worst-performing urban school district: 6 percent of its high schoolers were proficient in science and 4 percent were proficient in math. Roughly two-thirds of students were not reading as expected, based on their grade level. The district was under a crushing $483 million in debt for normal operating expenses and $1.5 billion in debt for construction.

But Bert didn't relent: "Detroit's schools had billion-dollar capacity bonding. They were issuing bonds to do innovative things in the Detroit public schools that were unheard of, and, then, at a record pace. It was a completely solvent school system until the state legislature and the governor, back in the late '90s, started interfering to tear the district apart and hand its bonding capability to white contractors who were eager to get their hands on that capacity."

After the COVID-19 pandemic, the city had its first net gain of residents since 1957. Though they were a mere 1,852, city officials and others found reason to celebrate. They hyped the increase, recorded between July 2022 and July 2023 and reported by the Census Bureau in 2024, bringing the population total to 633,218 and putting Detroit at No. 29 nationally in size. That, city officials touted, was bigger than Memphis, Louisville, and Portland.

"This day is for the Detroiters who stayed and for everyone who has put in the hard work to make Detroit a great place to live," said Mayor Duggan, a former Wayne County prosecutor. Elected in 2014, he was the first white man in the City of Detroit's top job since Coleman Young made history as the first Black mayor in 1974. In contrast to Coleman, whose administration was almost entirely peopled by Detroiters, 45 percent of the Duggan administration's top officials, including the deputy mayor, lived outside of Detroit, according to a *Detroit Free Press* analysis published in 2024. The head of public transit lived three hundred miles away, outside of Chicago. The head of property tax assessment—for a city whose property owners were overtaxed by at least $600 million between 2009 and 2016—lived one hundred miles away near Lansing.

"And it's not a new phenomenon," the *Free Press* wrote. "In 2020, almost half of Duggan's appointees lived elsewhere, records show. While a few of these employees with distant addresses say they have second homes in the city where they spend most of their time, some critics say the percentage of Duggan's staff who aren't full-time Detroiters undermines the mayor's narrative."

In other words, Duggan was talking out of both sides of his mouth. As the newspaper wrote, Duggan spent a decade "promoting Detroit as a thriving, comeback city that's attractive to both new and existing residents, including pinning his own success on growing the city's population."

The Duggan administration counted the population boost as another sign of Detroit's revival. He listed the increase alongside City Hall's multiyear $1 billion investment in thousands of units of public housing; the city's return to investment-grade bond status, which it last had in 2009; a $3 billion decade's worth of new wealth for Black homeowners; the fewest deaths by homicide in almost six decades; job growth by the tens of thousands; and a spectacular spotlight for Detroit in the form of the NFL draft.

It was, of course, all good news. What it did not capture were some of the tensions simmering under the surface. Months after the NFL draft, as Detroit was still basking in the afterglow of such a coup of an event, a white woman assigned to usher me, among others, into VIP seating for a Fourth of July affair peppered me with inane and borderline insulting questions. Instead of "Are you here for the Visit Detroit fireworks party?" she asked, "Where are you going?" Instead of "Can I help you find your seat?" she asked, "Are you sure you're in the right place?" I am a Black man, expressly invited to this private event. She is a white woman, in a position of supportive authority, in the until-recently Blackest major American city, and yet the default for her was still to assume I was out of place.

Subconsciously or not, she was mirroring the behavior of a growing number of new white city residents who seem hell-bent on doing an insultingly subpar job of recognizing that even amid a so-called revitalization, Detroit remains a city that is 75 percent Black. But that's the thing about neocolonization, known, by another name, as gentrification: It can be intractably toxic to the natives. As newcomers find a home in Detroit, paint, and decorate, many natives face erasure of their customs and norms, of their neighborhoods, of themselves as people. Not to overstate what was ultimately a banal interaction between me and the white greeter, but it was the type of thing that, perhaps for a relatively brief period in history, a Black Detroiter simply would not have been subjected to.

Black Detroit had some golden, and sadly abbreviated, years as a Chocolate City run by our kind of people. From 1974 through 2013, from Coleman Young through Dennis Archer, Detroit had Black mayors. For most of my life, it was as if Black people in this majority-Black town owned themselves. And it was glorious.

In 2023, analyzing the wonders of Black success in Detroit, despite what systemically was arrayed against it, Georgetown University's Sheila Foster wrote of her hometown, of its past and present, and of what's missing in the contemporary narrative about it: "It is important to emphasize that the early twentieth century was a golden age for Black businesses in the city. It seeded what would become a significant Black enterprise community in the city in later decades. . . . Black commercial and professional life flourished despite widespread exclusion and discrimination.

"The Black business community, leading into the 1930s, bonded together to survive economically. Collective organizations and ventures, such as business groups and associations, benefited the broader Black community by promoting self-help and boosting businesses and were crucial to maintaining Detroit's business community in a time of economic crisis."

Urban law and policy professor Foster wrote of our unfinished business—as Black strivers in business, public policy, academia, and grassroots activism in Detroit continue doing what the headlines don't always capture. Blacks own a good portion of TechTown Detroit, which the World Economic Forum has cited as part of Detroit's path forward. Spurred by Black clinicians and nonclinical health care executives, Henry Ford Health and Michigan State University have partnered to do never-before-conducted research to address health disparities and push a diversity of health care professionals into a pipeline already experiencing a critical shortage of workers.

Many who move about Detroit daily are aware of these strides and innovations. Those who hear Detroit's heartbeat are aware. Detroit cannot thoroughly, inclusively continue its revival without us, the constituents of the 13th Congressional District, the communities my father represented for so long, at the table.

At its peak, 705,000 people lived in the 13th, an amalgam of neighborhoods encircling, arching over, and jutting into adjacent congressional districts in Michigan's lower peninsula. Though it encompasses snatches of Wayne County—about 1 percent of the 13th is rural—mainly it comprises urban Detroit. Pop represented these people and their interests, which have remained largely the same over extended cycles of progress and regress.

As do other overwhelmingly Black electoral districts across the country, Michigan's 13th, initially etched in 1964 as the 1st Congressional District, resulted from the US Supreme Court's 1962 *Baker v. Carr* decision. Affirmed by six of the nine justices, the ruling declared that one individual's vote should hold the same value as another's—no more, no less, regardless of skin color, class, topography, or any other gauge. Then, and now, that notion of equals remains hypothetical. By mid-2021, eighteen US states controlled by conservative white lawmakers had passed laws making it tougher to vote and, thereby, diminishing that 1962 ruling from the high court. These new voting barriers are flagrant attacks against persons of color and others for whom full enfranchisement remains elusive.

Today, the 13th Congressional is 56.3 percent Black, 37.8 percent white, 7.1 percent Latinx, 1 percent Asian, and 0.4 percent Indigenous. By the most recent tally, the 13th's college graduation rate was 13 percent. Its annual household income was $30,273, compared to $48,699 statewide and $52,762 nationally. At the height of the pandemic, Detroit's unemployment rate was 48 percent, four times its pre-pandemic rate. By mid-2024, the rate had dropped to 4.3 percent, slightly higher than the statewide rate of 3.9 percent. Economists said the data likely did not capture the number of financially stressed workers whose paychecks shrunk as their hours on the job were cut.

Moreover, 62 percent of the total payroll—covering 1.2 million jobs—is concentrated in the Warren-Troy- Farmington employment center, part of Detroit Warren-Dearborn metropolitan area as defined by the Bureau of Labor Statistics. Detroit-Dearborn-Livonia, the other employment center, had 38 percent of the area's payroll employment, or 762,400 jobs. Blacks were 77.4 percent of Detroit's population of 632,464, 3.2 percent of Dearborn's 107,710 people, and 4.5 percent of Livonia's 93,779. Blacks were 19.8 percent of Warren's population, 4 percent of Troy's 87,294 people, and 8.3 percent of Farmington's 11,597 people. Proportionately, there were fewer jobs in the area where Black people were most concentrated, Detroit.

Congresswoman Rashida Tlaib, one of two in the US House's duo of first-ever Muslim women, succeeded my father in representing the 13th. Congresswoman Tlaib and Congressman Conyers represented different eras and somewhat different agendas. They had different styles. Pop and Congresswoman Tlaib, who has slowly built a reputation for working hard on behalf of her constituents, had not fostered a friendship, though, obviously, they did cross paths. She'd been a Democratic state lawmaker while Pop was in Washington. Both she and Pop deemed themselves as political progressives. And I do applaud some of her stances. Some, however, boggle the mind. For example, she voted against President Biden's proposed Build Back Better Act, which, with certainty, I can say Pop would never have done. Detroit's infrastructural and other economic needs are vast. Pop was a pragmatist when it came to issues of equity and the government's role in leveling the playing field, economically and otherwise. Relentlessly, he veered toward those things he believed would best serve the pocketbooks and everyday existence of the people of the 13th Congressional District.

Shri Thanedar, who succeeded Tlaib after redistricting moved her to the 12th Congressional District, has made a habit of not meeting with his constituents. I cannot begin to imagine what would be my father's take on him. Pop knew the potential value of Black people being represented by Black officials. Endlessly, Detroit had celebrated Coleman Young's election as Detroit's first, breakthrough Black mayor. It wasn't just about having a mayor who looked like them, it was about what he, during an unprecedented four terms, achieved. After he was elected in 1973, when crime and joblessness were raging, the former Michigan state senator and first Black on the Democratic National Committee kick-started a revitalization that attracted new businesses to Detroit. He reformed the police department. His administration created, launched, and oversaw such major projects as the Renaissance Center, Detroit People Mover light-rail system, and Louis Armstrong Stadium. (After Jimmy Carter lost the White House to Ronald Reagan, funding to expand the Mover beyond its original 2.9 miles was nixed and never resumed.)

Black folks tended to love Young. Many whites thought him

bombastic, rude, crude, and needlessly confrontational. Young couldn't care less about his critics. He'd made known his inclinations in the 1950s when he was one of a handful of labor unionists boldly rebuffing the infamous House Un-American Activities Committee, founded in 1938 by Texas congressman Martin Dies. "I consider the activities of this committee as un-American," Young told the House panel, whose anti-communist investigations of private citizens, public employees, and entire organizations came to be associated with US senator Joseph McCarthy's anti-communist crusade.

If you'd asked Young, Black political kingmaker Bob Millender, Erma Henderson (the first Black person elected to Detroit City Council), or my father to forecast forty years down the line, they might not have guessed Detroit, a bastion of Black political activity in America, would have a white mayor and no Black elected officials in Washington. As for my father, though, he was less concerned about guaranteeing Black-on-Black political representation than he was about representation that was proper and equitable, no matter the lawmaker's skin color. Pop might have been disappointed that Detroit no longer had Black representation, but if Thanedar, an immigrant from India, or Mayor Duggan, a white man, shared the right political ideology and delivered results to the people most in need, what did it matter?

My father would, of course, have held their feet to the fire: "What are you doing for Detroit? What are you doing about jobs, justice, and peace, especially for those who have the least and cannot bear to lose anything more? How are you ensuring that the people who weathered Detroit's lowest moments have a place as the city regains prominence and the rich get richer?"

During each election cycle, the people dictate who presides over them. People cast the ballot or they do not. Neither Detroit nor Michigan nor many among the United States have been ideal on that front. The list of top ten nations in voter turnout worldwide does not even include the United States. (Six of the ten are in Africa, two in South America, and one each in Southeast Asia and central Asia). By the last count, US voter turnout ranked thirty-third among the fifty member nations of the Organization for Economic Co-operation and Development. Just 37 percent of eligible US voters cast a ballot in the national elections of 2018 and 2022, with the 2020 Donald Trump–Joe Biden face-off clocking the highest turnout since 1900, a comparatively whopping 66.3 percent. In each of those same elections, 30 percent of those eligible didn't vote.

In Wayne County, Michigan, where Detroit is the county seat, there was in 2020 yet another dip in voter turnout, a decline of 6.6 percent.

Once, at length, Johnson and I mulled over the reasons why protests over the fact that a white mayor presides over a city with a Black majority are naive and hypocritical.

Johnson: We have a white mayor, who's been reelected three times. We have a white superintendent of schools, and I was in a room where people were saying, "He's been doing an astounding job." There are a lot of people who disagree with that. I'm not saying who's right or wrong. Still, we have a white superintendent of schools, an Arab woman in the 12th Congressional District, and an Indian man in the 13th Congressional District.

It's overly convenient, politically correct, maybe even politically relevant, but this idea of insisting on Black elected officials seems like a whole lot of pretty talk. When you say you need a Black person in Congress, that can just be aspirational. They're pretty, but empty words. People's behavior in the voting booth doesn't match the words. And, in Detroit, that's been true for multiple cycles now.

Me: You've got State Senator Mallory McMorrow, who is white, and Stephanie Chang, who represents Detroit.

Johnson: Regina Weiss, who represents Detroit. Mike McFall represents an area of Detroit and Highland Park. This insistent discussion about Black representation? There are enough asterisks to call it into question. Is it really what people want?

As a state senator, I got a mixed bag of responses. Black folks said, "Go up there, make it better for Blacks. Espouse Pan-Africanism, Black nationalism. Don't equivocate. Don't relent. Speak with the strident words and conversation that you know is appropriate. Don't talk soft. . . ." I took all that up there to the state capitol in Lansing, but I wasn't getting no backup. Like in the movies when they say, "Cover me." I tell you to cover me and you don't shoot your gun? Or they can focus on me when I'm running to get a better vantage point.

Me: That's like Congressman Jamaal Bowman in New York. Whether I agree with how he went about talking about Gaza and Israel, it didn't appear that he had any cover from the rest of the Congressional Black Caucus or its leadership.

Johnson: And no cover is a dangerous place to find yourself politically. You're out on a limb. You're risking something. Maybe you're using up your political capital. Maybe you're calling favors. For a lawmaker to wake up and ask himself, "Hey, man, am I doing the right thing? . . . Am I tripping? Is this what's most closely associated with what the people want? Is your voice necessary?" Whether it's Duggan finding out through a poll that people no longer want him. Or John Conyers III not getting the support from a group of people who were carrying a flag for his dad.

Me: Why do you think people talk that talk but aren't voting in the way they talk?

Johnson: It's what people think they're supposed to say. The easiest thing is to reach out and touch. There is no accountability in the words. As long as we, Black folks, are at least 51 percent of Detroit, someone will stand up and say, "Hey, we deserve Black representation." And that is true. But you've got to put something with that, behind that. Otherwise, it's just "faith without works"—which don't amount to nothing at all. It's pretty words without works or effort behind it. Try telling this strange realism of our people not electing our people *to* the people who worked so damn hard to get elected and raise and elevate our people in this space.

And I ask those same questions. How can we demand anything—anything—if we do not participate? If we don't back up all that talk with our time and our resources and our vote? Politicians oil the squeaky wheel. They attend to whoever facilitates or threatens their reelection. They ignore all the rest. They get away with, proverbially and figuratively speaking, murder.

Since its inception, politics has been a kind of blood sport, played by egotists and, on many levels, those who game our political system. Kilpatrick, a Black man, was called on the carpet and convicted of bid-rigging. But Duggan, a white man, wasn't taken down by an investigation of his alleged, similar malfeasances during his first year in office.

Under the Duggan administration, Gilbertville and the empires created by the Ilitch family, founders of Little Caesars Pizza, have gotten tax breaks to ease their moneymaking and, yes, employ people in Detroit's Downtown Development Area. But many a Detroiter—not just those who are Black—are upset by the unfairness of the rules benefiting the Gilbert and Ilitch enterprises. The Ilitch companies lied about hiring a quota of Black construction firms and workers to build Little Caesars Arena. And the company got away with that.

Those are exactly the fraudulent, self-serving dealings my father decried. Those are the dealings of men and women who are full of themselves. Pop worked hard to not lose himself in such arrogance. It leads to wanton greed.

By extension, I'd argue that Pop was less driven by ego than many of his colleagues in the entire hierarchy of pols who decide who gets a tax break, a dispensation, an open door into deep wells of opportunity.

"Eleven of us founded the Congressional Black Caucus in 1972. In 1965, when I was sworn into Congress, there were six of us," Pop said. "We'd traveled enough in the world—in our America—to know we had a job to do. We had to speak for and work for the people. Not one of us had the luxury of getting too full of ourselves. That is such a dangerous distraction."

Though Pop had leapfrogged over the Michigan State Legislature—a great many lawmakers, including Tlaib, got their start in local, county, and state governance—he had been weaned on a brand of Michigan politics that was Detroit-centric, by necessity. The bulk of Black Michiganders still reside in Detroit. Behind Atlanta and Jackson, Detroit is still the third-largest concentration of Blacks among the nation's cities whose populations exceed 100,000. Detroit and its 13th Congressional District are a bellwether. As goes Black Detroit, so go other pockets of Black America.

And my hometown is shape-shifting. Its recent influx of whites, including newcomers from outside of Michigan, are attracted to Detroit's relatively cheap housing; its boom in made-in-Motown retailing and micro-manufacturing; its locavore restaurants; and a billionaire-funded streetcar line.

White people are claiming more than their rightful share of redevelopment dollars dispensed by, among others, a City Hall presided over by Mayor Duggan, Detroit's first white mayor in four decades when voters chose him in 2013. During his most recent re-election, he garnered 75 percent of the vote. Apart from one Latina, the nine-member Detroit City Council is comprised of Black people who, in the main, represent a kind of new guard—at a time when the Blackest parts of Detroit, as ever, are reeling from blight, bad schools, blocks upon blocks of vacant land and abandoned buildings, and the lingering impacts of a municipal bankruptcy that Detroit declared in the same year that Duggan was elected. It's safe to say that many of Detroit's Blacks, Duggan supporters, were sick of City Hall's failings.

It's also fair to say that Detroit—like other gerrymandered, jury-rigged, and redlined locales—must face a necessary reconciliation in the coming years, both culturally and politically. That confrontation seems inevitable, as Detroit struggles to strike a balance. How will it preserve and propagate the cultural forces that make this place special—in large part because it reflects the still dominant Black-majority population—while pressing into a revitalization that excludes many in that popular majority?

CHAPTER 12

IN MY FATHER'S NAME

I was on a call in my bedroom in the house on Seven Mile, the one my father bought long before fatherhood and family were on his radar. More than I can remember what that call was about, I remember a river of sunlight pouring through the window. I remember the refracted gleaming of that October afternoon. I remember the shadows, lurking.

By now, Pop should have already walked past my room to head downstairs. By now, I was usually already down there. Pop and I had a routine that served us well since he came home, and our routine was off. He was late for telling me what he wanted for lunch, or for asking what I was already preparing. But even if he was taking it slow that day, I hadn't heard my father moving about as he normally would have. I hung up the phone and called out for him. "Pop?!"

It was normal for him not to answer the first callout; that was usually the prod that woke him from his nap. I called out a second time. Still nothing.

The house knew what today wrought before I did. It was almost like it swallowed all of the reverb its old construction normally provided. So I couldn't mistake the unnerving quiet for anything else. Panic began to set in. I moved out of my doorway toward the back stairs and called out again on my way up to his room.

"Dad . . . ?"

Silence.

I can count on my ten fingers and ten toes the few times I'd referred to Pop as "Dad." The word sounded strange, tumbling out of my mouth as I darted up those stairs, hit the landing, and rushed into his bedroom. My father was in a fetal position on his bed. He looked like he was sleeping. I nudged him with both my hands, trying to gently wake him. My father was not asleep. He'd slipped away.

I've not stopped wondering if Pop might have lived an hour, or a day, or a week longer had I gone upstairs sooner to tell him what I'd told him almost daily during the twenty-two months and twenty-two days since he'd retired from Congress: "It's time for lunch." To which he'd reply, "What are we having?" And I'd always say, "Whatever you want!"

Pop had come to the end of his road. Already his body was growing stiff and cold in his bed. He left here while I was in the early throes of paving my own path, one simultaneously merging with and diverging from his.

When my father's political journey started, back in the early 1960s, *Jet* magazine cost twenty cents an issue. On November 19, 1964, newly elected Pop was on the front cover of Black America's quintessential weekly, which arrived on newsstands and mailboxes from coast to coast. It chronicled the gains and developments of the Civil Rights Movement, Black high society, an upward-bound Black middle class, Blacks in entertainment, and other sectors. In words and pictures, *Jet* provided a panoramic view of our progression from Negro to Black-and-proud to, for those who choose it, African American and related honorifics we've attached to ourselves in a country so maniacally bent on denying us anything that might confer honor. *Jet* celebrated Blackness.

In the cover photo, my father clutched the receiver of a rotary telephone to his right ear, his mouth agape and animated as he spoke into its mouthpiece. His left shoulder was slightly pitched, balancing another phone's receiver, and making what he was saying audible to whoever was on the second line. His left hand clenched a third receiver, while yet another caller, or callers, waited for a turn to hear what had to have been Pop's unflinching triumph.

"NATION GETS SIXTH NEGRO CONGRESSMAN" blared the headline *Jet*'s editors overlaid on Pop's image in that black-and-white photo. Behind him was a screened-in replica of the US Capitol.

"JOHN CONYERS: DETROIT LAWYER IS THE SEC-OND NEGRO CONGRESSMAN FROM THE AUTO CAPITAL" read one of the subheads on that cover.

"HOW ELECTION RESULTS WILL HELP NEGROES" read a third subhead, teasing the findings from a survey of readers.

My father was thirty-five years old in the photo, just a few years older than I was when I started the heavy task of writing the biography Pop had insisted he was way too busy to stop and ink himself. I have interviews of Pop on tape, me peppering him with questions. As I've replayed conversation after conversation, I've asked myself, "How would Pop have told his story? If he had made time, been willing to talk at length about his own accomplishments, what would he have shared? Would he impart an inspiring story about an American family that, by its bootstraps, climbed higher, defying expectation? Would his lens be that of a military veteran, an activist, an advocate, a lawyer, a lawmaker, a rabble-rouser, a policy wonk, a good neighbor?" We contain multitudes.

I do wonder who my father truly thought he was. I wonder

which reflection he saw when he looked into a mirror. Of all our conversations, I especially cling to one we had as he was fine-tuning H.R.676, his Medicare for All proposal. "We're progressives," Pop told me, speaking about and summarizing himself but also anointing me, his son, the capitalist who shares my father's socialist moorings. Pop believed wealth should be more evenly distributed. Yet, in addition to being a politician, my father also had been a businessman. He'd partnered with his father and his brother, my uncle Nate, to open a barrier-breaking car dealership in Detroit. But Pop relinquished his stake in the partnership when my uncle and grandfather needed to apply for a federally backed loan to help the dealership to stay afloat. The business partnership became a political conflict of interest at that point. And my father fought hard to be an ethical man.

Whenever I pull out that *Jet* magazine cover photo to look again at my father's triumphant face, I also wonder what my father looked like in his parents' eyes. I'm not a parent, but I try to imagine some of the emotions they must have felt—pride, awe, adoration, gratitude, humility, maybe even fear—seeing Pop on that cover. They'd watched him morph from infant to boy to a magazine cover of a man. Could they have imagined the impact his work would have on Black Americans still seeking paradise inside a country to which our kidnapped, shackled forebears were dragged strictly to build a society for someone else's benefit?

There was so much work ahead for newly elected Pop, the neophyte lawmaker who, on a magazine cover, projected energy and vitality. Those twin engines reverberate inside of me, in the here and now. I can hear my father teaching, urging, and cautioning. No victory is written in stone, in perpetuity. Again and again, the victory must be reassessed. Perhaps, it also must be recalibrated. Most assuredly, it must be rewon. Out of the blocks, my father knew that.

As a people still seeking so much on so many American fronts, how do we proceed without my father and the countless individuals who'd spread out across our civil and human and economic battle-fields? How will we cross an ever-changing finish line, victoriously? What does victory look like, realistically? How do I best aid us in getting there? How do I, John Conyers III, proceed?

As he called the names of Pop's contemporaries—Shirley Chisholm, Fannie Lou Hamer, Jesse Jackson—author and activist Ta-Nehisi Coates once said those sheroes and heroes and what they stood for had been "pushed out the frame." The Democratic Party, once upon a time, seemed much more in league with oppressed peoples at home and abroad. As one example of the Dems many hypocrisies, Coates cited their silence regarding the innocence of the Central Park Five when they were maligned, falsely accused teenagers. Those now grown, exonerated, formerly imprisoned men were invited onstage during the Democrats' last national political convention. But gestures are just gestures. Much of what's critical to our everyday lives doesn't matter nearly enough to the Dems, not really. "I'm standing with people who've been pushed out the frame. . . ." Coates said, as Election 2024 approached. "What does 'never again' really mean? . . . That's a question for us, too. We've gotta hold folks accountable. I don't believe you get to take Shirley Chisholm, I don't think you get to say 'Fannie Lou Hamer' and then bankroll those bombs to be dropped on people."

In other words, the cause of Palestinian people and of oppressed peoples everywhere, at home and abroad, are one and the same. That's what I heard Coates saying. I lean in the direction of the questions he asks and the solutions he seeks on behalf of us all— and the knowledge that we cannot rely on the Democratic Party.

After losing the race for the congressional seat occupied by my father for more than a half century, I allowed myself time and space to ponder how I might help sustain his signature campaign mantra "Jobs, Justice, and Peace." He'd used that slogan for every congressional campaign he ran. He knew, of course, that folks couldn't make it without a paycheck. For him, and his time, when too many Black people were in menial and other low-paying jobs, making sure everyone had access to a job with better-paying wages was a primary concern. It is a need that persists today. I grasp that entirely. Indeed we need the jobs, but we also need to own the companies. Where my father and I diverged was in distinguishing the issue of jobs and fair employment from a much broader mandate. A job may help ensure the rent gets paid each month, but a job does not necessarily allow for a stockpiling of the kind of capital Black people need to be truly free in a fanatically capitalistic society. A job may let us exist with some level of comfort, perhaps, within someone else's nation. Wealth—true wealth—allows us to live comfortably inside a nation of our own. More than just a paycheck, we must have equity in education, housing, health care, corporate America, and every other indispensable aspect of life in this country that is our home, too. Money settles some of the issues. The changing of policy and systems—systemic upheaval, overhaul, and restructuring—settles the rest. Systems themselves dictate who gains wealth and who does not.

Regarding money and other forms of currency, from its founding, the United States of America has been transactional. From politics to culture to linguistic vernacular, everything that can be sold will be sold—whether or not any one individual or community likes it. It's been a favor-for-a-favor, barter-for-barter, product-for-a-price kind of place. Money is this country's mother tongue. It buys influence and protection; it brings power and respect. US policy is, so often, a reflection of the needs of the wealthy, not the needs of those of lesser means, even though, without their grinding work, our country would come to a halt. These problems are solved, in my mind, only by increasing the collective economic position of those with less money and means. Ownership and the equity that accompanies it are keys to that kind of wealth—the kind that will ultimately lead to Black liberation in America. Emphatically, that is what I believe.

And I believe it in light of the reality that politics—perhaps, the nation's greatest arbiter of wealth, of who gets a critical tax break, of who hides taxable wealth, etc.—also are for sale. Policy at local, state, and federal levels reflects the will of people, communities, corporations, and various institutions best positioned to make demands of politicians. The most influential among them can and do bankroll the governmental entities and leaders who best meet their demands: "If you will not represent our interests, we will fund a candidate who will." There should be consequences for politicians failing to competently represent Black constituencies. I believe we should hold our policymakers to account.

As a people, we must also position ourselves to field candidates who will satisfy our needs. We deserve to vote for candidates we believe will help us most, not just those we believe will harm us least. We must be proactive, not reactive, in the entire electoral process and post-process. How many of those candidates pander for our votes but, after Election Day, disregard our actual interests and our actual progress? I wish for Black people to be full partners, not pandered to in America's next chapters. I wish for us to not be mislabeled as people dependent on the largesse or charity of companies we don't own and governments we do not control—a reliance that, throughout much of our history here, has been more a myth than a fact. Hence, the myths of the Black welfare queen, the unqualified Black affirmative action hire, the Black Supreme Court justice who couldn't have gotten into Harvard Law without a special accommodation. We are much more than some wild herd to be corralled and leveraged at the whims of this or that election season, this or that candidate.

The Civil Rights Movement made immeasurable, mind-blowing

strides on behalf of all marginalized peoples. I would never denigrate the Movement's gains—who can?—and I hope that is clear. But the Movement was triaging the acute traumas of that time. Those Movement-makers were defending themselves against fire hoses, fists, and racist firearms. This far past the Civil Rights Movement, we can and we must forecast in a different way, using new tools designed for the current war that is new and old, at the same time. Today, the children of our oppressors, generally speaking, have replaced the lynchings with either an outright disdain for us or a feigned tolerance, thinly veiled, of Black people. But tolerance is at best a salve, at worst a distraction, and in neither case is it a cure. It's putting a Band-Aid on a bullet wound. So we've got to revisit and deeply excavate the strategies employed by Pop and his cohort. Then we must build on that. We've got to take it to the next level if we are to regain the ground we've been losing in recent years and reach new, never-realized, equity-focused goals.

While we demand real pain relief, we also must defend ourselves against the weapons causing the injury. The remedy, at least politically, is amassing and leveraging political capital and being politically educated. We've too rich and accomplished a political history to remain stunted, to not be far more mature politically. In both those areas, our lack is largely the fault of structural denial by entrenched systems and partly the fault our disillusionment and exhaustion over being so forcefully disregarded by those systems. Why vote if you can't readily derive a benefit from voting? That's a legitimate question. But not voting absolutely is not the answer. We must understand the rudiments and intricacies of town halls, city halls, county courthouses, state legislatures, the US House, the US Senate, federal courts, and other governmental offices dictating just about every aspect of how Americans live and who among us can thrive. And with that better understanding, we hit the ballot box. When we show up at venues where public officials are charged with doing the public's bidding, those elected officials will be compelled to represent us, not just out of duty, but also a healthy amount of fear. Not fear of physical violence, but fear of reprisal in the form of being voted out of office. We are, too often, *found money* to the political establishment. We are treated as a nice-to-have, not a need-to-have, when, in fact, without the Black vote, the Democratic Party, for one, would crater. For the establishment to value us, we must make ourselves a force to reckon with.

Our ability to build political capital is inextricably linked to our collective economic position. The US Supreme Court's Citizens United decision is a case in point. By allowing corporations and individuals to spend, without limits, on political campaigns, that ruling strengthened our politicians-for-hire system. Nevertheless, the game is the game; it's time we play it. Generation after generation of white Americans have been able to successfully pursue economic opportunity and have had their accumulation of wealth seen by their country as something they righteously earned. As if the wealth they amassed was something for the entire country to be proud of. In the early twentieth century, the country passed policy after policy aimed at expanding economic opportunity for the masses. A cornerstone of FDR's sweeping New Deal, launched in 1933, was its promise to prop up the middle class. The New Deal, though, bypassed plenty of people who were neither white nor middle class. "But many forget the crucial fact that black and brown workers across the country were systematically excluded from key programs like Social Security as well as protections afforded under the National Labor Relations Act," wrote Rockefeller Foundation analysts, critiquing the Biden White House's effort to shore up the US economy during COVID-19. "Also, the Home Owners Loan Corporation and the Federal Housing Administration promoted racial covenants and other instruments of segregation by refusing home loans for Black and Brown families.

"This move was not an accident: Roosevelt intentionally cut out occupations dominated by people of color, including domestic and agriculture workers, from New Deal initiatives as part of a strategy to win the support of Southern Democrats in Congress."

Despite those sorts of deliberate, discriminatory exclusions, Blacks have accumulated wealth and political power. Take Tulsa's iconic Black Wall Street. Instead of enacting de facto and de jure policy—policy enumerated by common but informal practice versus policy cemented in the law—to protect those thirty-five city blocks of Black entrepreneurship, it pardoned the racist whites who torched that commercial district. Similarly, whites in government seized Detroit's Black Bottom and Paradise Valley by eminent domain and bulldozed much of it. Then and now, Black people also have deserved the opportunity to live the same version of America and its promised dream that our white counterparts, by comparison, have come to know well.

Pop knew that, though he filtered that knowledge through a lens crafted in a different time. Still, his signature reparations bill aimed to ensure we receive our due while also creating a path toward equity. While I doubt that a single-check payment for, thus far, unpaid labors of the enslaved will be the silver bullet, end-all solution to our complex, compounding, and confounding problems and circumstances, I have serious trouble understanding those who argue that we are not owed restitution. We, the disenfranchised, dispossessed, and denied, are owed. In an unabashedly capitalist nation, where everything is for sale, how can the cost of centuries of wrongdoing be ignored? We filled this country's coffers and singularly marked its culture. Acres and mules at this point feel like a pittance.

Experts whose know-how was included in the *New York Times*'s Pulitzer Prize–winning *The 1619 Project*, the brainchild of journalist Nikole Hannah-Jones, asserted that Black culture is the only modern American culture, other than the Indigenous cultures that either remain alive, if in fragments, or are struggling to rebound from the effects of genocide. The discussion about reparations generally centers on the period of time between 1619 and 1877, when Black bodies went from boat to auction block to the fields to the grave, unpaid, their labor serving as the driving force behind the meteoric rise of the American economy. The period that followed saw policy and practice conspire to expand the exploitation of Blackness for commercial gain, if by different means.

Next on the auction block, in place of our bodies, was our culture, our aesthetic, our music, our food, our dance, the exuberant markers of our humanity, precious and ethereal assets often born from the inhumane treatment experienced. Like the corporeal commodity that preceded it, the people who make the most money from the sale of Black culture are not Black people. It's all connected, Pop would say. He knew that to protect it, we first needed to acknowledge Black art and culture as explicitly and undeniably both American and ours. That's why he fought for and won passage of the 100th Congress's H.R.57, "a concurrent resolution expressing the sense of Congress respecting the designation of jazz as a rare and valuable national American treasure." He was codifying that Black culture was intrinsically invaluable to America. He was laying the groundwork for the arguments we are still making, still in pursuit of our just due.

Opposite Pop's efforts to alter how Black people, still largely poor and huddled masses, experienced America, there have been concerted efforts from the opposite end of the social hierarchy to expand the systems of cultural control through economic influence. The year before he became a US Supreme Court justice, Lewis F. Powell Jr., in 1971, blueprinted what became known as the Powell Memorandum, a detailed memo to then US Chamber of Commerce chairman Eugene B. Sydnor Jr. The memo, titled

"Attack on American Free Enterprise System," for more than fifty years has served as a road map for long-term efforts of fiscal conservatives and members of the business class to fortify that system of so-called free enterprise. Powell's memo was a granular plan. On two separate points within the memo, Powell tells Sydnor that this plan will take time and a coordinated effort. First, he states, "But independent and uncoordinated activity by individual corporations . . . will not be sufficient. Strength lies in organization, in careful long-range planning and implementation, in consistency of action over an indefinite period of years, in the scale of financing available only through joint effort, and in the political power available only through united action and national organizations." Later in the memo, he reminds Sydnor, "This is a long road and not one for the fainthearted." What he and the business class were in pursuit of, Powell knew, would not happen overnight or even within one generation.

Recognizing the country's growing shift to the Left and a burgeoning socialist movement, Powell wrote, "The most disquieting voices . . . come from perfectly respectable elements of society: from the college campus, the pulpit, the media, the intellectual and literary journals, the arts and sciences, and from politicians." Clearly, he had readily identified where the plan should be enacted; he proceeded to walk through the how of it all. Ground zero for the shift was the college campus, controlling everything: teaching and research scholars, alumni associations, administrators, boards of directors, textbooks, and much more. Why were all of these positions so important? Influencing who was hired, what they taught, and the lens from which they taught meant being able to shape the future. Powell pointed out that American corporations were, at the time he wrote the memo, supporting and paying taxes that funded intellectuals diametrically opposed to corporate dominance. Corporations received the message; laid plans for a shift to the Right, regarding government regulation of businesses; and, with full-fledged assault, commenced sharing its message across media platforms.

He identified the neglected political arena and opportunities in the courts as among the most important. "One should not postpone more direct political action, while awaiting the gradual change in public opinion. . . . Business must learn the lesson . . . that political power is necessary; that such power must be assiduously cultivated; and that when necessary, it must be used aggressively and with determination—without embarrassment . . ." He continued: "Under our constitutional system, especially with an activist-minded Supreme Court, the judiciary may be the most important instrument for social, economic and political change."

With Powell's insistence in mind, my message to fellow millennials and Black people across generations is that in order to win, we must be this strategic. We must be as granular as Powell and his ilk and as committed over time to building economic and political capital, and exercising our power to create the country we wish to live in.

Some fifty years later, we see the effect on the country of those conservatives who heeded Powell's memo. I can't help but question whether Powell could have known how far his proposed strategy would take the country. In the hands of an ever-more-radical Right, his corporate manifesto has been incredibly effective. Effective enough that some would argue, myself among them, that our republic finds itself on the cliff's edge of catastrophe. In his blueprint, Powell stated, "There seems to be little awareness that the only alternatives to a free enterprise are varying degrees of bureaucratic regulation of individual freedom—ranging from that under moderate socialism to the iron heel of the leftist or rightist dictatorship."

While some January 6 insurrectionists were persons of pedigree, financial and other means, many were not. Rather than address the roots of their discontent, President Trump and his league of liars convinced the least moneyed and most uninformed January Sixers—mainly white people but also a smattering of people of color—that immigrants, affirmative action hires, DEI (Diversity, Equity, and Inclusion) programs, and such were the problem.

In *People of the Lie: The Hope for Healing Human Evil*, Dr. M. Scott Peck, a Christian thinker and psychiatrist, explained why some individuals and groups choose a flagrant untruth over reality, then embrace the havoc-creating lie. In part, it's their effort to ignore, rather than address, their failings. It's them transferring blame often to those who are victims. "With each step along the wrong road," Peck wrote, "it becomes increasingly difficult for them to admit that they are on the wrong road, often only because they have to admit that they must go back to the first wrong turn and must accept the fact that they have wasted energy and time."

People of the lie are deluded. They are self-sabotaging deniers. Deliberately, they tell, hear, and embrace the lie. They cling to it, believing it will save them from any number of more inconvenient truths. They would rather be wrong than hopeless. They would rather believe in grand conspiracies and supervillains than to grapple with the reality that their lives and circumstances are bleak. *Info Wars*'s Alex Jones was forced to sell his personal assets to finance a $1.5 billion court-ordered settlement to the parents of Sandy Hook Elementary School students slain by a twenty-year-old gunman. But lying conspiracy theorist Jones, who got rich saying Sandy Hook was a hoax and the kids were still alive, won the praise of Trump's 2024 vice presidential pick, Yale Law grad J. D. Vance, an Ohio congressman. People of the lie tend to cast their lot with the Donald Trumps of the world. They believe Trump will help them reach a range of ends, because he affirmed a worldview that doesn't demand that they confront those inconvenient truths. He validates the white supremacist ideologies that blame "white plight" and hardship on Black and Black-adjacent peoples. He gives voice to their grievances, founded or not, against a variety of American systems. He sees them struggling and in the most minor of ways pads their bank accounts, or makes them believe he will, even if not by very much. The people of the lie are stuck in the desert, thirsty. To them, bottles of arsenic-tainted water airdropped from Trump Force One are enough for them to excitedly call him President. This is especially true for many whites among Trump's supporters. Decades ago, LBJ explained why. "If you can convince the lowest white man he's better than the best colored man, he won't notice you're picking his pocket. Hell, give him somebody to look down on, and he'll empty his pockets for you."

Some Black folks are also people of the lie for various reasons, mostly still rooted in their own rejection of the inconvenient truths that their lives present, and the simplicity of the lies it feels easier to believe.

In the run-up to the 2024 presidential elections, Trump's support among Black voters was inching up. If a Black person wants to vote for Trump, that's a travesty. In his long history of race-baiting antagonism toward us, the US Justice Department sued him in the 1970s for refusing to rent his apartments to Black tenants whom he roundly dismissed as "welfare queens." In the 1980s, Black employees were said to be ordered off the floor of Trump Castle—its new owners renamed it the Golden Nugget Atlantic City—whenever Trump and his then wife, Ivana, showed up. When Barack Obama was running for president, Trump was among those not only alleging that the 44th president was not born in this country, but fundamentally accusing him of attempting to defraud the American people by presenting himself as a citizen. Those false claims not only attacked his viability as a candidate, they attempted to impugn his character. Xenophobes who embraced the false claims believe that Brown and Black people are less American than white people.

And yet, this man who has been a true friend to only himself—and who tolerates persons of color only when it serves his own purposes —has succeeded at making some of us pawns on his chessboard. And while I am vexed by this reality, I am not surprised by it. If you feel like you're about to die of thirst, arsenic poisoning may be a quicker and more appealing way to die than dehydration. Still, I wonder whether we would be so thirsty, and feel so deserted, if Pop's reparations bill had passed successfully. I wonder, in that case, if we would be so willing to sell our long-term health at a cost so much lower than our value.

Trump's bluster has centered around money—his real profits, and the ones he fabricated on paper. Money, of course, is a motivator. It's an invaluable tool. That cannot be truer for any group of people, anywhere, still struggling to gain their financial footing. Comedian Dick Gregory, a contemporary of my father who ran for mayor of Chicago and lost bookings because of his civil rights activism, used to say it costs money to finance any revolution. In "Bring It Back," the artist Trouble rapped, "Wanna go to war. But you ain't got no money." Trouble couched his lyrics in a context and time that didn't parallel Gregory's, but I've borrowed that snippet of lyrics to accentuate a point. Whether Trouble or Gregory are our guides, our North Star remains in the same location: Any economic, social, or political salvation we find in this land will rely upon our capacity to aggregate capital, deploy it responsibly, gain influence that dictates policy, and deliver outcomes with a lasting impact. We are a great distance from that place.

Based on the sluggish pace of change for Black people between 2011 and 2021, it would take more than three hundred years to close the gap between us and white people in housing, health, education, employment, and other quality of life and economic equity issues shaped by where people reside and what's available to them in those locations. In a 2023 report by the McKinsey Institute for

Black Economic Mobility, researchers highlight this economic disparity: "We find that America's suburbs and exurbs currently seem to have the nation's best balance of positive overall Black outcomes and parity. But even here, large disparities persist. Effectively, there is nowhere in the United States where outcomes for Black residents equal those of their white neighbors. Moreover, most places close to parity are small rural counties where outcomes are poor for all residents, regardless of race."

These persistent disparities formed the crux of my father's watershed proposal to study how and what sort of reparations should go to descendants of the US's enslaved, House Resolution 40. After my father died, Texas congresswoman Sheila Jackson Lee, while she was taking the lead legislatively on H.R.40, wrote: "With the rise and normalization of white supremacist expression during the Trump administration, the discussion of H.R.40 and the concept of restorative justice have gained more urgency, garnering the attention of mainstream commentators and illustrating the need for a national reckoning. . . . The designation of this legislation as H.R.40 is intended to memorialize the promise made by Gen. William T. Sherman . . . to redistribute 400,000 acres of formerly Confederate-owned coastal land in South Carolina and Florida, subdivided into 40-acre plots. In addition to the more well-known land redistribution, the order also established autonomous governance for the region and provided for protection by military authorities of the settlements. Though Southern sympathizer and former slaveholder President Andrew Johnson would later overturn the order, this plan represented the first systematic form of freedmen reparations."

Cities and counties in states including California, Georgia, Florida, Massachusetts, Missouri, North Carolina, and Rhode Island have established commissions to study the question of reparations for their residents. In 2023, the Detroit City Council established a reparations task force to examine how to create housing and economic equity for Black people.

"Reparations can mean a lot of things, but it must include no-strings-attached direct cash to Black people and systemic change throughout all levels," said Kofi Kenyatta, at the time UpTogether's senior policy director, as he phoned in his comments during the thirteen-member task force's inaugural meeting at Detroit City Hall. "Poverty plagued this majority Black city and has for far too long."

"Small-scale" government programming could never be a sufficient fix, he added.

"We are at a . . . moment of a political opportunity for paradigm change," said economist Darrick Hamilton, founding director of the Institute on Race, Power, and Political Economy at The New School in New York City, where I am enrolled. He was giving me a primer, situating my father's H.R.40 within the United States's recent political, economic, and cultural climate.

"The last fifty to sixty years is characterized by a neo-liberal paradigm that's grounded in an ethos of market fundamentalism . . . and the idea that market mechanisms are the fair, efficient, colorblind arbiter of our value and worth. As a result, when people have bad outcomes, some will argue that that's the result of their actions, inactions, attitudes, or norms. And that part is a lie. This is a culmination of a previous paradigm by which race was the weaponized mechanism to get us to what the socialist Eduardo Bonilla-Silva would characterize as racism without racists.

"We naturalized poverty by castigating people based on the action and inaction of the poor themselves. The poor were racialized, described in dastardly terms as deadbeats, welfare queens, super-predators. And government was villainized as tilting the scale in favor of these *undeserv-eds* and, worse, creating further dependencies that kept them in the positions they were in."

"Which is a long way from the New Deal," I interjected, noting the job-generating public works and other programs President Franklin D. Roosevelt designed to bring the poorest of the poor, especially, back from the brink during the Great Depression.

"Exactly," Hamilton told me. "Coming out of the New Deal and coming out of the Great Depression and coming out of World War II, there was a moment in history that opened up a different type of enlightenment. The 'rights of man' became more entrenched in a universal way. There was a United Nations Universal Declaration of Human Rights.

"That document is the result of a political culmination. And it reflects a great deal of the vision that was put forth by your father around a federal job guarantee . . . civil rights, political rights, social rights, cultural rights, and economic rights. The economic rights aspect of that declaration of human rights has been co-opted. It's been ignored over time. But what this country has done is totally and completely naturalize poverty as the fault of individuals who are poor. We've naturalized this notion of economic markets being colorblind, and that cultures of poverty are the fault of Black people with a lack of ethics and detrimental behaviors. We've pivoted to those types of narratives."

Hamilton and I discussed the broken promises, the social contract America has not kept. I asked the expert some of my most burning questions. How has that social contract been eroded? Did the contract cover Black folks to begin with? Have resources, subsidies, and benefits that rightfully belong to citizens, to taxpayers—including a wide-open avenue toward success—been transferred to governments and corporations?

"The government and the capital class have always been in cahoots," Hamilton said. "The notion that government should serve the people, if you ask me, is a fairly recent concept. . . . It ramped up because of events that took place in the world, frankly. The near destruction of humanity. The economic collapse of the Great Depression.

"Take property rights. If, today, we were to instill property rights without redressing how that property became distributed, that's immoral. It only solidifies and edifies and iterates oppression. Why? Because capital builds upon itself. Capital isolates and reiterates itself, amplifying the injustices by which property was distributed or captured in the first place."

Which means wealth begets more wealth. "If I have wealth," he continued, "I need not do any action, and I'll get a dividend in perpetuity. If I own land, I get rent. The difference between wealth and income is that income is exhaustive. And for the vast majority, income goes towards our subsistence, our consumption. Wealth is different. It's functional. . . ."

Wealth goes on for always. My father's mantra "Jobs, Justice, and Peace" was grounded in what Hamilton substantiated. Whether or not I seek political office again, I will be even more deeply immersed in politics, especially the economics and economy that drive it. Especially amid these rollbacks of hard-won provisions of an elusive American social contract with Blacks—the elimination of diversity, equity, and inclusion programs in public institutions, affirmative action in the public and private sectors—we've got to fight back on behalf of my father and MLK and Fannie Lou Hamer and the rest in that Black pantheon. We must pursue the sort of progress, economically and politically, that allows us to defend our wins. This is the only home we know. Our ancestors built this place.

Hopefully, in a world where we are able to achieve and then defend our wins with our dollars, we will also start to see a shift in how we measure ourselves as well. The key performance indicators by which we define ourselves need to be separate and distinct from our white counterparts. Too often, we're trying to achieve a standard someone else set, not one that is legitimately, remarkably ours. What does it look like to be successful as determined by Black standards? Black metrics? I'm not picking a fight with white people as much as I am forcefully working to win minds and hearts, to decenter whiteness and success in their systems as the metric. I am saying that I am less interested in a white standard, which we've yet to measure up to, anyhow, than I am in a Black one.

I'm saying that we—that I—must heed what leaders of the past professed and believed about Black achievement. And, I mean, achievement for all Black people. Whenever I hear the term "Black excellence," my skin crawls. For me, it's just W. E. B. Du Bois's "The Talented Tenth" rerocked. The iconic essay opens with this: "The Negro race, like all races, is going to be saved by its exceptional men. The problem of education, then, among Negroes must first of all deal with the Talented Tenth; it is the problem of developing the Best of this race that they may guide the Mass away from the contamination and death of the Worst, in their own and other races."

There are potential pitfalls and dangers in Du Bois's calculation. Who gets to decide who is the most exceptional? Based on what? Measured against what? What happens to the remaining 90 percent? What of the geniuses among that 90 percent who don't get to shoot their shot because the scouts didn't perceive their talent?

I've been astounded by how infrequently we champion our everyday heroes. It took some doing, some faith beyond fear, for Christian Smalls to organize a walkout of an Amazon distribution center in New York City, a COVID-19 epicenter, because the global giant wasn't supplying warehouse workers with adequate face masks and other protective gear. Now the founder and first president of the Amazon Labor Union, he'd been a rapper, touring with Meek Mill before choosing to support his family with his earnings from an everyday kind of job. How difficult and daring must it have been to organize a worker union at the second-largest company in the world?

To me, Smalls was playing above the rim. He was—and in his current role, still is—shooting for the stars. As my father would say, he was aiming to bring heaven down to the earth. Jesus, Pop believed, was love and an ultimate example of activism on behalf of the least and the lost. Jesus's name has gotten thrown around a lot these last few years, including by members of the Christian Right and Christian nationalists who seem to hate everyone except their kind. But, really, what would Jesus do? I'd have no problem with the United States declaring itself one nation under God if we were trying to give the poor a way out of poverty. If there were health care and paid family leave for all. If there were universal childcare and sufficient nurture for the babies who, in the name of Christianity, are being born against the will of women who wanted to make a different choice.

Black people have as much right as anyone to pick our battles and our preferences. In these recent years of being retested on battlefields where we'd already defended ourselves to the point of exhaustion, we find ourselves at war all over again. Whose side shall we choose, except our own? Which weapons can we best handle with dexterity and stealth?

How will I, John James Conyers III, arm myself? It's a question bigger than I am. It applies to an untold number of us during these last many politically fraught years. While speaking to a dear friend, Niles Heron, I gave this answer: "I'm progress over political affiliation. I believe in the progress of Black people. I'm a lifelong Democrat, but I'm a Democrat because being a Democrat best serves my personal political agenda. At such a time that the Democrat Party alignment no longer serves my political agenda, I'll have no interest. I've never had a deep allegiance to the Democratic Party beyond their willingness to promise to provide me and the people that I am concerned for a better life or a better chance at creating the lives that they want.

"I care about progress, first. Everything else is second."

Niles was a cofounder of and executive at one of the largest talent and brand management firms in gaming before leaving to, as he said, "get back to the soil," create economic opportunity in his own community, and with some of that cash, help underwrite this rebellion we've been waging since they unloaded us from those transcontinental slave ships. "Despite being raised by a socialist, I believe that the economic advancement of Black people is the single most stable way for Black peoples," he said, "to create defendable safety in this country that, for four hundred years, has been beset against that."

We are kith and kin, Niles and I, just as Pop and Mr. Featherstone were. We are iron sharpening iron. We are capitalists by necessity because we know its power. Capitalism picks up the tab. Capitalism pays the bills. We know that capitalism won't feed the soul. Community is what provides the spiritual sustenance needed for people to grow and to expand.

Even if my father, on paper, died a relative pauper, he also knew money was a necessity. But his generation made first things first. For them, it was the lynchman's noose, the KKK's burning cross, colored water fountains, and federal troops called up to facilitate the desegregation of white schools. On the backs of my father's generation, successive generations have crossed a bridge over to where we now find ourselves.

In the city that birthed me and Pop, we have a particular brand of Black privilege. Because Detroit has been such a Black city, the Black rich and Black poor, perhaps, are less separated from each other than they are elsewhere. Of course, one group lived in a nicer neighborhood than the other. And I don't applaud that or laud my family's home on a golf course over another person's home in less comfortable circumstances. What I do appreciate, though, is not growing predisposed to believing only white people could have wealth, access, and opportunity. The earliest imprints on my life were the Black lawyers, starting with my father, who handled all kinds of affairs for Black people and others. Within the 142 square miles of what remains a Chocolate City—Black flight and white newcomers, notwithstanding—a bunch of Black folks experienced a golden age of not having to "accept the scraps of whiteness," as Niles has put it.

At this point along the trajectory of being Black in America, we've got to fight to make sure no one is forced to accept anyone's discards. Racism exists only to the extent that those with power practice it and continue to profit from its necessary inequity. If there are no systemic imbalances, racism becomes simple prejudice, which everyone has. The difference is that the system of racism, propped up by its beneficiaries, is supremely self-sustaining. It can be stopped only by the hands of the system's gatekeepers. Were they to shuffle the deck and re-deal, we would still see lesser biases—not everyone wants to sit next to everyone else—but we wouldn't see the aggregate denial of a seat (and opportunity) at the proverbial table.

I proceed with all of these varied perspectives from my peers and advisers, and with lessons my father imparted. Some of Pop's lessons I am still trying to get my head and my heart around. We endure a period when we must proclaim and explain, as Dr. King did, *"Why We Can't Wait."*

My father kept that book of MLK's on his shelf. Pop shared his friend's immediacy, but Pop also was a slow-and-steady-wins-the-race kind of man. "Little by little, day by day," he'd often say. Sometimes, he'd remind me of that as I struggled with starting tasks, especially ones that seemed too large for me to even begin to tackle.

But Pop's measured pacing and MLK's urgency were not dueling concepts. They were tactics to be deployed based on the situation, selectively, carefully. MLK famously declared, "The arc of the moral universe is long, but it bends toward justice." That, too, is subjective. Fast is subjectively gauged. So is slow; the slowness of a thing also can be relative. And the ancients, after all, were not startled that Aesop's fabled slow-moving, persevering tortoise crossed the finish line as the victor.

True progress is measurable, sure, and undeniable. It is not mere rhetoric to pacify and anesthetize the people. Progress is an objective outcome, even when, on a micro level, we are left to subjectively assess its value. Making progress for me and those like me is my primary concern as I step into the next phases of my life, standing in the light and shadow of my father.

My father was an old man, sixty-one years my senior. He'd been born into what demographers call the Silent Generation, persons muted somehow by the economic pressures of the Great Depression and McCarthyism. They were, as a group, said to have kept their heads down, stayed on their grind, stayed focused on staying in line, and not caused much trouble. But that characterization doesn't capture Pop and his crew of changemakers.

He lived a long, full life. When I die, I hope my children can look back and say, "He did it all," the way I can say of my father. And though he could have, deservedly, he tended not to boast.

While I am at times sad due to his absence, I am a realist and think, "What else was there for him to do?" And that would have been the question he would be asking me.

It would have been a mandate, Pop handing off his blueprint because it was someone else's time, my time, our time to build.

And, in a way, he did leave that blueprint. He showed his work, and through the journey of trying to understand it through his words and the others reflected in the pages of this book, I have come to my own conclusions about the work still in front of us— inside and outside of government.

I will likely be a Democrat until my last breath, but I also unequivocally value our progress over any political affiliation. We do not have permanent enemies, only permanent interests. The Democratic Party has best served us during the lifetime of almost any Black person reading this book. And still, we have not positioned ourselves to demand that they cause our country to treat us as we deserve. Even without a desire to defect and no interest in suggesting that others should, I have no hesitation in saying I want more, and better, and now.

To that end, I aim to continue the work to educate, encourage, and evangelize the power of our economic impact. Our economic position allows us to protect the progress we make. The opportunity to grow our collective ownership, equity, and wealth to influence our political circumstance has eluded Black people for far too long, and we deserve more than to simply benefit or be burdened by someone else's needs and actions.

Even recognizing that alternatives might seem easier, I know that the best course is to remain steadfast in commitment to and pursuit of the truth. Opponents' tactics might lead some to believe that hyperbole and dishonesty are the paths to political and social progress. They are not. Neither I nor we can allow duplicity to become our modus operandi. If the truth does not land as a compelling enough argument, then we're saying it wrong, or there's a deeper problem to solve—still, the truth will guide us. It hasn't been wrong, yet.

I will always seek the best action for the task, learning from the work of the visionaries who preceded us in this struggle, and also assessing from a vantage point in the present. I understand, now, the question my father asked me and my friends all those years ago: "What shall we do, now, about all that's going on?" In asking, he was hoping that I, and we, might hear each section of the question posed. He wanted to make sure we understood what we sought to accomplish, specifically, and to understand the tactics appropriate for this moment in history as opposed to being irrevocably wed to the tactics of yesterday. And he was asking for our holistic assessment, suggesting that the measure comes before we move—that understanding *all* that is happening presents the best chance at success when attempting to treat, or attack, the disease and not simply temporarily alleviate the symptom. It is an inheritance, indeed, being able to proceed, benefited by the learnings of everyone that came before me, with respect to all we must do now.

Progress.

Truth.

Action.

ACKNOWLEDGMENTS

To my amazing editors, Abby West and Makayla Tabron, thank you for your patience, wisdom, grace, and belief in my story. Thank you for reinforcing your belief in the importance of not only my story but my father's. Thank you for helping me bring it to the world. I cannot overstate my gratitude!

Michael Eric Dyson, thank you for remaining as committed to this project as you have through the years. Thank you for eulogizing my father the way you did, and thank you for the beautiful foreword about Tab and our hometown.

To my teachers: From Mrs. Tower at Brookside Elementary, who nurtured me through my early reading struggles, to Ms. Woodfin, who ignited my passion for reading when she introduced my fourth-grade class to Lemony Snicket and Harry Potter. Mrs. Belinda Mitchell, my first Black teacher, oversaw my first book as a final assignment in fifth grade, and it was even bound. Who knew the young authors' tea would someday get me here? At Vaughn Middle School, Mr. Brewster Moore honed my love for language; while at Brewster Academy, Coach Rowley introduced me to annotated reading, forever changing how I interacted with literature. Finally, to Ms. Shea, who saw me in my loneliness and introduced me to Toni Morrison's *The Bluest Eye*, opening my eyes to characters who looked like me and paving the way for the perspective in *My Father's House*—your impact has been immeasurable.

Beyond my teachers, so many incredible people have taught me through conversations, examples, and actions—shoulders that I've stood on, enabling me to see the work still to be done. Nathan G. Conyers, Judge Damon Keith, Uncle Bill Clinton, Congresswoman Sheila Jackson Lee, Rev. Jesse Jackson, Congresswoman Maxine Waters, and Secretary Marcia Fudge—thank you for always being one phone call away. John W. Rogers Jr., R. Donahue Peebles Jr., Mark Cheatham, Lamell McMorris, Cedric Richmond, Rosa DeLauro, Greg Meeks, Anthony Scaramucci, Bakari Sellers, and the Dingells.

Thank you to every person who helped my father along his way, especially the staff that became like family and surrogate relatives and the voters.

Thank you to my family: the Conyerses, Esterses, Garretts, and Pughs. Gulinda Smiley, Rhonda Pugh, and Carla Whitley. To my brother, Carl, the reason why I work as hard as I do. Thank you to my brothers Jay John Henry, Dylan Warmack, and Chris Thomas. Bobbo, A.P., Mike and Will Polk, Harry Davies, Ken Montgomery, Rick and Ro, Reni George, BankReau, Ben Greger, Robert Boyle, Niles, Remmington, Terrence Smalls, Terrance Woodbury, Kazz, STL Juan, Shikeith, Khalid Elbakri, Bert Johnson, Yolanda Lipsey, Gabby, Xander, David Wachler, Morgan Fowler, Sunceria Garrett, Charlie Cavell, Shannon Smith, Holly Baird, Noah Schmidt, Noah Smith, Darren Sands, Vann Newkirk, Michael Hardaway, Adam Weiner, Michael Skolnik, Maura Chanz, Van Freeman, Illya Davis, John Brown, Chantel Watkins, Adam Friedman, Stephen and Blake Nemeth, the Lucas Family, Mitch Schuster, Kevin Hutzel, Ashley Lewis, Dan Weisman, Uncle J, Mike Posner, Coaches Tyree Fields, Don

Sellers, and Dwayne Bryant, Cousin Sonya, Gail Bean, Detroit Charlie, Caston, Langston, Akin Dairo, and Finally Famous— thank you all. Last but not least, the family that chose me, the House of Homage.

In memory of our brother Bydia B.Y. Wilson. #NNSOMOW

PS: If I forgot anyone, charge it to my head, not my heart.

ABOUT THE AUTHOR

John Conyers III is an accomplished entrepreneur and dedicated political organizer deeply rooted in the Detroit community, committed to revitalizing that city's economy through Jobs, Justice, and Peace. He is the son of former congressman John Conyers Jr. and former Detroit City Council president Monica Conyers, and brings a unique perspective to service and humanitarian causes given his family's generational civil rights accomplishments.